The New World of Economics
Explorations into the Human Experience

The Irwin Series in Economics

Consulting Editor
LLOYD G. REYNOLDS   *Yale University*

The New World of Economics
Explorations into the Human Experience

Richard B. McKenzie
Department of Economics
Appalachian State University

Gordon Tullock
Center for Study of Public Choice
Virginia Polytechnic Institute
and State University

 1975

Richard D. Irwin, Inc.   Homewood, Illinois   60430
Irwin-Dorsey International   London, England   WC2H 9NJ
Irwin-Dorsey Limited   Georgetown, Ontario   L7G 4B3

First Printing, February 1975

ISBN 0-256-01683-6
Library of Congress Catalog Card No. 74–24443

Printed in the United States of America

To
Mary Ann

Preface

Economics traditionally has been defined by both its method and its subject matter. That is to say, there are economic methods: models and statistical tests based on a set of assumptions about the way people interact. In addition, there is an area of human life, which is hard to describe in a brief phrase but is known to all economists, in which these methods are applied. We believe that the methods have a much wider scope than previously has been thought. This book is an attempt to introduce the student to the new work that has been done in applying economic methods to problems outside the traditional subject matter of economic study. This new field of research is, we think, more exciting, more interesting, and even more relevant than the more traditional applications to traditional economic problems.

Economics has developed over two centuries. During this 200 years, almost all of the places where a simple line of reasoning can be applied to an important and interesting problem have been explored. The remaining areas for economic research are, in general, those where the reasoning is difficult and the amount of progress made in each investigation is comparatively small. The result has been that more and more complex and sophisticated methods have been applied to smaller and smaller problems.

This book attempts to break out of the narrow confines of economic subject matter as traditionally defined, and seek out new and refreshing problems that can be dealt with in a simpler way. Although it is intended to be easily read by students, we sincerely hope that most teachers using it will find at least some of the material covered new and interesting. Indeed, many of the instructors, when they see how easy it is to apply economic reasoning outside the traditional field, may decide to try their hand at it.

There is a possible misunderstanding here. Economic method does not cover all phases of human life. Hence, when economics is applied to new areas (and in this book it is applied to many new areas), it does not give a complete picture. We study supply and demand without studying the consumer tastes which have so much to do with the demand schedule. This problem is left to the psychologists simply because we do not know enough to deal with it.[1] Similarly, in many of the areas we discuss in this book, our approach is a partial, rather than a complete, modeling of the real world. Nevertheless, we think that these economic models are enlightening, even if they do not give complete answers. The growth of human knowledge is a matter of step-by-step progress, and the fact that we are unable completely to explain crime by economic methods does not imply that these methods should be abandoned.

As the reader may deduce as he goes through the textbook, we have found it an interesting and exciting book to write, and we hope that both the professors and the students will also find it interesting and exciting. If it is merely used to teach elementary economics, we will have achieved only part of our goal. We hope that the readers of this book will learn enough so they can apply economic methods to various problems that occur, both in public life and in their own private lives, outside the traditional areas. We also hope that they will find the process more fun than more traditional economics.

A few of the chapters in this book are based upon articles which have appeared in the economic literature. Since we have not been deluged with critical comments on these articles, we assume that they contain no serious errors. The remainder of the book, which is largely original, has not undergone this test of publication. We have made every effort to eliminate all errors, but it is possible that we have missed some. We hope that professors and, for that matter, students who detect such errors will share them with their classes but will also let us know about them. This will make it possible for us to improve the quality of the book in future editions.

As a last note, the authors must admit frankly that this book is rather controversial. Both of us have been involved in controversy of one sort or another during our entire professional lives, so we, in any event, do not find this at all unusual. We have attempted to present the truth as we see it. But we should not be surprised if some of these chapters lead to very vigorous discussion. We only request that students reading the book attempt fully to understand our arguments. Perhaps, even after having fully understood them, they will prefer some other approach. But, at least they should

---

[1] Judging from their published results, neither do the psychologists.

give us that small benefit of doubt which involves reading carefully enough to understand before making a judgment.

In writing a book of this nature, the authors are, of necessity, indebted to others for ideas and criticisms which have improved the book. Accordingly, we would like to express our gratitude to James Buchanan, Stephen Buckles, Paul Combs, Lila Flory, Allan Freiden, Charles Haulk, Thomas Ireland, Alan Mandelstamm, Michael McPherson, Dennis O'Toole, Lloyd Reynolds, Robert Staaf, and Gilroy Zuckerman, for giving us their views on various portions of the manuscript. In addition, we would like to recognize the expert editorial assistance of Gloria Cline, Eva McClain, and Mary Ann McKenzie and the gracious way they handled these responsibilities. Finally, one of the authors (McKenzie) is indebted to his principles of economics students at Appalachian State University during the 1973–74 academic year. They were used as a test group for most of the material included in this book. It is because of their response that we are convinced the material can work very well in the classroom.

January 1975   RICHARD B. McKENZIE
                                            GORDON TULLOCK

Contents

part three
The Family

part four
Crime and Dishonesty

part one

Introduction

The economist's stock-in-trade—his tools—lies in his ability to and proclivity to think about all questions in terms of *alternatives*. The truth judgment of the moralist, which says that something is either wholly right or wholly wrong, is foreign to him. The win-lose, yes-no discussion of politics is not within his purview. He does not recognize the either-or, the all-or-nothing, situation as his own. His is not the world of the mutually exclusives. Instead, his is the world of adjustment, of coordinated conflict, of mutual gains.

From James M. Buchanan, "Economics and Its Scientific Neighbors," *The Structure of Economic Science: Essays on Methodology,* ed., Sherman Roy Krupp, Englewood Cliffs, N.J.: Prentice-Hall, Inc., 1966, p. 168.

1

The Economic Approach To
Human Behavior

Economics is not what it used to be! This can be said about most disciplines, but it is particularly applicable to economics. At one time students could think of economics as being neatly contained within the sphere of "commercial life," and most courses and books on the subject have traditionally revolved around such topics as money, taxes and tariffs, stocks and bonds, and the operation of the market as it pertains to the production and sale of automobiles and toothpaste. In recent years, however, economists have greatly expanded their field of concern, and, as a result, the boundaries of economics as a discipline are rapidly expanding outward, encroaching on areas of inquiry that have historically been the exclusive domain of other social sciences. The change in direction and scope of the discipline has been so dramatic that the economists who have been involved in bringing about the change are no longer inclined to debate the issue of what is or is not economic in nature. They merely ask "What can economics contribute to our understanding of this or that problem?"

This book reflects this expanded vision. Accordingly, we will introduce you to topics and points of discussion you may never have imagined would be included in an economics book. We will talk about family life, child rearing, dying, sex, crime, politics, and many other topics.[1] We do this not because such topics add a certain flair to the book, but rather because we believe that these are extraordinarily important areas of inquiry and that economic analysis can add much to our understanding of

---

[1] Actually, Adam Smith was concerned with several of these problem areas in *The Wealth of Nations*, which was published in 1776. He would not be surprised that economists are now giving such topics more attention.

them. In addition, we are convinced that you will learn a good deal about economics through their consideration.

In dealing with such topics, we cannot avoid coming to grips with human behavior and making it the focus of our concern. The simple reason is that crimes cannot be committed, children cannot be reared, sex cannot be had, and governments cannot operate without people "behaving" in one respect or another. We argue that before we can ever hope to understand social phenomena we must understand why people behave the way they do. To do this we must have some perception, or model, of how behavior is motivated and organized, from which the revealed actions of people can be interpreted. Economists have such a model, which has been developed and refined since the days of Adam Smith, and it is because we employ this model in our discussion that we consider this to be an economic treatise. All we intend to do here is to extend the application of this model into unconventional areas.

This is not to say, however, that economics can give a complete understanding of these problem areas. Other social scientists have long considered many of the topics included in this book, and their contributions to our understanding of human behavior cannot be overlooked. By viewing these topics through the thinking process of economists, we must be ever mindful that what we are dealing with is *one* particular point of view, which can be complemented by many of the findings in other disciplines.

You may at times have reservations about accepting what we have to say, but this is not necessarily unwelcome to us. We could easily write a book with which the reader would readily agree; however, we imagine that such a book might deal only with trivial issues and very well be a monumental bore. We take the view that at any given time there are many important issues that are to some degree unsettled; we believe that learning not only requires that an individual know the settled issues but also be able to explore those issues over which there may be some disagreement.

You do not need to have a large reservoir of economic knowledge in order to understand what we have to say. We will provide you with the necessary principles on which later discussion will be founded. Furthermore, we do not intend to waste your time with a lot of esoteric theory that will never be used. We understand that you want to make as efficient use of your time as possible, and we intend to cooperate with you. (Remember, this is a book on economics!) The principles that we do develop and the points that we make will at times be very subtle and a little tricky to handle—we cannot escape this. You may be pleasantly surprised, however, at how few in number these principles are and at how useful they will be in thinking about topics that are and are not included in this book. First, we need to lay the foundation—to explain how economists look at their subject and at human behavior.

THE MEANING OF ECONOMICS

For nearly two hundred years economists have periodically struggled with the problem of defining economics, and it is still a live issue. At times the subject has been defined as "what economists do," as that part of human experience that involves money, or as a study of how men attempt to maximize their material well-being. Different people perceive a discipline in different ways; therefore, no one can ever claim to offer readers *the* definition of the subject. All we can hope to accomplish is to lay out our own perception of the subject and in that way suggest how we will proceed.

The approach taken in this book is to define economics as a *mental skill* that incorporates a special view of human behavior characteristic of economists.[2] It is, in short, a thought process, or the manner in which economists approach problems, rather than an easily distinguishable group of problems that sets an economist apart from others. Sociologists and political scientists have dealt with many of the problems considered in this book, but the reader may notice that our approach to these problems is substantially different from theirs. This mental skill or approach has several distinctive characteristics that can be discussed as follows.

ABSTRACTIONS

First and foremost, the economist is prone to think, as are all other scientists, in terms of *abstractions*, not in the sense that the notions he handles are vague or nebulous, but rather in the sense that his first impulse is to reduce reality to the relationships that are important and that bring the inquiry down to manageable proportions. The ideal approach to the study of human and social phenomena would be to treat the world as we confront it. However, the world is terribly complex; at any point in time it encompasses literally billions of bits of information and tens of thousands (if not millions) of relationships. On the other hand, man's mind has a limited capacity to handle such data; it can only consider so much at any one time. It is, therefore, literally impossible for a person to think about the world in its totality and deduce anything meaningful. As a consequence, the scientist must restrict the information he does consider; he

---

[2] In fact, it is the thought process or the mental skill developed below that defines an economist. Indeed, in the context of the discussion that follows, there are no doubt many people who call themselves economists but who do not meet the description offered here, and there are many persons in other disciplines who can, according to our definition, accurately be classified as "economists." However, given the differences in policy conclusions of "economists" and "non-economists," it is apparent that the mental skill developed here is possessed by only a small fraction of the population.

must *abstract* in the sense that he pulls out from the total mass of information a limited number of relationships he thinks are important and he can handle.

This means that the analysis that then follows will lack a certain degree of realism. The analysis is based on abstractions that represent only a small portion of what we might call the "real world." The expectation is, however, that such an approach will increase man's understanding of the "real world" and will increase his ability to predict events in it. Economists heed the principle concisely laid out by Kenneth Boulding: "It is a very fundamental principle indeed that knowledge is always gained by the orderly loss of information; that is, by condensing and abstracting and indexing the great buzzing confusion of information that comes from the world around us into a form which we can appreciate and comprehend."[3] (Take a moment and think about this.) If you have difficulty understanding the world we live in, we suggest that your problem is likely to be that you are attempting to consider too much information, *not too little*.

Since the theory or model that is handled is by its very nature "unreal," the test of its acceptability is not the degree of its "realism" but the extent to which the model is able to accomplish its purpose; that is, to explain events in the real world and to make correct predictions. At times, the reader is likely to think to himself that our analysis is, in one respect or another, unreal or that the model we employ does not represent the "fullness of the human experience." To such a comment we agree, but we must follow with the question, "Are our conclusions not borne out in the real world?"

There is a story of an economics professor who was lecturing on a very esoteric topic before his graduate class. In the middle of the lecture, the professor was interrupted by a student who said, "Sir, I hate to break in, but in the real world. . ." The professor snapped back, "Mr. Waldorf, you must remember that the real world is special case and, therefore, we need not consider it!" Before one gets the impression that we may be taking the same view as this professor, let us emphasize that everything we say, although it may be discussed in terms of models, is directed at our understanding of the real world, and we believe that economics has a very efficient way of doing that.

VALUES

The approach of the economist is *amoral*. Economics is not concerned with what *should be*, or how individuals should behave, but rather with understanding why people behave the way they do. Accordingly, our

---

[3] Kenneth E. Boulding, *The Skills of the Economist*, Cleveland: Howard Allen, Inc., 1958, p. 2.

analysis is devoid (as much as possible) of our own personal values. We treat each topic as something that is to be analyzed and understood, and in order to do that we must avoid the temptation to judge a given form of behavior as contemptuous, immoral, good, or bad. Therefore, in the context of our analysis, the services of a prostitute are treated no differently than the services of a butcher; they are neither good nor bad—they exist and are subject to analysis. Criminal activity is considered in a manner similar to that of legitimate enterprise, and religion is treated as a "good" (for some) that is sought after and procured.

Our reason for taking this tack is that in this book we are not interested in telling people how they should behave or what is good or evil; we are interested in gaining understanding of the behavior of others, *given their values*. Further, we are interested in evaluating the effects of institutional settings on human behavior and in suggesting how institutions may be rearranged to accomplish whatever objective is desired. Note that our intention is to suggest changes in institutions and not in behavior.

Like everyone else, we have our own value systems, and we could easily make recommendations regarding how people's behavior *should be* changed to accomplish what we, as humanists, think is "right." We also recognize that you have your own values and we in no way wish to suggest that you dispense with them. You may violently disagree with prostitution or with political corruption—we do not quarrel with this. All we ask is that you allow us the opportunity to address the question of why such phenomena occur. In the process, you may find a solution to the problem that is more consistent with your values than the solution you now perceive.

THE INDIVIDUAL

The focal point of the study of economics is the *individual*. It is the individual who possess values, makes choices, and if given the freedom, takes actions. All group decisions and actions are thought of in terms of the collective decisions and actions of individuals. Social goals are considered only to the extent that they reflect the collective values or choices of individuals. All too often we hear such expressions as "society disapproves of this or that," "Congress is considering legislation," or "government has made a decision to enforce a given policy." If the expressions are meant to suggest that individuals are involved, we have no qualms; if, on the other hand, the expressions are intended to suggest that these bodies have a behavior of their own that is independent of the behavior of individuals, we must take issue. We ask how can a "group" act? What is group behavior if it is not the behavior of individuals? How can a society, as an independent organism, have a value? Where must the values come from?

Do not misinterpret us; we are interested in understanding group behavior. However, we argue that to do this, we must first understand
the behavior of the individuals that make up the group. We take it as
a given that only individuals can act.

RATIONAL BEHAVIOR

The economist begins his analysis of human behavior with the assertion
that *man acts* and he does so with a purpose. That purpose is to improve
his lot—to change his situation from something less desired to something
better, or as one economist put it:

> Acting man is eager to substitute a more satisfactory state of affairs for
> a less satisfactory. His mind imagines conditions which suit him better,
> and his actions aims at bringing about this desired state. The incentive that
> impels a man to act is always some uneasiness. A man perfectly content
> with the state of his affairs would have no incentive to change things. He
> would have neither wishes nor desires; he would be perfectly happy. He
> would not act; he would simply live free from care.[4]

This is the ultimate foundation of economics as a discipline. Philosophers
and social scientists in general still debate the issue of whether or not
man has "free will." We do not mean to detract from the importance of the
debate. From our point of view, it is not necessary to discuss it. Whether
man makes free decisions or whether he is "programmed" to make the
decisions is irrelevant from the economic standpoint. We only need note
that he does make decisions. Such a position has several implications.
First, in economics the individual is assumed to be "rational" in the sense
that he is able to determine within limits what he wants and will strive
to fulfill as many of his wants as possible. He is able to offset environmental, social, and biological forces that would otherwise determine what he
does. To what extent he is able to accomplish this depends on the resources
at his command and the intensity of his desire to overcome these forces.
Although taken for granted by many, these points need to be made because not all social scientists agree with this perspective. Many will argue,
at least for purposes of their theories, that a factor such as the environment
determines—not influences—man's behavior. The economist, on the other
hand, looks at such factors as constraints within which the individual's
preference can operate.

This position implies that the individual will always choose more of
what he wants rather than less. It also means that he will choose less of
what he does *not* want than more. For example, if the individual desires
beer and pretzels and is presented with two bundles of these goods, both

---

[4] Ludwig von Mises, *Human Action: A Treatise on Economics.* New Haven, Conn.:
Yale University Press, 1949, p. 13.

with the same amount of pretzels and one with more beers, the rational individual (i.e., college student!) will take the bundle with the greater number of beers. If he does not like beer, then that is another matter. In a similar vein, if one bundle contains a greater variety of goods or goods with a higher "quality" than the other bundle, the individual will choose that bundle with the greater variety or higher quality.[5]

If there is some uncertainty surrounding the available bundles, the individual will choose that bundle for which the *expected value* is greatest. People do make mistakes mainly because they have incomplete information, but this does not negate the assumption of rational behavior. We only assume that the individual's motivation is to do that which improves his station in life, not that he always accomplishes this. There are such things as losers.

Economists are often criticized for assuming that man is wholly materialistic—that man wants "material things." The criticism is unjustified. All we have assumed from the start of this section is that an *individual has desires*. These desires may be embodied in material things, such as cocktails and clothes; however, we also fully recognize that men *want* things that are aesthetic, intellectual, and spiritual in nature. Some people do want to read Shakespeare and Keats and to contemplate the idea of beauty. Others want to attend church and worship as they choose. Even a few may want to read this book! We have no quarrel with this (particularly with those who are interested in this book). We accept these as values with which we must deal in our analysis. They are a part of the data we handle. We emphasize, however, that what we have to say regarding "material things" is also applicable to those values that are not material. We may talk in terms of "goods," but what we really mean are those things people value.

COST

Another implication of our basic position is that as far as the individual is concerned, he will never reach Nirvana. He will never obtain a perfect world; and as a result, he must accept second best, which is to maximize his utility through his behavior. This suggests that the individual will undertake to do that for which there is some expected net gain. He will in this sense pursue his own self-interest. This does not mean that the individual will necessarily lack concern for his fellowman. One of the things that he may want is to give to others. Such behavior can yield as much pleasure as anything else, and if so, he will do it. Why do people give gifts, say, at Christmas time? There are many motives that can

---

[5] For all intents and purposes, goods of differing quality can be treated as distinctly different goods.

be separated out; however, we suggest that the overriding reason is that the person involved gets some pleasure (gain), in one form or another, from doing it. Even the Bible admonishes that "it is better to give than to receive," indicating that there are gains to be had for acts of charity. Can you think of anything you or anyone else has done for which you or they did not *expect* some gain? (Remember, you have, no doubt, made a mistake and lost, but this is not involved in the question.)

If the individual is seeking to maximize his utility, then it follows that he must make choices among relevant alternatives. It also follows that in the act of choosing to do one thing, the individual *must* forgo doing or having something else. There is no escaping this. Although often measured in terms of dollars, *the cost of doing or having something is that which is forgone.* Therefore, for every act there is a cost, and it is this cost that will determine whether or not (or how much) something will be done. Cost is the constraint on action. In other words, is there anything such as a "free lunch?" Free TV? Free love or sex? How can these things be had if choices are involved? No money may have changed hands, but, again, *cost is not money.* Money or, more properly, dollars—is just one means of *measuring* cost. To have such things, we have to give up something in the way of time, psychic benefits, and/or resources that may be used for other purposes.

In an attempt to explain social phenomena we will, throughout this book, address the question of the costs and benefits of any given form of behavior. In understanding behavior, cost is a very powerful explanatory factor as we will see. Consider the following problems:

1. Why do the poor tend to ride buses and the rich tend to fly? It may be that there are differences in the educational and experience levels of the two groups, resulting in different behavior patterns. It may also be that being rich, the rich can "afford" such "extravagancies" as airplane tickets. All these factors may explain *part* of the behavior; but we wish to stress that it may be cheaper for the poor to take a bus than to fly and for the rich to fly than take the bus. Both rich and poor pay the same price for their tickets; and, consequently, the difference in cost must lie partly in the difference in the value of the time of the rich and poor. If by rich person we mean someone whose wage rate is very high, it follows that the rich man's time is much more valuable (in terms of wages foregone) than the poor man's time. Since it generally takes longer to take a bus than to fly, the cost of taking the bus, which includes the value of one's time, can be greater to the rich than the cost of flying. The poor man's time may be worth, in terms of what he could have earned, very little. Therefore, the total cost of a bus ride can be quite inexpensive to him. As a case in point, consider Johnny Carson who makes over $1 million per year and a poor man who is unemployed. Determine the *total* cost for each to take the bus and plane from Washington to Chicago. You may think that

Johnny Carson has a lot of "free time" for sunbathing on the beach. Regardless of how you view the situation, it is still true that Carson can sell his time for a considerable sum to many willing buyers. Given your calculations, would you ever expect Carson to take the bus?

2. Why do the British use linen table napkins more often than Americans? In part, the answer may be that the differences in culture have had an effect on the willingness of people to use one form of napkins or another. However, one should also realize that the British have to import virtually all of their paper or pulpwood and that paper is relatively expensive there. Paper napkins are much less costly in the United States. Furthermore, linen napkins require washing and ironing; and since American wages are generally higher in the United States, the cost of using linen napkins is much greater to Americans than to people in Britain. Again, the differences in cost provides an explanation.

3. Why do some people resist cheating on their examinations? It may be that they fear being caught and suspended from school, which means they attribute a cost to cheating. Barring this, they may have a moral code that opposes cheating, at least in this form. If they cheat, they would have to bear the psychic cost of going against what they consider right. This does not mean that all those with a moral code or conscience will not cheat to some degree. (Why?)

4. Why do some men forgo asking women out on dates? They may be shy (or gay) but they may feel that the cost of the date in terms of the money and time expenditures, is too great. They may also be reluctant to ask women out because in doing so they have to incur the *risk cost* of being turned down.

5. Why are people as "courteous" as they are on the highway? They may have a streak of kindness in their hearts, but they may also be fully aware of the very high cost they can incur if their rudeness ends in an accident.

MARGINAL COST

In determining how many units of a *given good* he will consume, the individual must focus on the additional cost of each additional unit. Another name for this cost concept is *marginal cost*. In other words, before the rational individual can proceed to the consumption of the next unit, he must at each step along the way ask how much does that additional unit cost?

If the individual is allowed time to make choices, there is substantial reason to believe that, as a general rule, the marginal cost of successive units he provides for himself or others will rise. At any point where a choice must be made, the individual is likely to have a whole array of opportunities he can choose to forgo to do this one thing. These opportunities are likely to vary in their value to the individual. In making the choice to consume the *first* unit of a good, which opportunity will he give up? The rational man will forgo that opportunity he values least. Since cost, or, as in this case, marginal cost, is the value of that opportunity given up, this means that the cost of the first unit is as low as possible. If the individual then wishes to produce or consume a second unit, he will have to give up that opportunity that is second to the bottom in value. This means that the marginal cost of the second is greater than the first. Given this choice behavior, we should expect that the marginal cost of successive units to rise progressively. Therefore, if we were to describe the relationship between the unit of the good provided and the marginal cost, we would expect to have a curve that is upward sloping to the right as in Figure 1–1. In this graph marginal cost is on the

FIGURE 1–1

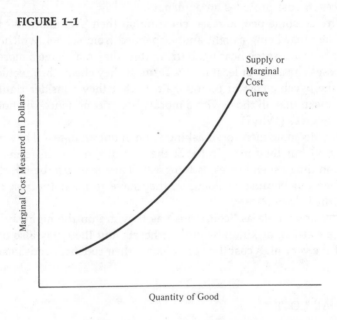

vertical axis and the quantity of the good is on the horizontal axis. We economists refer to such a curve as the *supply curve*. Because of this relationship, we can argue that the higher the benefits (or price) received per unit, the more units of the good that the individual can justify providing.

There are cases in which the marginal cost of providing additional units is constant. More units of the good can be provided by forgoing alternatives that are equal in value. (Can you think of such cases?) In this event the supply curve could be horizontal. See Figure 1–2.

There is no reason to believe that the supply curve will remain stationary over time and under all conditions. Basically, the curve is set where

FIGURE 1-2

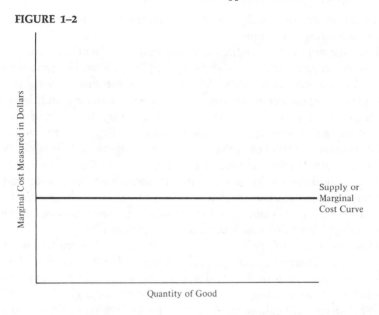

Supply or
Marginal
Cost Curve

Marginal Cost Measured in Dollars

Quantity of Good

it is because of a given cost structure of providing the good. It follows that anything that changes this cost structure will cause the curve to shift in one direction or the other. If the cost (which means the value of alternatives) of providing the good rises, then the curve will shift upward and to the left. If the cost goes down, the curve will move downward and to the right.[6] (Can you think of changes that would change the cost structure?)

DEMAND

The assumption that the rational individual maximizes his utility implies that he will fully allocate his income among those things he wants. When we say income, we mean *full income*, which includes not only what a person can earn on a conventional job and which may be *measured* in terms of dollars, but also what a person can earn by doing things for himself such as cooking meals, outside of his job. How can a person not fully allocate his income? Even when a person saves, the individual is allocating his income and is doing it for a purpose. That purpose may be to acquire a certain degree of security for himself or his family or to buy something

---

[6] For a more detailed discussion of the concept of supply, see any standard textbook on principles of economics. For example, see Armen A. Alchian and William R. Allen, *University Economics: Elements of Inquiry*, 3rd ed., Belmont, California: Wadsworth Publishing Company, Inc., 1972, or Campbell R. McConnell, *Economics: Principles, Problems, and Policies*, 5th ed., New York: McGraw-Hill Book Company, 1972, especially Chapter 4.

he wants in the future. By saving, we might rightfully argue that the person is buying something.

The assumption also implies that the individual will continue to consume a given good until the marginal cost (MC) of the last unit obtained is equal to the marginal utility (MU). (Like the concept of marginal cost, marginal utility (or benefit) is the additional utility on each additional unit of the good.) If this were not the case and the marginal cost of the next unit of the good were less than the marginal utility of it, the individual could increase his level of satisfaction by consuming additional units. He could get more additional satisfaction from the additional unit or units than he would forego by not consuming something else. Note that the marginal cost is the value of that which is foregone. If the marginal cost exceeds the marginal utility, the individual can increase his satisfaction by consuming at least one unit less. (Can you explain why?)

This rule is readily applicable to production and consumption decisions involving, say, carrots or candy; but we suggest that it has a much broader application than may be first realized. If you are a student, what rule do you follow in determining how much you study for a given course? We expect that you will follow the $MC = MU$ rule developed above. You will continue to study until the marginal cost of an additional minute spent studying is equal to the marginal utility gained from studying that unit of time. If the marginal utility of an additional minute is greater than the marginal cost, is not this another way of saying that you would gain more by studying this particular course than doing whatever else you could do with the time? Would you, therefore, not study that additional minute?

In determining the length of her skirt, what rule does a woman follow? Again, we argue that she will shorten the skirt until the marginal utility of taking it up one additional inch is equal to the additional cost. (What are the costs and benefits of shortening the skirt?) For different people in the same situation and for the same people in different situations, the costs and benefits of a skirt's length are different. Therefore, we would anticipate a variety of skirt lengths.

Consider a person—yourself, if you like—who is preparing to eat dinner. What rule does he use in determining how many beans he will dish onto this plate? By now, you should have it; he will add beans to his plate until the marginal cost of the additional bean is equal to the marginal utility.

No individual is really able to act in as precise a manner as the above discussion may imply. He may not have the capacity to do so, and the benefits to be gained from such precision may not be worthwhile. (Explain.) Actually, we are interested only in making the point that the individual will approximate this kind of behavior.

When considering more than one good, say, two goods such as beer and pretzels, the utility maximizing condition of $MC = MU$ translates into the following condition:

$$MU_b/P_b = MU_p/P_p$$

where

MU_b = marginal utility of beer
MU_p = marginal utility of pretzels
P_b = price of beer
P_p = price of pretzels

If this is not the case and MU_b/P_b is greater than MU_p/P_b, then we can show that the person will not be maximizing his utility. No one really knows what a "util" of satisfaction is, but for purposes of illustration, let us assume that utils exist and that the additional satisfaction acquired from the last unit of beer (MU_b) is 30 utils, the additional satisfaction of the last unit of pretzels (MU_p) consumed is 10 utils, and that the price of both beer and pretzels is $1. It follows that

$$MU_b/P_b > MU_p/P_p \qquad (30/\$1 > 10/\$1)$$

The individual can change his consumption behavior, consume one less unit of pretzels and use the $1 to consume one additional unit of beer. He would give up 10 utils of satisfaction in the consumption of pretzels, but he would gain 30 utils of satisfaction in beer. He would be better off, and he would continue to reorganize his purchases until the equality set forth above is met. (You may find this a little tricky. Do not hesitate re-reading what you have just finished. It is imperative that you understand what has been said above before going ahead to the next point.)

Now, let us suppose that the individual has fully maximized his satisfaction and that $MU_b/P_b = MU_p/P_p$. Further, suppose that MU of beer and of pretzels is 20 utils and that the price of beer falls to, say, $.50 and the price of pretzels remains at $1. This means that the individual can get two units of beer (40 utils) for the price of one unit of pretzels; he can gain utility by switching to beer. Notice what we have said: *if the price of beer goes down, the rational individual will buy more beer.* This all falls out of our general assumption that the individual is simply out to maximize his utility.

This inverse relationship between price and quantity is extremely important in economic theory and in the analysis of this book. It is so important that economists refer to it as the "law of demand." It is important because it adds predictive content to economic analysis. We can say with a great deal of confidence that if the price of a good or service falls, *ceteris paribus*, people will buy more of it. It is, perhaps, the strongest predictive statement a social scientist can make with regard to human behavior.[7] The law of demand can be graphically depicted by a downward sloping curve as in Figure 1–3.

Courses in economics generally deal with the law of demand in the context of conventional goods and services such as peanut butter, detergent, and meals at a restaurant. Although we agree with such application, we wish to stress that the law has a much broader application. In fact, we go so far as to assert that the law of demand applies to anything which people value and the procurement of which is revealed in human behavior.

FIGURE 1–3

Consequently, we argue that the law of demand is readily applicable to sex, honesty, dates, highway speeding, babies, and life itself! We predict that if the price of any one of these things goes up, the quantity demanded will diminish and vice versa.

We will spend much of our time in this book discussing how the law of demand applies to areas such as these; for purposes of illustration at this point, let us consider the demand for going to church. Many people do place a value on going to church, and as strange as it may seem there is a price to church attendance. The church may not have a box office outside its doors selling tickets, but people have to pay the price of their

---

[7] The relationship is held with such complete confidence that one prominent economist has reportedly argued that if an empirical study ever reveals that people buy more when the price is increased, there must be something wrong with the empirical investigation. Other economists, taking a more moderate view, may recognize possible exceptions to the rule, but argue that they are extremely few.

time and they do understand that they are expected to contribute something to the operations of the church. (How many well-established people in the community would feel comfortable taking their families to church week after week without contributing anything to the church?) Through stewardship sermons and visitations, the church does apply pressure, as mild as it might be, to get people to contribute. To that extent they extract a price. Suppose the minister and the board of elders decide to raise significantly their demands on the congregation. What do you think will happen to the church's membership, holding all other things constant? The membership may be on the rise for a number of reasons. What we maintain is that because of the greater price, the membership will rise by less than otherwise. In that sense the "price" increase reduces the membership. This does not necessarily mean that people would be less religious; it may only mean that some will react to the price change and make use of other ways of expressing and reinforcing their beliefs.

Suppose we return to the days when men were expected to be the ones who asked women out on dates. (In recent years, this social institution has broken down to a significant degree.) Given all the attributes of a given group of women, men placed, as they do now, some value on having dates with them. They in other words had a demand for dates. (In the event that you are concerned with the approach we are taking, we could easily reverse the example and talk about women's demand for dates. We only intend to use this situation as an example. We do not wish to judge it as being good or bad.)

Clearly, the utility maximizing men will date women, if they can get the dates, until the marginal utility of the last date during some specified period of time is equal to the marginal cost of the date. There is a price for dating. For the man, if they are expected to bear the expense, it is equal to the money spent on transportation, the entertainment, and refreshment plus the value of the individual's time. (There is also a price to the woman.) Suppose that during this epoch when men were expected to pay for dates, a group of women collude; they get together and decide that the humdrum dates of yesterday are no longer up to their standards. They decide to collectively require the men to spend more on them. They, in effect, agree to raise the price of dates. If such a collusive arrangement were to stick, what do you think would have happened to the number of invitations issued to this group of women? No doubt it would fall. It may fall because the men would then have an incentive to substitute other women for the women that were taking part in the cartel. Additionally, the increase in price of dates can induce several men to consume other goods such as watching Saturday night television or having a cold beer at a local tavern.

(As the number of calls for dates begins to fall off, there would very likely be women who would begin to chisel on the collusive agreement by effectively lowering their demands (i.e., price). Thus, the agreement would tend to break down. Competition, as we will see on a number of occasions, will play a role in determining exactly what demands are made in areas of social interaction.)

Many people value speeding in their cars. If caught speeding they may pay a fine of, say, $50. If they expect to be caught one out of every 100 times that they speed, the price they pay per time speeding averages out to $.50. Given this price, they will find a certain quantity of speeding desirable. Suppose, now, that the fine is raised to $10,000 per speeding conviction. The average price paid per time speeding would then raise to $100. Do you think that the people would speed less as the concept of demand predicts? (Suppose that the probability of being caught is increased. This can be accomplished by putting more patrolmen on the roads. What would be the effect?)

SUPPLY AND DEMAND

Measuring marginal costs and benefits in terms of dollars, we can draw both the demand and supply (i.e., marginal cost) curves on the same graph (see Figure 1–4). In taking this step we have constructed an *abstract* model of human behavior, but one that can be quite revealing and useful in many contexts. We will repeatedly demonstrate this throughout the book. For now, we need only point out that the maximizing individual will choose to produce and consume Q_1 units of this particular good. It does not matter what the good is or where the curves are positioned; the individual will choose that consumption level at the intersection of the two

FIGURE 1–4

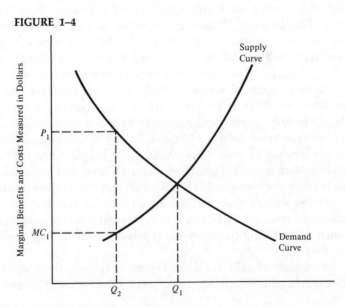

curves. It is at this point that marginal cost is equal to marginal utility. If the individual choses to restrict his consumption to Q_2, note that the marginal benefit, which is indicated by the demand curve and represented by P_1, is greater than the marginal cost, which is indicated by the supply curve and is MC_1. This is true of every unit between Q_2 and Q_1. Therefore, the maximizing individual can raise his utility by consuming them. Beyond Q_1, the reverse is true; the marginal cost is greater than the marginal benefit. (Can you see this?)

Quite often, people find that it is less costly to trade with someone else than to produce the good themselves. To understand a social setting in which there are many producers and consumers trading for a particular good, we need to construct a model involving a *market* supply curve and *market* demand curve. We can derive a market supply curve by adding together what all producers are willing to offer on the market at each possible price. If each individual producer is willing to offer a larger quantity at higher prices, the market supply curve, like the individuals' supply curves, will be upward sloping.[8] To obtain the market demand curve, we can add the amounts demanded by all consumers at each and every price. Since the individuals' demand curves are downward sloping, the same will be true of the market demand curve. The market supply and demand curves are depicted in Figure 1–5. The quantities involved in this graph are much greater than in Figure 1–4.

In a highly competitive market situation, one in which consumers have many sources for obtaining a given good, we will still expect the market to offer that quantity of the good (Q_1), which is at the intersection of the market supply and market demand curves. The simple reason is that if only Q_2 units (which is less than Q_1) are provided on the market, there will be many more units demanded (Q_3) than will be available (Q_2). Also, note that there are consumers who are willing to offer the producers a price that exceeds the marginal cost of producing the additional units. As a result the suppliers can be induced to expand their production from Q_2 to Q_1. Beyond Q_1, the marginal cost of providing an additional unit is greater than what any consumer is willing to pay for it. If one producer refuses to expand production to Q_1, the consumers can, since we are talking about a competitive market, turn to other producers who may be in the market or may be enticed into it. In a monopoly market, one in which there is only one producer of the good, the consumers do not have the option of turning to another producer (i.e., competitor). To that extent, the monopolist has control over the market: he can restrict the number of units provided and thereby, demand a higher price from the consumer.

---

[8] Strictly speaking, the market supply curve is not equal to the horizontal summation of the individuals' supply curves. Nothing is lost for our purposes, however, by leaving this refinement for more advanced treatments of the theory of supply.

By restricting output, the monopolist can reduce his total cost of production and can receive greater revenues. (Why?)

Similarly, suppose that the suppliers offer more than Q_1. The only way they can justify doing that is to charge a price higher than what consumers are willing to pay. Note that at Q_3 the marginal cost of the last unit is

FIGURE 1–5

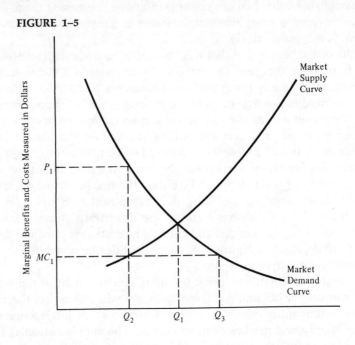

greater than the price the consumers are willing to pay for it. There will, as a result, be more units offered than will be purchased by consumers. Hence, the suppliers will be in a dilemma. They can either cut back on production and lower the price to the point that consumers will buy what is produced, or they can continue to produce more than can be sold at the price necessary to cover the cost of production. The suppliers can also produce the good and sell it at a price less than the cost incurred. Which option do you think the rational producers will choose? They will cut production back to Q_1, of course. To the extent that the competitive market produces where marginal cost equals marginal benefit, which is the optimizing condition of individual's as explained above, economists say that it is "efficient."

Now that we have outlined the basic framework of the economist's model, we can use it to consider *changes* in market conditions (meaning environmental, social, or whatever). We consider such changes in the discussion of most topics in this book.

CONCLUDING COMMENTS

How a person views the world and interprets the information he receives from it depends upon the preconceived model he has of it. The preceding has been an outline of how the economist perceives the real world. For sure, this has been an incomplete description of the economist's way of thinking; there are many more refinements that can be made. (Because of space restrictions a book of this nature forces upon the authors, we have attempted to extend and refine the model until we thought the marginal benefits of an additional point was equal to the marginal cost of making the point.)

Because of this model—because of the concepts of supply and demand—the economist never thinks in terms of absolutes, of whether or not something will be done or left undone, or whether or not a goal will be sought.[9] Everything has a price at which it may be obtained, and adjustments in behavior are made according to the price (benefits) that is charged (received). By concentrating on the general goal of utility maximization (and when talking about the firm, profit maximization) rather than on specific objectives, the economist is continuously seeking out new and non-obvious alternatives and thinking in terms of the substitutability, on the margin, of specific means of reaching the general goal. Years of life are, therefore, viewed as a possible substitute for cigarette smoking; low quality medical service in large quantities is one alternative to high quality service in more limited quantities; ice cream is a possible substitute for good dental care. Because the economist views the individual as fundamentally seeking ways of gaining, whenever a person proposes a solution for any problems, the economist instinctively asks: Are there private interests involved? The economist is trained to separate private interests from the fabric of proposals offered as solutions for social concerns, and he is trained to pull out value judgments from arguments that are put forth as matters of logic. The economist's proclivity to think in this way sets him and his discipline apart from others.

QUESTIONS TO PONDER

1. What role does utility maximization play in economic theory? Why does the economist not assume that the individual strives for something less than maximum utility?

2. What is the decision rule an individual will follow, while driving, in determining how far behind he will follow another car? What will be the impact of a reduction in the speed limit on the distance between cars? Explain.

---

[9] See the quote by James Buchanan at the beginning of this section.

3. Many university libraries across the country provide duplicating facilities and charge a nominal fee. Many lose money by doing this. Why do they charge low prices, knowing that they will go in the hole? What does this suggest about the demand for honesty?

4. If in the so-called "economy size" box of detergent, a consumer can actually get more detergent per penny, why do people buy smaller boxes? What are the costs and benefits of various box sizes?

5. The authors could provide the readers with a more highly complicated and sophisticated economic theory. What are the costs and benefits of doing so? Why do they not do it? How complicated should a theory be?

6. "If a theory can explain everything then it can predict nothing." Do you agree? Explain.

RECOMMENDED READINGS

Kenneth Boulding, *Beyond Economics: Essays on Society, Religion, and Ethics,* Ann Arbor, Mich.: The University of Michigan Press, Ann Arbor Paperbacks, 1970.
————, *Economics as a Science,* New York: McGraw-Hill Book Company, 1970.
Israel M. Kirzner, *The Economic Point of View,* New York: Van Nostrand, 1960.
Ludwig von Mises, *Human Action: A Treatise on Economics,* New Haven, Connecticut: Yale University Press, 1949.
Mancur Olson, Jr., "Economics, Sociology, and the Best of All Possible Worlds," *The Public Interest,* 12 (Summer 1968), 96–118.

2

Anything Worth Doing Is
Not Necessarily Worth
Doing Well

In the previous chapter we stressed the role cost plays in guiding human behavior. In this chapter we offer specific examples of the influence of cost.

ANYTHING WORTH DOING

From early childhood most of us have been taught that "anything worth doing is worth doing well." If we were asked today if we still agree with the statement, many of us would say that we do.[1] It is only natural for a person to prefer a job that has been done well to one that has been done not so well, indeed, such a preference is fully consistent with the basic assumption in economics that more (quality) is preferred to less (quality). It is also easy to see why a person may not like to re-do something that has already been done, particularly if the combined time involved is greater than the time that would have been required to do it right in the first place.

Obviously, people do not behave the way they profess they should. There is probably not a minister around who has not written what he considered at the time to be a poor sermon, and one of the authors recently built a bookcase that was more-or-less thrown together. Housewives (and

---

[1] James Buchanan has suggested that an economist can be distinguished from a non-economist by his reaction to the statement. "Economics and Its Scientific Neighbors," *The Structure of Economic Science: Essays on Methodology*, ed., Sherman Roy Krupp. Englewood Cliffs, N.J.: Prentice-Hall, Inc., 1966, p. 168.

husbands) have cooked dinners they knew in their hearts were seriously deficient in one respect or another. Students regularly choose to work for a grade of a C (or a GPA far less than 4.0) instead of going all out for an A. This is true even though the A is the preferred grade. How many, do you suppose, of the students who are reading this have written a paper that by their own standards fell far short of a "well done" paper? In fact, can you say at this point that you have read the last few pages "well"?

Admittedly, people do some things well, but the point we wish to emphasize is that they frequently do things less than well, not because they do not want to do better, but because of the *additional* cost involved in improving the quality of whatever they are doing. Given the student's ability —which, as a matter of fact, is limited at any point in time—writing a "good" A paper generally requires more effort and time than writing a C paper. If the student spends additional time on the paper, he has less time for doing other things. He has less time to study the subject matter in other courses, in which case he may do less well or even fail; he cannot use the time for physical exercise; he cannot spend the time in bed or out on dates. To reiterate, there is usually an additional cost that must be borne for a higher quality paper, and it is because of this cost that he may rationally choose to turn in a paper that may "just get by." (Even so, the student may still hope for an A. Can you explain why?)

If the cost is not greater for higher quality work, then one must wonder why the job may be done poorly. The student will be able to have a higher quality paper without giving up anything. The problem of the poorly done work may be one of perception; that is, the student may perceive the additional cost to be greater than what it actually is, in which case he should respond appropriately if provided with accurate information. He may, in addition, inaccurately assess the benefits of a better performance.

Quite often one person will admonish another to do a good job. For example, a professor may be distressed at the quality of the papers that he receives, and may honestly feel that if his students are going to write a paper, they should write a good one. He may be even more upset if he finds out that his students spent the last few days doing very little or having a "good time."

The values the professor and students place on different activities obviously differ. The professor may view the paper as being of greater value than the students do; he may view the "other activities" as being of less value. Consequently, he believes it is in the student's best interest to do a better paper. However, since students view the value of the other activities as being higher, they, in effect, view the cost of doing the better paper as being higher. Of course, it is clearly rational for the professor to want the students to turn in better papers, but if he had to bear the cost, he might change his mind.

The same line of argument can be used to explain why the preacher's sermon is of low quality even though he may have the ability to do better.

If he writes a better sermon, he may have to bear the cost of not seeing his parishoners at the hospital or of giving up something else that he considers valuable. The housewife may have to forgo writing letters, discussions with neighbors, or cooking a better meal.

What should be the "quality level" toward which a person should strive? The utility maximizing individual should raise the quality of whatever he does until the marginal benefit received from an additional unit of quality is equal to its marginal cost. Suppose that the marginal benefits for units of quality diminishes as the total quality of the work goes up. Assume also that the marginal cost of additional units increases as the quality level is raised. The diminishing marginal utility assumption is represented by the downward curve (which is equivalent to the demand curve) in Figure 2–1. The upward sloping curve

FIGURE 2–1

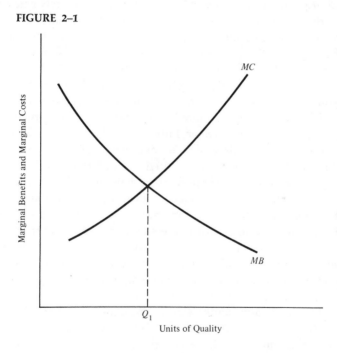

Q_1

Units of Quality

represents the increasing marginal cost. Notice that we have labeled the horizontal axis as "units of quality." (The actual good or service involved can be anything.) The utility maximizing quality level is Q_1. Before Q_1 the marginal utility of an additional unit of quality is greater than the marginal (or additional) cost.[2] By expanding the quality toward Q_1, the

---

[2] Marginal cost can be viewed as the utility foregone in some alternative activity. Therefore, by consuming more quality, the individual can, when $MU > MC$, acquire more utility than he gives up in some other activity.

utility of the individual can rise. If the person extends the quality level beyond Q_1, notice that the marginal cost of doing so will be greater than the marginal utility. The result is that the person's total utility level will be less than it would be at Q_1. An outside observer (such as a teacher) may feel that the quality of the work done by the student, Q_1, may be quite low—and it may even be low by the standards of the individual student— but this does not make his behavior any less rational. In other words, anything worth doing is not necessarily worth doing "well."

WHY THE YOUNG GO TO COLLEGE

College classes are predominantly made up of young adults, between the ages of 18 to 22 years old. A small percentage are in their middle or late 20s, but people who are over 50 constitute an extremely small minority. Why do the young go to college whereas older adults, as a general rule, do not? The list of answers conventionally cited may include (1) the young, having recently graduated from high school, are more accustomed to the routine and peculiar demands of the educational process, (2) the young do not have the family responsibilities that the older people have, (3) the young, as a rule, realize the value of education more than do their elders, and (4) the young are more intellectually alive than their parents.

All of these factors can have an influence in determining the composition of college classes, although our experience suggests the last two reasons are invalid. Although rarely cited, the difference in the cost to the two groups may be equally important in explaining the composition of college classes. The cost of a college education is more than the direct monetary expenditures made by the student at the start of each year or academic session. The total cost is the summation of all that the student must forgo; in addition to university charges, this total may include the loss of income one may experience while in the classroom and studying, the transportation expense associated with going to and from the campus, the additional postal and telephone expenditures one must make to stay in contact with friends and family, the cost of books and materials, and the cost of "fitting in" culturally with the college community.

Although there may be differences, the essential one to the young and old is the opportunity cost of one's time. This, of course, will mean that the total costs will differ. Suppose, for example, that total university charges are $2,000 (approximately the average for all public universities in the country in 1974) and that all costs other than opportunity cost of time are $500 per year. (We realize that the older people *may* be inclined to spend less on such things as "fitting in.") A younger person, just out of high school, can over the course of the following four years probably earn at the best job that he can get about $20,000 for an average of $5,000 per year. On the other hand, the man who is 45 years old can conceivably earn twice as much, $40,000, or even more. This means that the total cost to the young adult, totals about $30,000 for four years of college education; the cost to the older person is approximately $50,000.

Four Years	Young Adult	Middle-aged Adult
University Charges	$ 8,000	$ 8,000
Opportunity Cost	20,000	40,000
Other Costs	2,000	2,000
Total Costs	$30,000	$50,000

Even if we assume that the two groups have the same values and are equal in every respect with regard to college education, we would expect a larger quantity of education to be demanded by the young than by the old. For example—and only as an example—assume that the demand for college by the young is exactly equal to the demand of the old, as depicted in Figure 2–2A and 2B. Since the price of a college education to the older

FIGURE 2–2

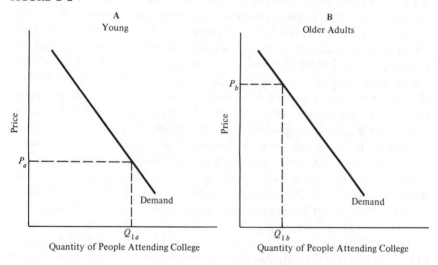

A
Young

B
Older Adults

Quantity of People Attending College

Quantity of People Attending College

person (P_b) is far greater than the price paid by the young (P_a), we would expect that the quantity of education demanded by the young would be greater. In the example of Figure 2–2, the quantity of education demanded by the young would be Q_{1a}, which is greater than the quantity demanded by the old, Q_{1b}.

In addition, the young have a much longer period of time to reap the benefits of a college education. The 45 year old man or woman has only 20 years left in his or her working life, whereas the 22 year old college graduate has 43 years until retirement. Therefore, the investment expenditure by the young is likely to be much more profitable. Finally, we should note that the total cost to the young can be much less than we calculated since their parents may foot the university bills. This is less likely to be the case of the much older persons.

WHY PEOPLE WALK ON THE GRASS

Walking on the grass may not appear to have anything to do with economics or to be sufficiently important to warrant discussion. We suggest, on the contrary, that the decision to walk on the grass, for example, on the campus mall, is an aspect of human behavior and, therefore, economics. A study of the decision to walk on the grass can be revealing about the causes of pollution and human action in general.

Why do people walk on the grass? Why do people who may dislike to see paths form on campus or courthouse lawns walk in places where paths exist or are likely to exist? To answer these questions, one must begin by recognizing that there are benefits to walking on the grass. It can be a short-cut across campus and save time; the walk may also be personally gratifying, particularly in the spring and without shoes. The individual, who may strongly favor campus beautification must, in making the decision to walk on the grass, weigh the expected benefits against the expected costs. Before stepping onto the grass he must quickly reflect on the benefits and then calculate the costs involved. He may calculate that if he walks on the grass, he will be responsible for killing several blades of grass, but it is very unlikely that anyone will be able to notice, even if he regularly walked in the same places. Even if the individual dislikes paths on lawns, he may reasonably expect the cost of his walk to approximate zero, since his individual walk does not materially affect, under normal circumstances, the environment. Consequently, the calculated benefits exceed the costs, so he walks—and he does it rationally![3]

The problem is that everyone, independently and making similar calculations, may do the same thing. The result is that a path forms, an eyesore is created. This does not mean that it is rational for any one individual *not* to walk even after the path has formed. Since he cannot control the walking of everyone else and his walking cannot be detected by anyone, the rational choice is to take the benefits of cutting across the lawn. If the path is there, he can reason that if he does not walk, no one will be able to tell that he did not—that is, the nature of the path will not be affected. So, he walks and everyone else walks, and the path remains and continues to deepen and, possibly, spread. This in miniature illustrates evolvement of a form of pollution.

---

[3] Before the reader becomes unduly disturbed by this statement, he should check the economic meaning of "rational action" in Chapter 1.

Following this line of argument, one can deduce that if a *private* cost is incurred by the individual then the logical thing to do may be to take the sidewalk or another route. If the lawn or path is prone to become a quagmire when it rains, then private costs *are* imposed for walking. The individual will have to clean his shoes and since time is involved in doing that, there is a cost. The cost for some may still not be as great as the benefits, but significantly when such conditions exist, there is less walking on the lawns than on sunshiny days. The connection between walking on lawns and pollution of other forms should be clear. A person or firm may litter because he calculates that there are certain benefits to getting rid of a piece of paper. He may reason that one piece of paper by itself will not significantly affect the environment or materially affect anyone's sensibilities. Therefore, he discards the paper. The problem, again, is that if everyone follows suit, an environmental problem will develop. If the individual can control the behavior of all others, he may not pollute himself, but given his inability to control others, polluting may be rational. Also, cleaning up can be irrational; one may reason he cannot do enough to affect the general environment, particularly since others will be littering as he cleans up. (In fact, his attempts to clean up can reduce the cost of polluting to everyone else—the environment is less affected—and, therefore, one might anticipate, without an intervening change in people's values, more littering by some.) As a result he does not receive the full benefits of his actions and to that degree is less likely to clean up.

The analysis can be extended to conversations at a crowded cocktail party. If the reader has ever been at such a gathering, he probably remembers that often the sound level starts off at a low level and then increases, even though the number of people in the room has not changed. The reason for the crescendo in conversation volume is that at the start people may be able to understand one another at a low volume. However, as everyone else begins to talk, the general volume begins to rise; this means that the volume that any one individual must use in order to be understood by the person standing next to him must be increased. Because he and everyone else increases his volume, talking louder can be rational. The result may be (as it has time and time again) that all persons in the room end up virtually shouting at one another. *If* each were to lower his own individual volume then all could have a more pleasant conversation. But, the question is whether or not it is rational for any one individual to lower *his* volume. The answer is no; he could not be heard, because he cannot control the volume of the others in the room. In addition, he may not significantly affect the general volume level. Therefore, no one changes his volume.[4]

---

[4] One qualification: as the volume goes up, several may decide to leave the room, keeping the volume from going as high as it otherwise would. Additionally, the higher general volume can make the party more tiring and can cause it to end more

These problem areas point to the usefulness of some form of collective action, the purpose of which may be to impose private costs on the actions of individuals so that they may be expected to act in the general interest (which can also be in their own interest). In the case of walking on the grass, the "government" can plant hedges or thorny bushes along the edges of the sidewalks. If people want to walk on the grass, they will have to incur the cost of jumping the bushes or of runs in stockings. In the case of industrial pollution, taxes or fines for polluting can be imposed. Since people's demands for these activities slope downward, the quantity demanded will be reduced.

THE DILEMMA OF ALTERNATE WAYS OF CONSERVATION OF ENERGY

Most people are concerned about the developing shortage of energy. Many are attempting to conserve energy by cutting down their thermostats a few degrees and, perhaps, driving a little slower. The effects of such voluntary actions is, however, not expected to be sufficiently great to eliminate the shortage. Drastic government action is expected by many to be necessary to remedy fully the situation. Why will people who are concerned about the energy crisis leave their lights burning and continue to zip along the highways at high speeds? Is it solely because people do not care (as many do not)?

Imagine, for the moment, someone sitting in an overstuffed chair, watching television. He knows that a light has been left on in an adjoining room, but he does not get up and turn it off.[5] Leaving the light on for, say, an additional half hour until he happens to walk by the room will increase his electric bill, but we must also recognize that getting up requires effort and diminishes the entertainment value of the television program. In other terms, cutting the light off is costly. Moreover, given relatively low rates on the use of electric power, the television watcher may calculate that the cost of turning the light off is greater than the increase in his electric bill. If he is concerned about the total community consumption of fuel through the generation of electric power, he may still reasonably assume that his decision to leave the light on, or even leave every light in his house on, will not appreciably affect the total amount of fuel consumed by the power company. The problem, as in previous examples, is that many people, viewing the situation only in individualistic terms, may decide to leave

---

quickly for some. The host could conceivably get up and ask that everyone quiet down; the immediate effect can be a sharp reduction in volume. This is, however, likely to be a short interlude before the sound increases.

[5] We recognize that there are times when a person will get up and turn the light off; our purpose here, however, is to explain why at times he may not.

their lights on, in which case more fuel will be consumed by the generating facilities. The reader should understand that we do not necessarily condone this behavior; we are merely attempting to explore the logic of what can be considered a deplorable circumstance. If you question the legitimacy of this explanation, suppose then that the television watcher knew that leaving lights on for the duration of the program would cost him $50. Would you expect him to get up and turn it off?

When the shortage of gasoline began emerging in the spring and summer of 1973, Exxon and other petroleum companies advertised a saving in gas consumption if a driver were to drive at 50 miles per hour instead of 70. The Exxon commercial demonstrated that a car going 70 mph will use a 20 gallon tank in 253 miles; if the car went 50, the 253 miles could be covered with four gallons of gas to spare. Should Exxon or anyone else have expected the ad to make a significant dent in total gasoline consumption? Not really, because it would take the driver approximately one and a half hours longer to travel the 253 miles at 50 than it would at 70. The value of the gasoline saving is, at $.50 per gallon, approximately $2.00. This means that the driver would have had to value his time at approximately $1.33 per hour, or less than the minimum wage, to justify (on purely economic grounds) slowing down. If he has the public interest at heart, he may slow down, but he will have done so without materially affecting the long-run fuel problem of the United States. It is also very difficult for anyone to slow down in the public interest while others including public officials, are cruising along at higher speeds.

If the price of gasoline were to rise to, say, $2.00 per gallon, several effects can be predicted. First, and as a generality, a greater private cost will be incurred for energy consumption. Second, the saving from going 50 miles per hour (instead of 70) would be $8.00 (four gallons times $2.00). This means that anyone who would then value his time at less than $5.32 per hour would find going slower economical; economists would expect more to do so. (Why?) Third, economists would also expect that, since the demand curve for travel is downward sloping, people will drive fewer miles; they will buy more smaller cars, use more car pools, and make greater use of mass transit. All this will further reduce the amount of energy consumed. Fourth, since people will be going slower and the highway fatality rate declines with lower speed, there should be fewer deaths on the highways. The dollar value of damage per wreck should also fall, causing a reduction in insurance rates. Not having made a detailed study of the possible effects, we cannot say *how great* the effects will be, but we can predict with confidence the favorable direction of the effects and that the "shortage" will be eliminated with some increase in price. (Why? What will be the effects of an increase in the price of heating oil?)

No one likes to see the prices of things he buys increase. The problem is that when the quantity demanded exceeds the quantity supplied, how is the shortage to be eliminated? How is the available quantity of gasoline and fuel oil going to be distributed among the potential buyers? The pricing system has drawbacks. The real income of many people is going to be reduced; most will be unable to buy as much. The question is not, however, whether or not the pricing system is perfect for allocating supplies, but rather how its advantages and disadvantages stack up against alternative systems.

The pricing system may not be "fair," but is a formal coupon-type rationing system "fairer," by your own definition? Do we distribute the coupons according to the number of cars that a person has? If we do, more wealthy people who tend to have more cars, will be getting disproportionate shares of the gasoline. Do we give the people who live two miles from work more than the people who live 20 miles away? Do we give the family with six children and one car less gasoline than the person with two children and two cars? Do salesmen get more gasoline than college students who commute to and from school? Can we really say that being able to go to work for a middle aged man is "more important," in some ultimate sense, than an afternoon ride for an elderly couple who may have no other principal form of entertainment? These questions have no easy answers but, if the pricing system is not employed, these questions and many, many others like them must be addressed. If we do adopt a non-market rationing system, then it follows that the price of the good will be kept lower than otherwise but that there will still be people who are willing to violate the rules and sell the gas on the black market at a higher price. Control of black markets are likely to be necessary.

If an economist ever suggests that the price should be raised to reduce the quantity demanded, he will normally be confronted by the argument that the rich will be able to continue to buy all the gas that they need, but the poor will not; and the poor "need" the gasoline to go to work. We are inclined to believe that both rich and poor will cut back on their gasoline consumption. In addition, it is not at all certain that the poor will, under a coupon system, end up with the gasoline.[6] If the price of gasoline goes to $2.00 per gallon and the poor are unwilling to buy at that price, will they not be willing to sell their coupons at that price? If they do, they will have more money, but they will not have the gasoline which, as suggested, they "need."

---

[6] If the government is interested in setting up a coupon system to minimize people's disutility under a bad situation, then they should permit people to sell their coupons. By the fact that people freely choose to buy or sell coupons, we must conclude that they are better off by doing so. Otherwise, we must wonder why they make the trade. If coupons are sold, it means that the price of gasoline will in effect rise.

RECKLESS DRIVING

There are many drivers on streets and highways who are, for all practical purposes, numbskulls. They do not know how to drive, are drunk when they do, or generally do not think about what they are doing when behind the wheel. Others take out all of their pent-up aggressions when driving their cars.

We can attribute a large percentage of the deaths that occur each year from automobile accidents to these types of drivers. There are, on the other hand, many conscientious people who are careful and continually think about the consequences of their driving behavior. They are the ones who purposefully stay on their side of the road, observe speed limits, do not tailgate, or, in general, do other things which may be deemed reckless because they calculate the costs of having an accident to themselves and the other people in the car. They are "careful" because the costs of being less careful are greater than the benefits that can be achieved.

Actually, the cost of driving recklessly is not *necessarily* equal to the cost incurred from any given accident, but, rather, is equal to the cost of the accident discounted by the probability of having the accident. Granted, the probability of having an accident under such conditions, is very close to one; however, under other conditions, for example, driving 85 miles an hour on a freeway, the probability of having an accident can be far removed from unity. The calculated costs of reckless driving is correspondingly lower. The reader should think in terms of the probability of having an accident as well as the cost of the accident if it occurs. When discussing reckless driving, too often people tend to think only in terms of the cost of the accident if it occurs; consequently, they tend to overestimate the cost and fail to understand why so many people drive recklessly.

Those people who weigh the costs and benefits of driving "recklessly" should respond in a predictable way to changes in the expected costs and benefits. If the benefits of going faster, making U-turns in the middle of the street, and driving on the wrong side of the road were to increase, then obviously driving of this nature from drivers as a group would increase. For example, if a child were to have a serious head injury requiring immediate medical attention, would you not expect the parents to break speed limits, ignore stop signs, and generally take more chances, attempting to get the child to the emergency room, than they otherwise would? This is a clear example of an increase in benefits from reckless driving; we suggest that similar responses will occur even if the change in the benefits were less dramatic. Take, for example, a person who may be late for an important meeting. How would he behave, relatively speaking, behind the wheel? At least, would you not expect drivers as a group to respond in the way an economist would predict?

In a similar manner, we would expect people to respond to changes in the expected costs of reckless driving. There should be less reckless driving when the expected cost of doing so goes up and more when the cost goes down. If these statements are reasonable, the reader should agree that *one* reason for the large volume of accidents on highways is that the expected cost to the drivers is relatively low.[7] This is simply another application of the law of demand.

Admittedly, not everyone will respond to changes in cost—for example, those who do not think about what they are doing and those who do not consider cost as a factor—but so long as there are people who do consider cost as a factor, the downward sloping demand curve should hold. The number of people who think or act randomly will determine the position of the demand curve and not the slope. To illustrate this basic point, would the reader not agree that students have more collisions in the hallways of their classroom buildings than they do on the streets when they are in their cars? It appears clear to us that, although students are involved in large numbers of automobile accidents, the number of "hallway accidents" is far greater. One explanation for the difference in the accident rate is possibly that bumping in the halls does not cost the individual very much; whereas, automobile collisions can be considerably more costly. If the student knew that if he bumped into someone in the hall he would be fined $50, would you expect the same amount or less bumping? Would your answer not apply to people's behavior in traffic?

Finally, there is an ironic implication of our argument. Safety devices such as seat belts, padded dashes, and air bags reduce considerably the probability of death and severity of injury in the event of an accident. The government, by making such equipment mandatory, is in effect reducing the expected total cost of an accident to those in the car and, thereby, of reckless driving. (The total cost of an accident is the damage done to the car plus the personal injury.)

Therefore, required seat belts and other similar internal safety devices should, contrary to the good intentions of those who supported the legislation, increase the amount of reckless driving. The effect may not be very great (just how great it is will depend upon the elasticity of demand), *but it should still be positive.* This means that there will be a tendency for people who have such devices to inflict a greater cost on the drivers around them, which was not, undoubtedly, what the Congress had in mind when it passed the legislation.[8]

---

[7] We recognize that in an absolute sense the cost of an accident may be quite high. The cost that the driver will operate on, however, is the cost of the accident discounted by the probability of having the accident. Besides, we are merely suggesting in different words that if the costs were even higher, the quantity of reckless driving would be lower.

[8] We have suggested that seat belts will reduce the private cost incurred from

PROBLEMS

1. Is life priceless? What evidence can you offer to support your contention?

2. In the fall and winter of 1973, gasoline production was falling behind consumption partially because of the Arab embargo of oil shipments to the U.S. State governments were beginning to order cutbacks in speed limits for cars to 50 miles per hour. CBS News reported (November 28, 1973) that the cutback in speed could result in approximately 14,000 fewer deaths on the highways. Given this benefit, why would the states not reduce the speed limits under more normal circumstances?

3. By the end of 1970, the federal government had spent more than $700 million on the development of the SST (supersonic transport). The reader may know that Congress in December 1970 cut off funds for the project; however, should the Congress have considered the $700 million they had already spent in their decision on whether or not the project should at that point be completed?

4. In most democratic organizations such as student governments and faculty senates, motions will pass and candidates will be elected if they secure a simple majority of all votes. Provide an economic explanation as to why such organizations would generally be opposed to the adoption of a rule that required unanimous consent.

5. Explain why there is congestion on highways.

---

driving recklessly and increase the social cost, that is, the cost of one's own reckless driving borne by others. If the government is interested in reducing the *social cost* from automobile travel, then it should develop requirements for proper headlights and brakes and annual safety inspections. Internally, the car can be made less safe, thereby increasing the private cost of an accident to the driver. As an extreme example, suppose the driver had a dagger mounted on the steering column and pointed at his chest. Would he not be inclined to drive more safely? We are not proposing that such devices be required; we are merely attempting to make general points concerning how people may respond as a result of automobiles which are made less safe.

3

Basic Needs and Human Behavior: A Digression Into Psychology

A. H. Maslow, a psychologist, argued that basic human needs can be specified with reasonable clarity and can be ranked according to their importance in providing motivation and influencing behavior.[1] Embedded in Maslow's hierarchy of needs is a theory of human behavior that is to some degree foreign to the economist's way of thinking. In this section, Maslow's system will be outlined so that we may be able to use it for comparative purposes. This, admittedly, is a digression of sorts, but we think it is an important one because we have a suspicion that Maslow's system (at least, in terms of its basic structure) is not terribly dissimilar from the views of many laymen in economics.

Maslow's need hierarchy is pictured in Figure 3–1. The importance of the needs, in terms of how powerful or demanding they are in affecting human behavior, ascends as one moves downward through the pyramid; that is, the most fundamental or prepotent needs, which are physiological in nature, are on the bottom. This category of needs includes on one level all attempts of the body to maintain certain chemical balances (such as water, oxygen, hydrogen-ion levels) within the body. On a higher level, the physiological needs include the individual's desires for food, sex, sleep, sensory pleasures, and sheer activity (meaning the need to be busy).

The need for safety, which is next in prepotence, may include the desires of the individual for security, order, protection, and family stabil-

---

[1] A. H. Maslow, *Motivation and Personality*, New York: Harper and Row, 1954. See primarily Chapter 5.

FIGURE 3–1
Maslow's Hierarchy of Needs

ity. The next category, belongingness and love needs, may include among other things the desire for companionship, acceptance, and affection. Maslow lists under the heading of esteem needs the individual's desire for achievement, adequacy, reputation, dominance, recognition, attention, appreciation, and importance. He argues that the need for self-actualization "refers to man's desire for self-fulfillment, namely, to the tendency for him to become actualized in what he is potentially. This tendency might be phrased as the desire to become more and more what one is, to become everything that one is capable of becoming."[2]

Maslow stresses that such an individual may indicate he is striving after one need when in fact he is pursuing something else. For example, the individual may say that he is hungry because by doing so and going out to dinner, he can acquire companionship, affection, and attention. This may be the case because the individual may find it useful to deceive another person or because he does not *consciously* know what his true motivation is. In addition, Maslow argues that certain preconditions, such as the freedom to express oneself, are necessary before basic needs can be satisfied. Consequently, the individual can be motivated to establish the necessary preconditions; he may not appear to be attempting to satisfy basic needs.

Maslow does not hold rigidly to the ordering of needs as indicated in Figure 3–1. He specifies this particular ranking because it appears to him to be descriptive of the people with whom he has associated and because it appears to be a reasonably good generality concerning human motivation. Because of cultural or environmental factors or because, for example, love has been denied in the past, some people may place more emphasis on esteem needs than on the need for love. He also suggests that "There are other apparently innately creative people in whom the drive to creativeness seems to be more important than any other counterdeterminant. Their

2 Maslow, *Motivation*, pp. 90–92.

creativeness might appear not as self-actualization released by basic satisfaction, but in spite of the lack of basic satisfaction."[3]

Although he qualifies his argument, the core proposition in Maslow's theory of human behavior is the argument that a person will first satisfy his most basic needs (i.e., physiological needs) before he attempts to satisfy needs of higher order. He writes:

> If all the needs are unsatisfied, the organism is then dominated by the physiological needs, all other needs may become simply nonexistent or be pushed into the background. It is then fair to characterize the whole organism by saying simply it is hungry, for consciousness is almost completely preempted by hunger. All capacities are put into the service of hunger-satisfaction, and the organization of these capacities is almost entirely determined by the one purpose of satisfying hunger. . . . Capacities that are not useful for this purpose lie dormant, or are pushed into the background.[4]

If the most basic needs are satisfied, "At once other (and higher) needs emerge and these, rather than physiological hungers, dominate the organism. And when these in turn are satisfied, again new (and still higher) needs emerge, and so on."[5] One gets the impression from reading Maslow that the individual will not attempt to satisfy his second most prepotent needs until the most prepotent needs are (almost) fully satisfied; he will not move to the third tier in the hierarchy until the needs at the second tier are (almost) fully satisfied.[6] Apparently, the individual will not attempt to effect any self-actualization until he has moved through all former tiers. If any tier in the hierarchy is skipped entirely, it is because of insurmountable environmental or physiological barriers.[7]

Maslow's approach to human motivation and behavior resembles the approach of economists in several respects. First, they are similar because the essence of both theories is an assumption that the individual is able to rank all of his wants (or needs) according to their importance to him. In the Maslow system, anything that is not directly a basic need is ranked according to how close it is to a basic need; and other needs beyond the five categories mentioned, such as the need to know and/or understand

---

[3] Maslow, *Motivation*, p. 98.

[4] Maslow, *Motivation*, p. 92.

[5] Maslow, *Motivation*, p. 83.

[6] We use the terms "are (almost) fully satisfied" because of such statements as "If both the physiological and safety needs are fairly well gratified, there will emerge the love and affection and belongingness needs" (Maslow, *Motivation*, p. 89). Maslow never explains what will keep the individual from fully satisfying any given need level before moving on to a higher tier.

[7] Admittedly, this is an interpretation of Maslow and may be an unfair statement of what his true position is; however, he does tend to write in black or white terms— either the barriers are there or they are not.

and the need for esthetic quality, can be handled by adding additional tiers.[8] As pointed out in Chapter 1, the economist simply starts with an assumption that the individual knows what he wants and is able to rank all possible goods and services that are able to satisfy his wants.

The two systems are dissimilar, however, when it comes to the specification of the ranking. Maslow is willing to argue that in general the basic needs and their ranking can also be identified; that is, he can say what the individual's needs are and is willing to venture a statement about their relative importance. On the other hand, an economist would generally take the position that the relative importance of the needs varies so much from person to person that a hierarchy of needs, although insightful for some limited purposes, does not move us very far in our understanding of human behavior. The economist may specify whether a good or service may add to or subtract from the individual's utility and will argue that more of something that gives positive utility is preferred to less; but, he would be unwilling to try to say exactly where the good (or need) may lie on some relative scale. We must presume that the specificity Maslow seeks is to him a useful, if not necessary, basis for predicting human behavior. Economists believe that they can say a great deal about human behavior without actually specifying the relative importance of the things people want. We certainly admit that the economist's inability to specify the relative importance of needs is a limitation to economic theory. (Given some of the areas into which economists are now delving, more and more economists are beginning to wish that they could somehow specify the ordering of people's preferences.)

Both systems are similar to the extent that they view the individual as consuming those things that give him the greatest satisfaction. Even in the Maslow system, which lacks a direct statement to the effect, there is the implicit assumption that the individual is a utility maximizer. Maslow also assumes diminishing marginal utility as more of the need is consumed; if this is not the case, it is difficult to understand how the individual can become fully or almost fully satisfied at any need level.

The systems are different because of their views of the constraints that operate on the ability of the individual to maximize his utility. The constraints in the Maslow hierarchy include environmental and cultural factors and the individual's character, or his beliefs about what is right and wrong. There is no mention of the individual's productive ability or income (unless these are implied in the environmental or cultural constraints) or of the costs of the means by which his basic needs can be fulfilled. These considerations are basic constraints in the economist's view of human

---

[8] Maslow, in his 1954 book, is less certain about the relative positions of the need to know and the need for esthetic quality because of the limited research that had been done on the subject at the time he wrote the book.

behavior. By not considering cost, Maslow appears to assume that either there is no cost to need gratification and/or (in spite of an implicit assumption concerning diminishing marginal utility) the demand curve for any need is vertical (or perfectly inelastic). This means that the quantity of the need fulfilled is unaffected by the cost. An implied assumption of the vertical demand curve is that the basic needs are independent of one another. They are not substitutes; for example, a unit of an esteem need fulfilled does not appear in the Maslow system to be able to take the place of even a small fraction of a unit of physiological need.

Maslow recognizes that most people only partially fulfill their needs at each level. He writes:

> So far, our theoretical discussion may have given the impression that these five sets of needs are somehow in such terms as the following: If one need is satisfied, then another emerges. This statement might give the false impression that a need must be satisfied 100 percent before the next need emerges. In actual fact, most members of our society who are normal are partially satisfied in all their basic needs and partially unsatisfied in all their basic needs at the same time. A more realistic description of the hierarchy would be in terms of decreasing percentages of satisfaction as we go up the hierarchy of prepotency. For instance, . . . it is as if the average citizen is satisfied 85 percent in his physiological needs, 70 percent in his safety needs, 50 percent in his love needs, 40 percent in his self-esteem needs, and 10 percent in his self-actualization needs.[9]

Maslow does not, however, explain why this will be the case, nor does he provide an explanation as to why a person will not fully satisfy the higher needs before he moves to the next tier.

The economist might concede for purposes of argument, as we do, that the demand for a physiological need is greater (and more inelastic) than the demand for a safety need, which in turn is greater than the demand for a love need. However, it does not follow that, as Maslow suggests, the love need will be less fulfilled in percentage terms than the safety or physiological needs. To what extent the different needs are gratified depends upon the cost or price of each unit of the means for satisfying a need and the elasticity of demand of each need. To illustrate, consider Figure 3–2. The demand for a means of a gratifying a physiological need is depicted as being greater (meaning it is further out to the right) than the other demands. (For the sake of simplicity we consider only three needs.) We assume that any given need is fully satisfied if the quantity of the need "purchased" is equal to the quantity at the point where the respective demand curves intersect the horizontal axis.[10]

---

[9] Maslow, *Motivation*, pp. 100–101.

[10] At that quantity the marginal utility is zero, implying that the person's utility level from the consumption of that need is at its maximum.

FIGURE 3–2

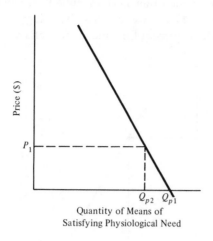

Quantity of Means of
Satisfying Physiological Need

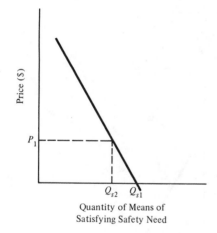

Quantity of Means of
Satisfying Safety Need

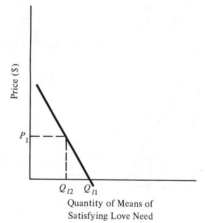

Quantity of Means of
Satisfying Love Need

If, as in this example, the cost of satisfying each need is the same, P_1, the individual will consume Q_{P1} of the means of satisfying his physiological need. As far as units are concerned, this is greater than the quantity of units consumed of the other needs; however, the percentage of the need gratified does not have to be greater. If demand for the physiological need were sufficiently inelastic, the percent of the need gratified could be greater.

It is doubtful, however, that the costs of satisfying the different needs are the same. The availability of the resources needed for satisfying the different needs can easily be different; consequently, the costs of need gratification can be different. If the cost of fulfilling the physiological need were substantially greater, even though the demand for the need were greater, the percentage of the physiological need fulfilled could be less than the percentage of the other needs fulfilled. In Figure 3–3 the prices (or cost per unit) of the means by which a physiological need can be satisfied (P_p) are less than the prices of the means for satisfying the other needs.

FIGURE 3–3

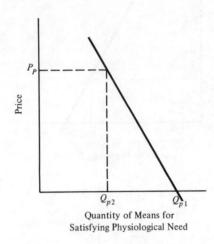

Quantity of Means for
Satisfying Physiological Need

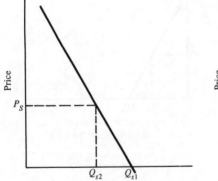

Quantity of Means for
Satisfying Safety Need

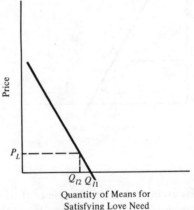

Quantity of Means for
Satisfying Love Need

The price of satisfying the safety need (P_s) is also assumed to be greater than the price of satisfying the love need (P_l). The result in this case is what we suggested could be: the individual will fulfill a lower percentage of his physiological need than he will fulfill of his other needs. In fact the order of need fulfillment is reversed from the order suggested by Maslow: the individual fulfills a higher percentage of his love need than the other needs.

Maslow apparently has observed that people fulfill a higher percentage of their physiological needs than other needs. Our line of argument suggests that this may have been the case because the price of physiological need fulfillment is lower than the prices of fulfilling the other needs.[11] The point we wish to make is that a change in the price (or cost) structure can bring about a change in the extent of need gratification at each level. In such an event our (and psychologists') definition of what may be considered "normal," as far as need gratification is concerned, should be reconsidered. People's behavior need not have changed in any fundamental sense; they may merely be responding to different prices, while their basic preferences and attitudes remain the same.

---

[11] It may also be that the demand for physiological satisfaction is more inelastic than the other demands. This could be considered "normal," as far as need gratification is concerned.

4

The Wonderful
"One-Hoss Shay"[1]

Have you heard of the wonderful one-hoss shay,
That was built in such a logical way
It ran a hundred years to a day,
And then, of a sudden, it—ah, but stay,
I'll tell you what happened without delay,
Scaring the parson into fits,
Frightening people out of their wits,—
Have you ever heard of that, I say?

Now in building of chaises, I tell you what,
There is always *somewhere* a weakest spot,—
In hub, tire, felloe, in spring or thill,
In panel, or crossbar, or floor, or sill,
In screw, bolt, thoroughbrace,—lurking still,
Find it somewhere you must and will,—
Above or below, or within or without,—
And that's the reason, beyond a doubt,
That a chaise *breaks down*, but doesn't wear out.

So the Deacon inquired of the village folk
Where he could find the strongest oak,
That couldn't be split nor bent nor broke,—
That was for spokes and floor and sills;

---

[1] The full title of the poem is "The Deacon's Masterpiece or, The Wonderful 'One-Hoss Shay.'"

He sent for lancewood to make the thills;
The crossbars were ash, from the straightest trees,
The panels of white-wood, that cuts like cheese,
But lasts like iron for things like these;
The hubs of logs from the 'Settler's ellum,'—
Last of its timber,—they couldn't sell 'em,
Never an axe had seen their chips,
And the wedges flew from between their lips,
Their blunt ends frizzled like celery-tips;
Step and prop-iron, bolt and screw,
Spring, tire, axle, and linchpin too,
Steel of the finest, bright and blue;
Thoroughbrace bison-skin, thick and wide;
Boot, top, dasher, from tough old hide
Found in the pit when the tanner died.
That was the way he 'put her through.'
'There!' said the Deacon, 'naow she'll dew!'

First of November,—the Earthquake day,—
There are traces of age in the one-hoss shay,
A general flavor of mild decay,
But nothing local, as one may say.
There couldn't be,—for the Deacon's art
Had made it so like in every part
That there wasn't a chance for one to start.
For the wheels were just as strong as the thills,
And the floor was just as strong as the sills,
And the panels just as strong as the floor,
And the whipple-tree neither less nor more,
And the back-crossbar as strong as the fore,
And spring and axle and hub *encore*.
And yet, *as a whole*, it is past a doubt
In another hour it will be *worn out!*

First of November, 'Fifty-five!
This morning the parson takes a drive.
Now, small boys, get out of the way!
Here comes the wonderful one-hoss shay,
Drawn by a rat-tailed, ewe-necked bay.
'Huddup!' said the parson.—Off went they.
Had got to *fifthly*, and stopped perplexed
At what the—Moses—was coming next.
All at once the horse stood still,
Close by the meet'n'-house on the hill.

First a shiver, and then a thrill,
Then something decidedly like a spill,—
And the parson was sitting upon a rock,
At half past nine by the meet'n'-house clock,—
Just the hour of the Earthquake shock!
What do you think the parson found,
When he got up and stared around?
The poor old chaise in a heap or mound,
As it if had been to the mill and ground!
You see, of course, if you're not a dunce,
How it went to pieces all at once,—
Just as bubbles do when they burst.

End of the wonderful one-hoss shay.
Logic is logic. That's all I say.

Oliver Wendell Holmes

QUESTION TO PONDER

Holmes' poem was actually intended as a satire on the Calvinistic theology. Setting its satirical purpose aside and considering the poem only as a tale of the construction of a "one-hoss shay," is there an economic lesson to be learned from the poem?

part two
Sex

5

Sexual Behavior

To those who may be unfamiliar with developments within the field of economics over the past decade, sex—or human sexuality—may appear to be a peculiar topic for discussion among economists and for inclusion in an introductory book on economics. However, for those who view economics as a study of human behavior (as do the authors), concern with sex is not at all peculiar, bizarre, or sensational. Clearly, a major impetus for human action is the sexual drive, and concern with matters relating to sex in one way or another occupies a significant portion of most people's time. Indeed, given the dominance of sex in human experience, one must wonder how economists have been able to avoid the topic in their classes and books for so long.

If one thinks about what is normally considered to be within the traditional boundaries of economic science and considers the ramifications of sex as a part of human experience, the discussion in this and the succeeding chapter may not appear to be at all out of place. To the layman, economics may be thought of as a discipline which (1) is founded on the study of goods and services that yield benefits or, in the jargon of the profession, utility to the buyers; (2) concentrates on the give-and-take, exchange, or trading relationships between and among people; (3) deals with scarce resources and, thereby, with goods and services that involve costs in their production and can command payments from persons who desire them; (4) is grounded in such concepts as opportunity cost and on such laws as the laws of supply and demand, diminishing marginal utility, and diminishing marginal returns; and (5) is concerned primarily with that domain of human behavior in which the individual is rational; that is, attempts to maximize his well-being.

Consequently, economics is normally associated with the development of a theory that is readily applicable to such goods and services as football games, peanut butter, ice cream, brickmaking machines, Rembrandt paintings, and, perhaps, on occasion, with prostitution as an institutionalized profession. In the remaining portions of this chapter, an attempt will be made to show how the sexual behavior of people other than prostitutes or buyers of the services of prostitutes can be discussed, analyzed, and understood within the context of economic concepts and theory. No claim is made to the effect that economic theory can explain all aspects of human sexual behavior.

CHARACTERISTICS OF SEX

Sex as a Service

Sex is a classification of a whole range of services one person provides for himself or another and yields utility to the recipients. The list of services provided under the heading of sex may include such normal heterosexual experiences as holding hands, kissing, petting, and intercourse. A sexual experience (or service) may also include the stimulation one receives from watching the girls (or boys) go by, from reading *Playboy, Playgirl,* or *National Geographic,* and from the tales of those who write to "Dear Abby" or Dr. David Reuben. For junior high school boys and girls, a gratifying (and permissible) sexual experience may be nothing more than the frequent and purposeful bumping and shoving that goes on outside the class. The list of sexual services can be considerably lengthened.

Many people are quick to condemn one sexual practice or another as "inhuman" or "immoral." Although the authors, and most everyone else, have their own sexual preferences, they submit that they are just that— their preferences. The issue of what is immoral will not be our concern, mainly because such a discussion is likely to be worthless to anyone who disagrees with the writers. Moreover, it would be an unnecessary diversion from the central purpose of this chapter, which is to explore the question of *how people do behave* and not how they should behave.

The utility that one receives from a satisfying sexual experience may in the psychic realm be similar, if not identical, to the satisfaction a person receives from eating a good peanut butter sandwich, drinking a chocolate milkshake, or watching a performance of Sir Laurence Olivier in a Shakespearean play. Indeed, for most people the distinctive, but not the only, difference between a sexual experience and other more "normal" goods and services consumed may be the intensity of the pleasure received. For most persons, sexual intercourse and all the trappings that go with it probably give the recipient more satisfaction than a peanut butter sandwich; this is evidenced by the cost that a person is willing to incur for sex relative to the cost he is willing to incur to obtain the sandwich. For some people, however, the sandwich can deliver more utility than intercourse:

everyone may not consider sex to be within his own choice domain just as everyone may not wish to purchase pickled pigs feet. Oddly enough, even the person who never engages in sexual activity can receive considerable utility from sex; he (or she) may refrain from engaging in sexual activities because of the extent of the cost. Because of this, it is extremely risky (if not impossible) to make interpersonal utility comparisons regarding the absolute psychic value of sex just as it is risky to suggest that the people who attend Shakespearean plays "enjoy the plays more" than those who never attend.

Given that sexual experiences can yield utility like other goods, it follows that the quantity of sex demanded is an inverse function of the price; that is, the demand curve is downward sloping as in Figure 5–1. If

FIGURE 5–1

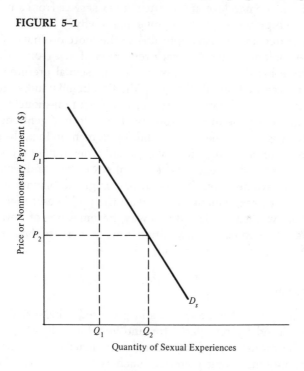

Quantity of Sexual Experiences

the price goes up, the quantity demanded goes down; if the price goes down, the quantity goes up. This means in effect that given the price of sex, the "consumer" will want only so much sex supplied by another and will vary his consumption with the price that is charged. The reason for this relationship is simply that the rational individual will consume sex up to the point that the marginal benefits equal the marginal costs (or until $MU_s/P_s = MU_a/P_a = \ldots = MU_n/P_n$, where MU and P denote marginal utility and price, respectively, and where s represents sex and a and n, other goods). If the price of sex rises relative to other goods, the consumer will "rationally" choose to consume more of other goods and less sex. (Ice cream, as well as many other goods, can substitute for sex if the relative prices require it.)

The law of demand, as stated above, is a fundamental principle of business operations the prostitute cannot ignore. By raising her (or his[1]) price, the prostitute will not only sell fewer "tricks," but *may* find that if there are a number of other readily available competitors, the quantity demanded from her can fall to the point that her total revenues will fall. Her revenues can rise if the demand she faces is inelastic. In other words, the prostitute (he or she) must remember that although the demand for sex in general may be inelastic because of the relative necessity of the service to those who want it, the demand for any particular sex service from any particular person can be highly elastic. (Can you explain why?)

The law of demand is also applicable to the more ordinary sexual relationships. A male may demand very few units of sex from the girl he is dating or from his wife, in part because of his sexual preferences. However, closer examination of the individual's circumstances may reveal that the price he would have to pay—although in non-monetary terms—may be so great that he must rationally choose to be "gentlemanly" and ask for very little. The same may be said for women; in fact, the difference in the quantity of sex demanded by men and women may reflect in large measure the relative difference in the cost of sex to men and women. If the price of sex to women were lowered, one might anticipate a relatively larger quantity of sex demanded by them; the problem of men obtaining more sex from women, if viewed this way, becomes one of how to reduce the cost of sex to women (or, in addition, how to increase their preferences for it; that is, increase their demand).

The Cost of Sex

Sex is a service that is produced and procured. The sexual experience must be produced by one party for another. Like all other production processes, the production of any sexual experience entails costs. This is because not only may some materials, such as contraceptives, be required and a direct expenditure made, as in the case of the prostitute, but also because the participants must generally forgo some opportunity which has value to them and which by definition is the cost. The actual experience, requires at least a few minutes and this, or course implies that one cannot normally do anything else of consequence at the same time. (One can, perhaps, imagine eating an apple or reading a book while producing

---

[1] The reader should recognize that there are male prostitutes, although they may presently account for a relatively minor portion of the total membership in the profession.

sex for someone else, but it may be difficult indeed to imagine playing a successful game of pool or efficiently carrying on one's normal business operations.)

The opportunity cost of the time spent in the sexual act in most instances may be a trivial part of the total cost involved in either the production or procurement of sex.

The total cost may include such items as the cost of the "wining and dining," which, contrary to the general impression, may often be heavily born by females. Consider for example, the number of times the girl may invite her male companion in for coffee and a snack after a date or over to dinner; or consider the possibility that she may be purposefully and skillfully arranging the situation in which the wining and dining may take place. Because the man may pick up the check, he is credited with the wining and dining. However, one must wonder who wined and dined whom. This is not meant to suggest that all such efforts by one party or the other are intended to procure or produce a sexual experience; the motive can simply be to have an enjoyable evening out. We are suggesting, however, that the wining and dining can for some be a part of the calculated cost of obtaining or producing a gratifying sexual experience.

The cost may also include the risk cost of pregnancy, which may be disproportionately born by the female; the expenditure of effort (male orgasm alone requires approximately 200 calories); the psychic cost of violating one's own moral standards; the damaged reputation cost which may be incurred if one's family or friends find out about the sexual relationship; and lastly there is the cost incurred in the time spent plotting and maneuvering into a position in which the type of sex desired can be had. Both female and male must assess the "market" to determine which persons and sexual experiences are within their choice domain and must develop a strategy tailored to the selected party(ies). The selected strategy may require a considerable expenditure on clothes, hairdos, makeup, and education; it may also require a time expenditure on being in the right places. The producer may also require the recipient to become "involved" emotionally as well as physically; coupling marriage with sex is, perhaps, the ultimate form of contracted involvements. The value of one's time, as approximated by his wage rate, will determine the cost of the sexual experience. The higher the opportunity wage, the higher the cost of the experience. Because of the different effects of higher income on sex consumption (and, perhaps, the associated education levels and lifetime experiences) and the different preferences between the high and low income groups, one cannot say theoretically which income group should be expected to have the higher rate of sexual activity. The economist can say, however, that the difference in the cost to the two groups, due to the fact that sex is labor intensive, can partly explain the difference in the level of sexual activity that may exist.

Studies have generally revealed that the higher income groups consume as a group more sex than the lower groups. They tend to be more "open minded," are more educated, and have fewer psychological hangups regarding sex.

We can explain these facts by arguing that the demand for sex, because of the non-price factors, is greater for the higher income groups. This situation is described in Figure 5–2A and 2B. The demand in 5–2A for

FIGURE 5–2

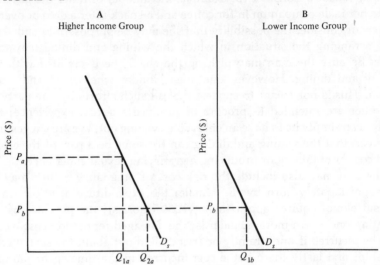

A
Higher Income Group

B
Lower Income Group

the higher income groups is greater than the demand in 5–2B; given the differences in cost—P_a for the higher income group and P_b for the other group—the difference in revealed sexual activity is $Q_{1a} - Q_{1b}$, where $Q_{1a} > Q_{1b}$. If the opportunity wage cost had been the same, and equal to the wage of the lower income group, the difference would have been greater, $Q_{2a} - Q_{1b}$. The difference in the opportunity wage cost explains $Q_1 - Q_{2a}$ of the difference in sexual activity of the two groups.

In summary, a gratifying sexual experience can be quite costly. In economics there is an adage that is probably repeated in almost all principles courses: "there is no such thing as a free lunch"; we suggest with equal conviction that there is no such thing as "free love" or "free sex."

Sex as an Exchange Relationship

The sexual experience involves exchange, one person doing something for someone else in return for something. Generally, the relationship is a barter one—no money is involved. One person provides sex to another in exchange for a similar sexual experience. However, the exchange is not always in kind; one party can provide sex in exchange for security, clothing, candy, kindness, marriage, interesting company, conversation, being a part of the crowd, and entertainment. How many times has one person said, or, perhaps, indicated in more subtle terms: (1) "I will give you sex if you will marry me or go out with no one else"; (2) "I will give you sex if you carry out the garbage or vacuum the house for me"; (3) "I will give you sex if you will stay home with me." In the courting ritual, therefore, implicit dealing is frequently, although not always, present. All such bargains imply non-monetary payments; since, as we believe, the supply of sex is upward sloping, the payments should result in a greater quantity of sex provided than otherwise.

Because money is not normally a permissible part of the deal, people who desire heterosexual or homosexual experiences must have double coincidences of wants: one party must be able to provide what the other party wants and must want what the other party has to offer. This implies that the search cost of both parties can be considerable and can result in less sex being exchanged than otherwise. It is because of such search costs alone that people may be willing to make monetary payments to prostitutes.

Sex as a Marketed Product

Sex can be molded, packaged, advertised, and promoted like most other product groups. In the case of *Playboy* and *Penthouse*, the marketing process is direct and open; people know clearly what is being sold. In other instances, such as Dr. David Reuben's column, the intentions, which may include the simulation of a sexual experience, are not so obvious. Most watchers of television realize that sex is the medium through which other products are sold. Joe Namath's testimonial in the "Brute" cologne commercial which ends with "If you aren't going to go all the way, man, why go at all?" is a less than subtle form of selling "Brute" by selling sex.

On a personal level, people use many of the same marketing techniques as do major manufacturers; they *do* package and advertise their sexual products. Short skirts, padded bras, no-bras, tight slacks, deodorant, and body shirts are all forms of presenting one's sexual services in the best possible light and methods of attracting the attention of possible buyers. By using such devices and techniques, the individuals involved may be as guilty of fraudulant packaging and advertising as are producers of cosmetics, soaps, and toys. If one views much of the advertising of such products as "wasteful," then it would be consistent to view much expenditure on make-up and clothing in the same light.

Why do people incur the costs associated with personal beautification? We must, at the start, admit that there is the prevalent "honorable" reason that people just want to "look nice" and/or "feel good." Be that as it may, we wish to suggest that there are other reasons (which are no less "honorable" except in an individualistic sense). An individual may want to increase the number of buyers for what he has to offer in order to have a larger quantity of sex and a larger group from which to select the services that he desires. With an increased choice domain, the individual in all probability can select a higher "quality" service, *as he assesses quality.*

By looking attractive, a person can also possibly increase the non-money payment received for the sex services that he himself produces, or he can possibly lower the non-money payment that he will have to make for the sex services of others. All of these possible benefits make expenditures on personal beautification rational.[2]

In other words, people may attempt to look more attractive for the same reason that the professional prostitute does, although not necessarily in the same ways; and how much expenditures are made depends upon the costs, the benefits, *and market conditions.* The girl (or boy) with no competitors may be expected to expend, *ceteris paribus,* less on improving the quality of her (his) sexual services.

There is one other economic explanation for looking attractive. The human mind has a limited capacity to absorb facts and information, such as who may be in our presence and their characteristics. On the other hand, an individual is bombarded by tens of thousands of bits of information. The mind is incapable of absorbing, analyzing, and registering all of the information. The individual must, by absolute necessity, make decision rules regarding the facts and information which will be permitted to register in the brain. As a result he may decide to ignore some information as a general rule, meaning that he may not notice all people around him. Before a person can have a meaningful relationship in any dimension with someone else, the fact that he exists as a distinct entity must register in the mind of the other person. Because of the construction of decision rules regarding which bits of information will actually be allowed to register, the person desiring the relationship must not only be present, but must be able to somehow break through the decision rule in the event that it actually presents a barrier to him. This may mean that his actions have to be dramatic or flashy; a simple statement that "I'm present" can be ineffective. The extra nice clothes, the short skirts, the makeup, and the exceptonally nice manners may be means of breaking through the barrier of decision rules;[3] once this has been accomplished—that is, presence has

---

[2] Personal beautification, once produced, becomes a public good because persons other than the one who is more beautiful receive benefits in the sense that their surroundings are more pleasant. This may mean that since the individual may consider only the private benefits from personal beautification, and not the total social benefits, there may be an underinvestment in such beautification.

[3] For some, breaking through the decision rules of those with whom they wish to associate may mean that they "dress down," "dress hippy," or dress in such a way that they may be considered a part of the anti-establishment.

registered—and the relationship has been established, the individual can drop back in his own manner of dressing and behavior.

A MODEL OF SEXUAL BEHAVIOR

The amount of sex that is produced and consumed is not in our view determined by the gods. Granted, men and women have biological drives and there are bodily constraints on sexual behavior. Men and women, however, have some control over these drives (as a general rule) and do not engage in sex to the extent of their biological capabilities. The amount of sex produced and consumed is the result of the interaction of individuals within what we might call social space (or the market). For an explanation of how the amount of sex actually consumed and produced is determined, we must look to the forces which these individuals bring to bear on this interaction process.

A restatement of principles that have been intrinsic in much of the discussion that has gone before would be helpful. These principles are the laws of demand and supply. We assume that the demand curve for sex by either males or females is downward sloping and that, as a reasonable generality, the market supply curve of sex is upward sloping. Therefore, the quantity of sex supplied will increase with the price paid for it. As in Figure 5–3, which depicts the demand for sex by men and the supply of sex

FIGURE 5–3

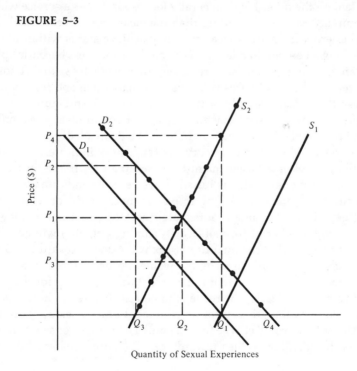

Quantity of Sexual Experiences

by women, the relative positions of these curves depend upon such factors as the relative preferences of the sexes and the relative costs of the sexual experience(s) borne by them.

If the supply and demand for sex were determined solely by biological drives, and if these drives were equal for men and women (which may or may not be the case), the supply and demand curves could be so positioned on the graph that their intersection is on the horizontal axis; the price, or non-money payment, paid for the sex would be zero, as is the case with S_1 and D_1 in Figure 5–3. This does not mean that no costs are involved to the parties; there are, as discussed above. It only means that there will be no need for extra non-money payments or direct money payments made by one party to the other. The gratification one receives from the experience will compensate him (her) for the cost incurred in providing the sex.

Such a circumstance does not, however, realistically reflect the general state of the world. Women are restricted from fully revealing their biological drives. They bear a substantial portion of the risk cost associated with pregnancy (men, it must not be forgotten, bear a part of the cost). Although general standards are changing, many women still view sex as an activity in which they are not supposed to engage except under the umbrella of marriage; many, because of their training from childhood, look upon sex as something dirty and not to be enjoyed. Virginity, in and of itself, can have positive value, entailing giving it up is an added cost of sex. Men, on the other hand, generally look upon sex as a service which is to be pursued for purposes other than the pleasure received directly from the experience. In tribal Africa, men may achieve status within the tribe from killing a lion barehanded; in more modern and "less barbaric" places, men can achieve the same stature among their peers by sexual conquests. The effect of these pressures is to raise the male's demand for sex and to decrease the female's supply of it (to say, S_2 and D_2 in Figure 5–3). At a zero price, there will then exist a shortage of sex to men, since only Q_3 sex will be supplied by females and Q_4 will be demanded.

The upward sloping supply curve of female sex indicates that women are willing to offer a larger quantity of sex than Q_3 if the "price" (not necessarily in money form) is raised above zero. As indicated by the demand curve, D_2, men are willing to pay as much as P_2 for an additional sexual experience. We might anticipate, therefore, that non-money payments in any number of forms (security, dining out, etc.) will be offered. The result will be that the quantity of sex will expand toward Q_2. Beyond Q_2 the side-payment required by the women to bring forth an additional unit of sex is greater than what the men are willing to pay for the experience. (To see this clearly, the reader should ask themselves how much the men would be willing to pay for an additional unit of sex at Q_1 and how much the women would charge for the unit.) The market for sex is changing along with individual values toward sex. The supply of sex by women is expanding. The availability of contraceptives is reducing the potential pregnancy cost of intercourse to women; virginity is no longer as important to many[4] and more and more the message is getting out that women are capable of enjoying sex. Abortions are becoming more common, cheaper, and more acceptable. Assuming that these changes in cost and values have no effect on the demand side of the market, we can conclude that the quantity of sexual activity will increase and the price or non-money payment made to women can fall.[5] We are frankly uncertain as to what is happening to the demand for sex by men. If the demand rises, but by less than the supply increases, the same general predictions as the ones above would follow; the price, however, would not fall as much, but the quantity of sexual activity would rise by more than in the case above. (What may be the consequence of a drop in the men's demand for sex?)

We have been speaking in terms of generalities; and, of course, an oversupply of sex for some women does not hold for all women. For some women—for example, the not-so-pretty and the old—there can be a shortage of sex, and they may have to make the non-money payments to obtain the desired quantity of sex.[6] In fact, if we individualize the market, we can postulate that what the woman may view as her "standards" may really be a mirror image of her relative market position. That is, because a woman is beautiful she can maintain higher standards than the woman who is less endowed and who has no offsetting differences.

PROSTITUTION

Why does prostitution exist? Once the existence of the cost of sexual intercourse and of the positive equilibrium price in Figure 5–3 are recognized, the question is easily answered. The price of the prostitute, even though it may be $50, can be much lower than the cost the man (woman) would have to bear in order to obtain the same pleasure from other "more legitimate" sources.[7] The man can pay the $50, and by doing so he does not

---

[4] Remaining a virgin for some women may now be considered a negative value; some women may feel that it indicates they are not desirable or are in such limited demand that the "price" offered by men has not been high enough to seduce them into giving up their virginity.

[5] It is possible that the price will become negative. This would mean a reversal of roles: the women would be paying the men. For more on the emergence of male prostitution, see Thomas R. Ireland, "The Supply and Demand of Sex," paper presented at the Western Economics Association meeting, June 1974.

[6] From some points of view, such women may be viewed as "deviates." However, such a designation may be inappropriate. These women can be behaving, in a sense, like everyone else; the only difference is the location of their equilibrium in the social market.

[7] On the other hand, by adding in the cost of venereal disease, we can understand why some men do not engage prostitutes; for some $50 plus the cost of contacting VD can be a greater cost than the possible benefits (and lower than the benefits to others).

have to spend the time that may be required to seduce the non-prostitute. He does not have to send her flowers or other gifts and, more importantly, does not have to become involved emotionally or otherwise. He can satisfy his needs and leave anonymously.

Another reason why a man may seek the services of a prostitute is that the quality of the service can be higher. The prostitute is a professional; she may not only have had more experience than the conventional sex partner, but she can prorate the cost of "training" and improving the quality of her service over a larger number of sexual experiences. The investment cost per "trick" can be trivial if she operates in large quantities.

Legalizing prostitution can have several predictable effects. First, since the penalties of being caught soliciting buyers will be eliminated and the cost of searching for buyers (streetwalkers have to keep on the move) will be substantially reduced, the supply of prostitutes should increase. This should result in a larger quantity of output. The quality of the product should also rise, bringing about in part a reduction in the threat of VD. Houses of prostitution would be able to justify more expenditures on medical check-ups for the prostitutes since the quantity of their business would reflect their reputation for cleanliness, just as in the case of Holiday Inns.

Furthermore, if we assume that the price or non-money payment charged for sex is competitively determined in the normal sex markets, the existence of clean, legalized prostitutes means a larger number of competitors for non-prostitutes, including housewives. Legalization of prostitution should, where non-money payments are charged, reduce the non-money payments. Housewives may be against legalized prostitution because of moral convictions; our analysis indicates, in addition, that they may (or should) be opposed to its legalization on the grounds that it can reduce their competitive position. In a similar vein, prostitutes probably do not look upon the changing values of women in general with much favor; to the degree that the price of non-prostitutes goes down, the price that the prostitute can charge must fall.

SEX AND LOVE

Our analysis has proceeded as if sex can be completely divorced from love. In many people's minds sex and love go together in much the same way as hotdogs and hotdog buns and razors and razor blades. Love and sex are viewed by many as complementary goods. This does not mean, however, that our assumptions concerning the normal slope of supply and demand for sex are upset; the demand can still be downward sloping and the supply can be upward sloping. The existence of the connection (although imperfect) between sex and love can determine the positions of the curves (and, possibly, their elasticities to a degree). A person's demand for sex can influence his demand for a "loving relationship," and the intensity of one's love for another can affect his demand for sex. Generally speaking, the common "requirement" among women that sex be coupled with a feeling of love is a statement that their supply curve of sex is further back toward the vertical axis than would be if the "requirement" did not exist. However, as a group, they can still be expected to respond positively to an increase in non-money payments as we have been using the term.

Admittedly, there are women (and men) who adopt the decision rule that they will not engage in sex unless they are married or have established a strong bond with someone else. They, in effect, rationally *choose* to ignore costs and benefits and changes in costs and benefits. Even though such people exist (and they may be quite large in number), the downward sloping demand curve and upward sloping supply curve hold so long as there are people who do weigh in their consumption decisions the costs and benefits of sexual experiences.

SOME DATA

There are probably some readers who at this point remain unconvinced about the validity of the assumptions underlying the foregoing analysis, particularly the assumptions of the downward sloping demand curve and upward sloping supply curve. In an attempt to settle the issue of whether or not people behave the way we suggest they do, we undertook a modest survey of students in two college level sociology classes. The total number of students was 64; 27 women and 37 men. One class was an introductory course and the other was an advanced, senior level course. (The purist will not find our survey satisfactory, and we fully recognize its limitations; however, it does serve the limited purposes we have in mind.)

The mean age was 22 for men and 20 for women. Twenty-one percent of the men and 8 percent of the women were married. Fifty-two percent of the single women were virgins, whereas only 10 percent of the unmarried men fell into the same category. Some of the differential is partly explained by the differences in age.

In order to determine the nature of supply and demand for sex, we posed the following problem:

> Consider the following hypothetical situation: You bump into some female (male) college student on campus whom you do not know. She (he) is about your height, or a little shorter (taller), and you consider her (him) to be reasonably attractive. There is nothing obnoxious about her (him); and you are not, nor do you expect to become, emotionally involved (either negatively or positively) with her (him). If you have sexual intercourse with her (him), there is absolutely no chance of her (your) becoming pregnant or of your contacting any disease, and there is absolutely no possibility that anyone else will find out about the relationship.

We understand that the conditions specified are somewhat idealistic, and the results should be interpreted accordingly. We believe, however, that the findings are still revealing about human behavior.

FIGURE 5–4
Light Petting

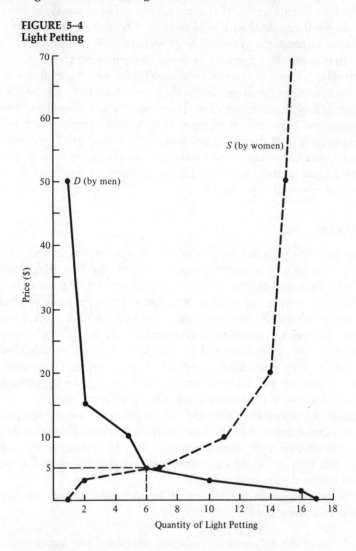

Given these conditions, we asked the women, "If he were to offer to pay you to engage in light petting (as distinguished from heavy petting and intercourse), what would be the *minimum* amount of money that you would be willing to accept for one and only one session of forty-five minutes?" We asked similar questions concerning heavy petting and intercourse, and each time we stressed that the amount could be as high (infinity) or as low (zero) as they wished. (Women were also told that they could give negative amounts, meaning that they would be willing to pay the male.)

The men were asked "What would be the *maximum* amount that you would be willing to pay her to engage in light petting for a period of forty-five minutes?" Again, similar questions were posed with regards to heavy petting and intercourse, and they, too, were told that the amount could be anything.

The results, as depicted in Figures 5–4, 5–5, and 5–6, tend to support, but do not confirm the realism of our assumptions. Because the men and women who responded to the questionnaire constituted different sexual

FIGURE 5–5
Heavy Petting

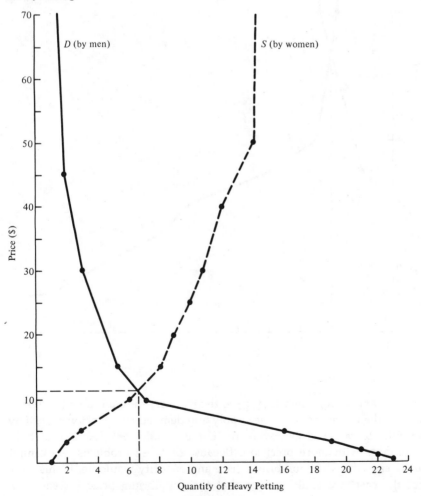

FIGURE 5–6
Intercourse

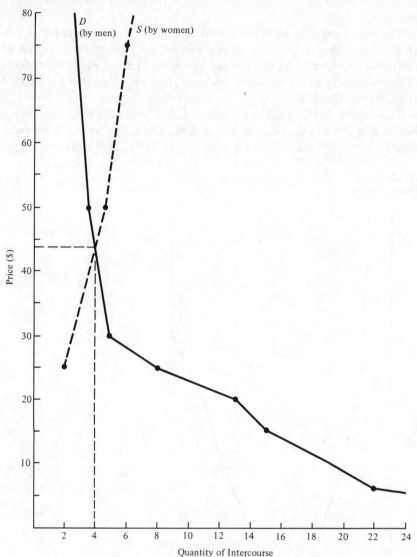

services and were, when they gave their prices, thinking about different people, the curves are not true supply and demand curves. However, they do indicate rather clearly what the curves would look like if the study were done with more precision. Because of these problems, we cannot really say what the equilibrium price and quantity would be. If this were not the case, we could deduce that the equilibrium price for each sex service is positive. Furthermore, we could note that at a zero price there would be a shortage of sex for men. We could note that as the service changes from light petting to heavy petting and then to intercourse, the demand increases and the supply contracts; that is, goes down. The equilibrium price of intercourse—which, if we could assume that the functions are continuous—is approximately $44[8] and is much higher than the price of light petting, which is approximately $5.

Although they may behave differently if an actual offer were made, 55 percent of the women said the price of intercourse would have to be infinity; in other words, they would not accept any deal. (Sixty-four percent of the non-virgin females and only 46 percent of the virgins would charge a price of infinity for intercourse.) Several of these same women, on the other hand, would have engaged in light or heavy petting for a price. Although there were a very few women who indicated very high prices (but far below infinity) for their services, most prices given were, as can be seen in the graphs, less than $100. Lastly, one of the two married women would have charged $25 for intercourse, and 75 percent of the married men would have paid an average $20 for intercourse.

Given that 90 percent of the single men were not virgins, it may be understandable why the demand for sex is as low as it is and that several of the men were unwilling to pay anything for light petting or intercourse. The old adage that "if you can get it free, why pay?" probably applies. The fact that many men were unwilling to pay very much for the sexual services might reflect the limited income of the male students and the fact that the marginal cost of acquiring the sexual services for them is not as great as one might expect. They were very likely indicating in their responses the values of one additional unit. One cannot forget the influence personal values may have in positioning the supply and demand curves.

We have admitted that the questions were asked, assuming highly restrictive conditions. Suppose that we had indicated that the probability of catching VD was two percent, what effect would this have had on the market? Suppose we had introduced "love," what would have been the effect? Suppose the market were expanded to include the whole university?

---

[8] This price is not far removed from what a reasonably attractive streetwalker would charge. The conditions of employment would not be the same.

6

Exploitation of Affection

The strength of most personal relationships is founded, to a significant degree, upon the affection one person has for another.[1] This is particularly true of the relationship between a man and a woman. The relationship works for two reasons. First, each person is concerned about the welfare of the other and is willing to do things for him. In this sense the relationship is largely charitable in nature; each person is both a donor of "gifts," broadly defined as any form of charitable expression, and a recipient of such expressions from the other.

Second, both persons understand that there is a need for implicitly defined limits to their own behavior and the behavior of the other person. These limits form the basis of the unwritten social contract between the two. Each person may then proceed in his own behavior, responding to the needs of the other, in the trust that the contract is being obeyed. This latter presumption makes possible behavior on the part of either person that is inconsistent with the agreed-on contract, implicit as it may be. It permits one party to, in a sense, "exploit" the other.

We intend to explain the logic behind this statement in the few pages that follow. We discuss the problem of exploitation under the general topic of "Sex" because most of what is said has a direct application to man-woman relationships. We stress, however, that the argument is really very general in nature and can be applied to the personal relationship between parent and child and between close friends. The analysis provides an explanation of the breakdown in many personal relationships,

---

[1] As we intend to discuss in considerable detail throughout the book, such relationships can also be founded upon individual private interests that have nothing to do with affection. However, in this chapter we want to focus on the affection aspect of the relationship.

and in general, why friends and loved ones can be "used." First, we briefly review the argument for what we call "charitable exploitation."[2]

THE MODEL

The basic proposition underlying the charitable exploitation argument is that the donor of the gifts receives utility from giving to the recipient. This implies that he has a downward sloping demand curve for making gifts. Also, the rational donor will *freely choose* to extend his gifts until the marginal benefits of doing so are equal to the marginal costs. We give "gifts" a very broad meaning here. A gift can, as is conventionally thought, be in the form of money or a material object. However, it can be the time one person spends doing something for someone else, and this can simply mean the time spent listening to another person. A gift can also be allowing the other person to listen to a record of his choice, scratching another's back, or providing him with a sexual experience of one form or another.

In Figure 6–1 we have placed marginal costs and benefits on the vertical axis and the quantity of the gift (which may be any single gift or a gift which represents a combination of gifts) on the horizontal axis. If we assume that the donor's demand curve (D_1) is downward sloping and, for simplification, that the marginal cost of units of the gift is constant at P_1 in Figure 6–1, then we can conclude that the donor will *choose* on his own to make gifts up to point Y or a quantity of Q_1. At Y the marginal cost is equal to the marginal benefits.

Notice that it is only for the last unit—the Q_1th unit—that the marginal costs and benefits are equal. Up to that point, the marginal benefits to the donor, as indicated by the demand curve, are greater than the marginal cost of each unit of the gift. As we have explained in Chapter 1, *the cost of something is the value of that which is foregone.* This means that the individual donor is getting more value in making each unit of the gift up to Q_1 than he could have gotten from the use of his resources in their best alternative. This excess value, referred to as "surplus value" by economists, can be described by the shaded area (P_1XY) in the graph. In simple language, when we do one thing we often say that we are "better off" in some sense; in terms of our graph we would say that the donor is "better off" to the extent of the shaded area.[3]

Given the extent of the consumer surplus indicated by the shaded area P_1XY, the recipient, if he is the only recipient (or if all recipients act collu-

---

[2] This chapter is based on a short article by Wilson E. Schmidt, "Charitable Exploitation," *Public Choice*, 10 (Spring 1969), 103–104.

[3] In more detailed terms, the total value that the donor receives from making Q_1 gifts is equal to $OXYQ_1$. The total cost is equal to OP_1YQ_1. The difference between the total costs and total benefits is equal to P_1XY, or the shaded area, which we have called "consumer surplus."

FIGURE 6–1

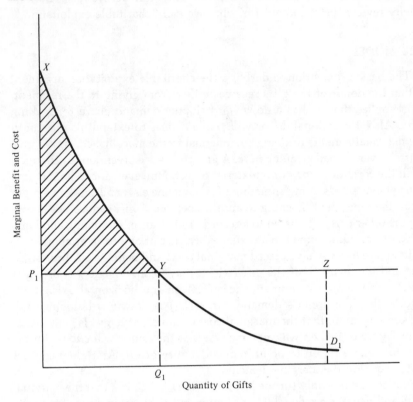

Quantity of Gifts

sively), can force the donor to increase his gifts beyond Y by merely refusing to accept anything unless the donor abides by the recipient's wishes, which is for more units of the gift. Notice that we have not said that the recipient threatens overt harm to the donor, but only threatens not to accept anything unless the donor gives more. The recipient in effect presents an all-or-nothing deal to the donor: "Either you give me more or I'll accept nothing."

If the recipient is able to pose the deal subtly, without the donor actually detecting the scheme he has in mind, the donor is presented with a choice problem. If he refuses to give more, then he must give nothing, which means that he must give up the surplus value he would have received by giving Q_1 units of the gift. If he gives more, the marginal cost of each unit, P_1, will be greater than the marginal benefits of each additional unit. There is what we might call a "negative surplus value" attached to these additional units. As a result, the donor's total satisfaction level will be lowered by giving more. We can postulate that if the negative surplus value is greater than the shaded area in the graph, the donor will be better off by not giving anything at all. If the negative surplus value is less, the donor will be better off by extending this gifts.

This means that the recipient's ability to extract additional units of the gift, and in that sense "exploit" the donor, is not limitless. If at point Z in the graph the negative surplus value (area YZD_1) is just equal to the surplus value (P_1XY), then the smart recipient will ask for an amount of gifts equal to something *just short* of point Z. In this way, he will insure that the negative surplus value is less than the surplus value and that the donor will give more. If the recipient asks for more than Z, the negative surplus value is greater than the surplus value, and the donor will be better off by not giving anything. If he asks for Z, the donor will be *indifferent* to continuing the gift-giving and may, on some whim, stop giving. Therefore, the closer the recipient trys to come to Z, the more risk he must assume that he has misjudged the charitable feelings of the donor, and he may end up getting nothing. Remember it is not likely that the recipient will be able to make the calculations that are implied here with a great deal of precision and certainty.

Two points need to be stressed. The first is that the ability of the recipient to extract a larger quantity of gifts depends on the number of alternative recipients of the gift; that is, the number of what we might call competitors for the gift. If the recipient is one of many possible equal recipients and he attempts to impose the all-or-nothing deal considered here, the donor can turn to someone else and in the end receive the full (or almost full) extent of the consumer surplus. He need not go beyond Y in Figure 6-1. The demand curve in Figure 6-1 is, in this case, the demand for giving in general and is not the demand for giving to any one individual.[4] If, on the other hand, the recipient is the only possible recipient *in the mind of the donor*, the recipient is, in essence, a monopolist; the donor must in this circumstance either accept the deal or turn to buying goods which yield less satisfaction.

Second, exploitation of the donor will occur only to the extent that the recipient is unconcerned about the welfare of the donor. If the recipient "cares" about the donor, then the recipient will be worse off to the extent that donor is worse off. By exploiting the donor, the recipient reduces the donor's welfare and, consequently, his own welfare.

ROMANTIC RELATIONSHIPS

Wilson Schmidt, who formulated the foregoing argument, suggested that the argument can be useful in understanding the behavior of welfare

---

[4] The donor's demand for making gifts to any one of the possible recipients under highly competitive conditions (that is, a large number of alternative recipients) will essentially be horizontal.

recipients under the conditions prevailing during the late 1960s. At the time, many welfare recipients were demonstrating against the welfare offices around the country, "demanding" larger checks. One might reason that the recipients were in effect threatening the government with the disruption of the welfare system. In such event, the government would have been unable to make the "charitable" payments. The protesting welfare recipients could have understood our argument to this point in an intuitive sense, recognizing that there may have been some consumer surplus that could be drawn out of the government bureaucrats and those who are in favor of giving to the poor.

We believe that the argument on charitable exploitation has a much broader application than originally conceived and is, perhaps, even more readily applicable to personal relationships. To show this we turn to romantic relationships between men and women. A romantic relationship is, almost by definition, a charitable one in the sense that the man's utility is related to the utility level of the woman and vice versa. The relationship is built on the presumption that this is; to some degree, the case; and as a result, a certain amount of trust develops concerning the intentions of the other party.

In a romantic relationship, the woman or man has a demand for "giving" in any number of dimensions. However, she or he will choose to freely give only so much, and that will be Y in our example, Figure 6–1. In the case of the woman, she may be willing to give Y because she feels confident in the man's feelings toward her. However, if she has been deceived, she can be "exploited" because of the existence of the surplus value. The man can drain the surplus value out of the woman in any number of ways: He can, to a limited degree, generally abuse her. He can make her go places and do things that she would not freely choose to do, and he can make her put up with quirks in his own behavior that he may find costly to change. In this sense he can make her go further in "giving" in to him than she would otherwise choose to go. If, however, he pushes too hard—that is, asks her to go beyond Z—he will be dropped. The irony of this may be that the woman may still "love" the man, but she drops him because he has asked for too much. All of this can also be placed in the context of the woman exploiting the man, which occurs perhaps as frequently as the case of the man exploiting the woman.

SEXUAL EXPLOITATION

The reader may sense that all of what we have said here can be readily applied to the physical-sexual relationship between a woman and a man. There may be activities in which a woman may freely choose to engage because they may give her direct pleasure or, more importantly for our purposes, may contribute to the pleasure of the man she is dating. Because of the woman's value system, however, and because there may be psychic costs associated with many forms of sexual activities, there are limits to the number of times in which she may *freely* engage in sexual activity (that is, make the gift). Because of the surplus value, the man, if he wishes and if he is her only boyfriend, can make the woman go further than she freely chooses to go. He can extract the surplus either in terms of an increased rate of specific, more readily acceptable activities (such as petting) or can draw the surplus out in the form of an activity in which the woman may not *freely choose* to engage (such as intercourse). This does not mean necessarily that the man can "force" the woman to have sexual intercourse, because the size of the consumer surplus may not be great enough to push her to that point. But, it does suggest that regardless of the level or kind of activity the woman chooses, the man *can*, in a sense and under the condition that he is a monopolist with respect to the woman's affection, exploit the woman to some degree. If the man is only one of many possible dates for the woman—that is, the relationship has not been permanently established—the all-or-nothing deal cannot work as effectively. In the event the man tries to make the woman go further than she desires, she can merely turn to one of her other possible dates and retain the full consumer surplus from giving to the opposite sex. She, in this event, has bargaining power.

The typical male may intuitively sense the essence of the foregoing discussion and realize that he can obtain more of what he wants if he is "the only one" as far as the woman is concerned. This line of analysis may explain why the man may refrain from trying anything on the first few dates. On the first few dates, he may intuitively understand that he is one of a number of candidates for the (charitable) affections of the woman, and if he attempts anything physical, she can turn to someone else to whom she may at that point receive equal pleasure in the sense we have been using the term and can ultimately receive the full extent of the consumer surplus from giving. By waiting and putting on his "best manners," he effectively may be able to eliminate the competition in the *mind of the woman* and, by the delay, more accurately assess the size of the woman's consumer surplus. He may also be investing the time for the purpose of increasing the woman's charitable demand for him, in which case she will of her own accord go further, and he may be attempting to determine what would be the most appropriate way of presenting the all-or-nothing deal.

The reader must remember that if the deal is not carefully posed—verbally, by facial expression, or otherwise—the woman's preferences for giving to the man can be damaged, implying a reduction in her demand for him. In other words, a deal clumsily made can reduce the woman's demand to the point that her demand curve intersects the vertical axis at P_1. In such case she will decide to give nothing.

Women do trade sex for other goods, such as security, and the subject was covered in some detail in the preceding chapter. This, however, is not what is meant by sexual exploitation here; by the term we mean one party "forcing" the other party to go further sexually than he or she would freely choose to go. Many readers may believe—by thinking in terms of the over-sexed, male stereotype—that if women do in fact find it necessary to make men go further sexually than they would freely choose to go, it is only of interest as a peculiarity of the relationships between nympho-maniacs and highly religious men.

The possibility of the female sexually exploiting the male becomes much more plausible if the male stereotype is set aside and if specific circumstances are considered. First, it should be realized that men can bear a cost by engaging in, say, intercourse; they may be liable for child support and/or may be forced, because of personal values, into marrying someone who under other circumstances they would not choose. The existence of such costs and the fact that once the woman is aroused, she may not want to stop short of intercourse, may partially explain why the woman may have to say, or subtly indicate, that "If you don't go all the way, then you may do nothing at all." Because of the male's surplus value from engaging in petting or from stimulating the woman, he may go all the way because by doing so he will be better off than he would be if he were not allowed to touch. (He could be even better off if he could touch without assuming the risk of pregnancy.)

Second, a married man may want to establish a rather impermanent, now-and-then relationship with some woman other than his wife. He gets pleasure out of doing things for her, but he still does not want the relation-ship to seriously encrouch on his family life. The woman may require that he see her more often—engage in sexual relations more frequently—than he would freely choose. He may consent, again, because of the sur-plus value acquired from the first few "units" of the relationship con-sumed.

Lastly, one party may need to resort to sexual exploitation when his or her appetite for sex differs from the appetite of the other party. In any continuing relationship, it is quite possible that there will be times when the female appetite is greater than the appetite of the male. In such a cir-cumstance, the female may find it necessary to exploit the male; and before closing, it should, perhaps be noted that male foreplay may be one means by which the women have sexually exploited the men. They in effect say that "Either you arouse me, or I will not be interested in anything you have in mind."

CONCLUDING COMMENTS

By suggesting that the woman (or man) can be exploited if she (he) has a "monopolist" for a boyfriend (girlfriend), we have been saying, in effect, that exploitation can more likely occur if the relationship is a well-established, permanent one: that is, if the woman and man are "going steady" or are engaged. We submit that the analysis supports many of the fears of parents in seeing their teenage son or daughter becoming tied down into a permanent relationship. In concluding, we emphasize that the analysis indicates what the man (woman) can do, not what he (or she) will do. What either does is, again, dependent upon their consideration of the other's welfare.

PROBLEMS

1. Does the argument in the chapter suggest an explanation as to how children (and college students) can "exploit" their parents—that is, get more from their parents than their parents would freely choose to give?

2. Does the analysis suggest an explanation as to why an "only child" may more likely be "spoiled" than children who have several sisters and brothers?

7

Equal Pay for Equal Work

By most conventional measures, women as a group do not have the same economic clout as do men. Many have known this simple fact for some time; it has only been, however, since the publications of such books as *The Feminine Mystique* by Betty Frieden and *Sexual Politics* by Kate Millet that the inequality of the sexes has been anything more than a passing concern to a substantial portion of the population. Currently, conversations on the subject are often emotional; and frequently, the important questions of what exactly is the relative economic positions of women and what will be the effect of proposed remedies are lost in the heat of the argument. The purpose of this chapter is simply to clarify the status of women and the issues in the debate. We will pay particular attention to the probable effects of equal-pay-for-equal-work legislation. First, a look at the data.

THE ECONOMIC STATUS OF WOMEN

Historically, the proportion of women in the population has never been fully mirrored in the labor force. (The reader should recognize that the concept of the labor force, as defined by the Department of Labor, does not include housework.[1]) However, the labor force participation rate of women has been changing as indicated in Table 7–1. In 1970 women con-

---

[1] The reason for the exclusion of housewives from the definition of the labor force is basically that since housewives do not enter any formal market in which a price for their work is set, it is difficult to determine the monetary value of work of women in the home. This is particularly true if differences in the quality of labor is recognized. Housework is also not included in the computation of Gross National Product, which means that such data understates the total value of productive activity in the country.

74

TABLE 7–1
Women in the Labor Force, Selected Years, 1900–72

Year	Women in Labor Force (thousands)	Women in Labor Force as Percentage of	
		Total Labor Force	All Women of Working Age
1900	5,114	18.1	20.4
1910	7,889	20.9	25.2
1920	8,430	20.4	23.3
1930	10,679	22.0	24.3
1940	12,845	24.3	25.4
1945	19,270	29.6	35.7
1950	18,412	28.8	33.9
1955	20,584	30.2	35.7
1960	23,272	32.3	37.8
1965	26,232	34.0	39.3
1970	31,560	36.7	43.4
1972	33,320	37.4	43.8

Data for 1900 to 1940 are from decennial censuses and refer to a single date; beginning 1945 data are annual averages.

For 1900 to 1945 data include women 14 years of age and over; beginning 1950 data include women 16 years of age and over.

Labor force data for 1900 to 1930 refer to gainfully employed workers.

Data for 1972 reflect adjustments to 1970 census benchmarks.

Sources: *Economics Report of the President, 1973,* Department of Commerce, Bureau of the Census, and Department of Labor, Bureau of Labor Statistics.

stituted just over 18 percent of the total labor force; by 1972 this figure had risen to 37.4 percent. Notice that the majority of the change has occurred since 1940 and that the percentage of all women (16 years and older) who are working has also more than doubled since the beginning of the century, from 20.4 percent to 43.8 percent.[2] It is also clear that, in spite of recent attention given to the plight of women, the *trend* in the labor force participation of *women as a group* has not changed dramatically over, say, the past decade. As indicated in Table 7–1, what change there has been in the participation rates since 1950 has been due substantially to the greater participation of married women and younger women who have remained single or have been divorced, widowed, or are separated from their husbands. The change in the participation rates of younger women is shown more clearly in Figure 7–1. Women, for example, who may now be in college have had an initial participation rate approximately equal to the peak rate of women born much earlier, 1906–15, and could have been their mothers.

By reclassifying employment data collected by the Bureau of Labor

---

[2] Because the category of "all women of working age" includes females who are 16 years and older and that most women of high school and college age are likely to be in school, no one would expect the percentage of women working to be close to 100 percent.

FIGURE 7–1
Labor Force Participation over a Working Life of Cohorts of Women Born in Selected Time Intervals, 1886–1955

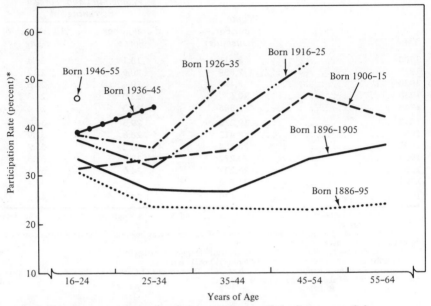

* Total labor force as percentage of total noninstitutional population in group specified.

For women born between 1886 and 1915, the first age plotted is 14–24 years. Cohorts reach each age interval according to the midpoint of their birth years. Thus, the cohort born 1886–95 reached ages 25–34 in 1920 and ages 55–64 in 1950; the cohort born 1916–25 reached ages 25–34 in 1950 and ages 45–54 in 1970.

Source: *Economic Report of the President, 1973;* Department of Commerce.

Statistics, Barbara R. Bergman and Irma Adelman are able to make the interesting observation that the overall employment pattern of women changed very little during the decade of the 1960s.[3] (See Table 7–2.) The "overrepresented" category—that is, occupations in which women account for more than 45 percent of the labor force—includes, as may be expected, such occupations as librarian, nursing, religious work, social work, elementary school teaching, and bookkeeping.[4] The percent of women in this occupational category changed only slightly, from 73.3 percent of all women workers in 1960 to 72.6 percent in 1970. By use of another statistical device, the Council of Economic Advisors drew a similar conclusion regarding the occupational shifts of women. If the reader has paid much attention to television and newspaper reports of "breakthroughs" in

---

[3] Barbara R. Bergman and Irma Adelman, "The 1973 Report of the President's Council of Economic Advisors: The Economic Role of Women," *American Economic Review,* 63 (September 1973), 509–14.

[4] The "well represented" category includes such occupations as authors and retail managers.

TABLE 7-2
Employment of Women in Occupations Classified by Extent of Women's
Representation in 1960

Occupations in which Women Were (in 1960)	1960		1971	
	Number in Thousands	Percentage of all Women Workers	Number in Thousands	Percentage of all Women Workers
Underrepresented (0–25%)	2,110	10.0	3,315	11.6
Well represented (25–45%)	3,503	16.7	4,470	15.8
Overrepresented (45–100%)	15,394	73.3	20,670	72.6
Total	21,007	100.0	28,455	100.0

Source: Barbara R. Bergman and Irma Adelman, "The 1973 Report of the President's Council of Economic Advisors: The Economic Role of Women," *American Economic Review* (September 1973), p. 510.

women employment and have accordingly formed an impression about what has been happening over the past few years, the data just presented is probably somewhat surprising.

There are several reasons that can be given for the growth in the labor force participation of women. First, real wages have been going up over time, and, consequently, the cost of staying at home has become greater. Also, the cost of "home produced" goods (since they are generally labor intensive) have become greater. Second, technological advances (in the form of such equipment as automatic washing machines) have occurred in housework. Women can now accomplish their work in less time. They can use a portion of their "greater real income" by going into the labor market, earning a money income, and buying clothes or other things they may want. They can thereby reap benefits from specialization.

Third, the divorce rate has been on the rise for some time. Since the divorce rate is currently somewhere in the neighborhood of one out of every three marriages, a married woman is assuming a considerable risk if she relies on her husband's income and stays at home. By staying at home, her education (or human capital stock) may depreciate for lack of use and can easily become obsolete with the changing times. If she is divorced after 15 years of marriage, she can find herself with very little earning power. She, therefore, may rationally go to work and self-insure herself against such consequences.

Fourth, there has been a disproportionate expansion of the service sector in the overall economy; and since women are disproportionately represented in that sector, one might expect a rise in the labor force participation rate of women. In other words, more employment opportunities could have arisen for women and, perhaps, more importantly, the real wage in the sector has risen, attracting women out of the home.

Fifth, and finally, there have probably been some long-run changes in the values of women (as well as men). Women's attitudes toward work and careers have been changing and their demand for children has been falling, causing a greater willingness to go out into and stay in the working world. (We should note here that these changes in values should have kept women's wages from rising as much as they otherwise would have. Can you explain why?)

We have said nothing that would explain the data that reflects very little change in the employment pattern of women among occupations within the working world; we have only attempted to explain the change in the employment pattern between home and the working world. The fact that the distribution of women workers among occupations has changed very little may indicate that (1) the types of jobs women as a group want has not changed very much; (2) the relative demand for women in "female occupations" has increased and the relative wages of women are greater by remaining in those occupations; or (3) the discriminatory barrier against women entering non-traditional fields are still as strong as ever. We suspect that all three forces are at work to some degree; which one is the most important is a question we feel cannot be answered with much conviction at this point in time. People in the forefront of the women's liberation movement, of course, are inclined to argue the case of the discriminatory barriers. It is also clear that the relative wage of people in the service sectors has been on the rise, and, as noted above, women are disproportionately represented in the service sector.

Unemployment

Table 7–3 illustrates the point that women have consistently experienced a higher rate of unemployment than men, 6.6 percent for women as opposed to 4.9 percent for men in 1972. Not only that, but the differential

TABLE 7–3
Unemployment Rates by Sex and Age, Selected Years, 1956–72*

Sex and Age	1956	1961	1965	1969	1972
All workers	4.1	6.7	4.5	3.5	5.6
Men	3.8	6.4	4.0	2.8	4.9
16–19 years	11.1	17.1	14.1	11.4	15.9
20–24 years	6.9	10.8	6.4	5.1	9.2
25–54 years	3.0	5.1	2.7	1.6	3.1
55 years and over	3.5	5.7	3.3	1.9	3.3
Women	4.9	7.2	5.5	4.7	6.6
16–19 years	11.2	16.3	15.7	13.3	16.7
20–24 years	6.3	9.8	7.3	6.3	9.3
25–54 years	4.1	6.2	4.3	3.5	4.9
55 years and over	3.3	4.4	2.8	2.2	3.4

* Unemployment as percentage of civilian labor force in group specified.
Source: *Economic Report of the President, 1973;* Department of Labor, Bureau of Labor Statistics.

in the employment rate has been rising over time, from 1.1 percentage points in 1956 to 1.7 percentage points in 1972. (This differential, however, went down between 1969 and 1972.) The reasons for the higher unemployment rates of women may include (1) layoffs, which tend to hit hardest among those who have the lowest seniority levels and women tend to be on the bottom rung of the ladder in terms of seniority; (2) a man who is employed and looking for work is not classified as unemployed whereas a woman working in the home who is looking for work is, because of the definition of the "unemployed," considered to be unemployed; (3) women are being discriminated against in employment opportunities; and (4) women are generally in the lower skilled occupations (by choice or force) and the unemployment rates are typically higher in such categories. Many of these same reasons can be given for why the differential in the unemployment rates of the sexes has been increasing and why the unemployment rates of women tend to fluctuate more with changes in general economic activity and with such public policy changes as increases in the minimum wage rate.

Earnings

There is, perhaps, no aspect of the economic status of women which can generate more emotional outrage than the wage differential between men as a group and women as a group. Table 7–4 and Figure 7–2 give a reasonably clear picture of the differential in earnings. At almost all occupational levels women do indeed earn substantially less than men. In 1971 the ratio of the women's earnings to men's earnings was 66.1 percent, after adjustments have been made. (See the Table notes for a description of the adjustments.) This means that the gross differential is approximately 34 percentage points and that men on average earned about 50 percent more than women. Note that the differential over time has not changed very much; the gross differential for all women actually went down between 1956 and 1971. Figure 7–2 reveals that in the past college women could expect to earn for most of their working life less than men with high school degrees.

What explains the differentials? First, it should be recognized that the computed annual earnings of women *could be* less because, for example, they have less education or are in lower skill jobs,[5] women have fewer years of seniority, and the working women are concentrated in regions that as a general rule have lower pay. These are possibilities, and the point

---

[5] Many will argue that women are in lower skilled jobs because of prejudice, as we have recognized, and because they are in lower skilled jobs their human capital does not rise as much as men, causing a greater differential in earnings as men and women become older.

TABLE 7–4
Ratio of Total Money Earnings of Civilian Women Workers to Earnings of Civilian Men Workers, Selected Years, 1956–71

Occupational Group	Actual Ratios					Adjusted Ratios*	
	1956	1960	1965	1969	1971	1969	1971
Total†	63.3	60.7	59.9	58.9	59.5	65.9	66.1
Professional and technical workers	62.4	61.3	65.2	62.2	66.4	67.9	72.4
Teachers, primary and secondary schools	(‡)	75.6	79.9	72.4	82.0	(‡)	(‡)
Managers, officials, and proprietors	59.1	52.9	53.2	53.1	53.0	57.2	56.8
Clerical workers	71.7	67.6	67.2	65.0	62.4	70.0	66.9
Sales workers	41.8	40.9	40.5	40.2	42.1	45.7	47.4
Craftsmen and foremen	(§)	(§)	56.7	56.7	56.4	60.8	60.2
Operatives	62.1	59.4	56.6	58.7	60.5	65.4	66.6
Service workers excluding private household workers	55.4	57.2	55.4	57.4	58.5	62.5	63.2

* Adjusted or differences in average full-time hours worked since full-time hours for women are typically less than full-time hours for men.
† Total includes occupational groups not shown separately.
‡ Not available.
§ Base too small to be statistically significant.
Data relate to civilian workers who are employed full-time, year round. Data for 1956 include salaried workers only, while data for later years include both salaried and self-employed workers.
Sources: *Economic Report of the President, 1973;* Department of Commerce, Bureau of the Census, Department of Labor, Bureau of Labor Statistics, and Council of Economic Advisers.

FIGURE 7–2
Annual Income by Age, for Male and Female High School and College Graduates

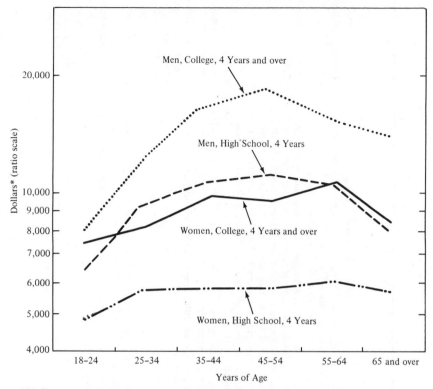

* Median income of full-time, year-round workers, 1971.
Source: *Economic Report of the President, 1973*, Department of Commerce.

that needs to be made is that before we can accept the argument that the gross differential in men and women wages reflects the amount or degree of discrimination, statistical manipulations must be performed on the data to account for the differences in the characteristics of the two groups. Because this is not a book on statistical inference and because of space limitations, we will not discuss how these adjustments can be made.[6]

Several studies have tackled the problem of accounting for the differential in the annual earnings of the sexes. Table 7–5 summarizes the results. Because the different studies were undertaken in different years, used different samples, and adjusted for different variables, the gross and net

---

[6] Actually, this is just a polite way of saying that the benefits of discussing methods used in statistically adjusting the data are not as great as the costs of doing so. This is also what other writers mean when they make similar statements. Would you expect the authors to use a few pages to add the necessary explanation if you or someone else would give them $10,000 to do so? Would you do it?

TABLE 7-5
Summary of Findings on Sex Wage Differentials

Author	Gross Earnings Differential*	Net Earnings Differential*	Variables Analyzed	Data Base
Sanborn	.42	.12	Detailed occupations, hours, age, education, color, and urban-ness within detailed occupations. Rough estimate of effects of turnover, absenteeism, and experience.	Experienced civilian labor force, 1950.
Morgan et al.	.36	.37	Broad occupation, education and age, population of city, urban-rural migration, movement out of Deep South, extent of unemployment in state, supervisory responsibility, attitude toward hard work and need achievement score, race, interviewers' assessment of ability to communicate, geographic mobility, physical condition, rank and progress in school.	Heads of household, 1959.
Fuchs	.40	.34	Color, schooling, age, city size, marital status, class of worker, length of trip.	Nonfarm employed persons, 1960.
Cohen	.45	.31†	Hours, fringe benefits, absenteeism, seniority, education, unionization.	Nonprofessional employees, aged 22–64, with a steady job, working 35 or more hours per week, 1969.
Oaxaca	.35	.29	Experience, health, migration, hours, marital status, city size, region.	Urban whites, 1967.
Suter and Miller	.57	.31	Education, occupation, work experience in 1966 life-time career experience.	Male wage and salary workers, 1967, plus special longitudinal subsample of women, aged 30–44.

Sawhill	.46	.57	Age, education, race, region, hours and weeks worked, and time spent in the labor force.	Employed wage and salary workers in civilian labor force, 1967.
Council of Economic Advisors	NA	20	Training, continuity at work, lifelong work experience, and others.	Sample is unspecified.
Department of Labor	NA	close to 0	Detailed job classifications and being within the same establishment, and other factors.	Sample is unspecified.

* The earnings differential is equal to 1 = F/M where F and M represent female and male earnings in some form (varying from study to study). The Morgan *et al.* and Fuchs differentials are based on hourly earnings.

† Calculated by present author as 1 = F*/M where F* is female earnings adjusted for hours, fringe benefits and absenteeism, seniority, education, and unionization. NA—data unavailable.

Sources: The summaries of the first seven studies were taken from Isabell V. Sawhill, "The Economics of Discrimination Against Women: Some New Findings," *Journal of Human Resources* (Summer 1973), 382–96. The primary sources are:

Henry Sanborn, "Pay Differences Between Men and Women," *Industrial and Labor Relations Review* (July 1964).

James N. Morgan et. al., *Income and Welfare in the United States*, New York: McGraw-Hill, 1962.

Victor Fuchs, "Differences in Hourly Earnings between Men and Women," *Monthly Labor Review* (May 1971).

Malcohm S. Cohen, "Sex Differences in Competition," *Journal of Human Resources* (Fall 1971).

Ronald Oaxaca, "Sex Differences in Wages," paper presented at a conference sponsored by the Woodrow Wilson School of Public and International Affairs, October 1971.

Larry E. Suter and Herman P. Miller, "Components of Income Differences between Men and Career Women," paper presented at the American Sociological Association meetings, September 1971.

Isabel V. Sawhill, "The Economics of Discrimination Against Women: Some New Findings," *Journal of Human Resources*, 8 (Summer 1973), 383–396. The secondary source of last two studies is *Economic Report of the President*, 1973, Washington: U.S. Government Printing Office, 1973.

differentials (that is, the differentials that remain after adjustments) are different. The gross differentials vary from 0.57 to 0.35 (the gross differentials in the studies conducted by the Council of Economic Advisors and Department of Labor could not be pinned down with precision in the sources that were used). The net differentials run from a low of approximately zero to a high of 0.57. In the case of the study by Sawhill the differential went up substantially after adjustments.

How much of a differential is there between sexes? Bergman and Adelman emphasize the importance of the findings in the second through seventh studies.[7] The Council of Economic Advisors concluded, "Some studies have succeeded in narrowing the male-female differential well below 20 percent. Indeed, Department of Labor surveys have found that the differential almost disappears when men's and women's earnings are compared within the same establishment. In the very narrow sense of equal pay for the same job in the same plant there may be little difference between women and men. However, in this way the focus of the problem is shifted but not eliminated, for then we must explain why women have such a different job structure and why they are employed in different types of establishments."[8]

WHY THE NET DIFFERENTIAL

A net differential between men's and women's earnings can remain after adjustments because not all relevant variables are considered. It may also be that the quantitative data used may not accurately represent the qualitative differentials. For example, a group of men and women may have worked for the same number of years, but the quality of the work experience, or the human capital acquired, can be dramatically different. As pointed out by Bergman and Adelman, the male management trainee has surely acquired more human capital after ten years on the job than the female clerical worker. It may also be true that the number of years in college glosses over the quality differences in men and women's education.

There is also the pure and simple fact that women are often discriminated against. This may be because the employers have a definite preference for working with male employees; women employers can have the same preferences. Because of the lack of controls on their behavior, they are able to express their preferences in their hiring practices. Customers, who are the ultimate employers, may also have a preference for buying from men, which means that the marginal value of men is greater than the

---

[7] Bergman and Adelman, *1973 Report*, p. 509.

[8] *Economic Report of the President, 1973*, p. 106.

marginal value of women.[9] The demand for men is greater and their wage is correspondingly higher.

Many persons who discuss the topic point the real world fact that employers are inclined to presume that certain jobs are for women and certain jobs are for men. Women are, therefore, because of the decision rules that are formulated, crowded into typically "female occupations." The crowding results in the wages of the workers (mostly female) in those occupations to be depressed. (The crowding can also be partly the result of women choosing, because of inculturated attitudes or independent preferences, to go into those occupations.)

Decision rules can, from the standpoint of the employers, be rationally formulated. Hiring people is an expensive process at best, and obtaining more information about each individual person who applies is progressively more costly. By not obtaining the more detailed information on prospective employees, the employer can make mistakes. He can hire people who are not productive, and he may after a short while have to incur the cost of replacing them. Likewise, the employer may incur less cost by formulating a decision rule and making mistakes than he would incur if he obtained more information on each applicant[10] and made fewer mistakes.

As an illustration of the point being made, consider the continuum shown (Figure 7–3), which represents the "quality of work" (in any dimension that the reader would like) for a given job. Let us assume, just for purposes of illustration, that the distribution of women is to the left of the distribution of men. This can be either because the employer *knows* where the distributions lie or because he believes, and may be wrong, that they lie in the indicated positions. There are some women who are of higher quality than some men, and vice versa. The mean for the women is still to the left of the mean for men. If the wages of men and women were the same and the cost of acquiring sufficient information to accurately place each applicant on the spectrum were quite high, the employer may find it profitable (in what sense?) to formulate the rule that men will be hired if a choice is to be made.[11] *On average,* the employer would receive (or would believe that he is receiving) a higher quality of work. This, of course, means that some women, particularly those who are of higher quality than the mean for men, would be discriminated against. This does not mean, however, that the employer is acting out of any sinister motive.

---

[9] Is this a pure form of discrimination in the sense in which the term is normally used? What other aspects of customer behavior can we classify as discriminatory?

[10] Remember that the probability of the information obtained being correct is likely to be less than one. (What will this do to the employer's willingness to obtain the information?)

[11] The reader should understand that the whole field of social science has been developed, at least, in part, to derive beneficial decision rules.

FIGURE 7–3
(Perceived) Quality Distributions of Women and Men

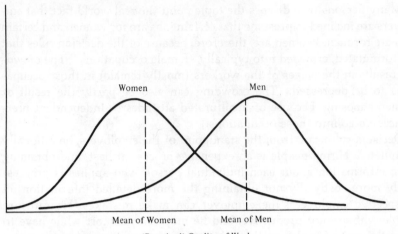

He is merely attempting to maximize the accomplishment of his objectives, which may not include "putting women down." When the wage differential results, it becomes rational for the employer to hire the women even though they are of less quality or are believed to be of less quality on average. (Why?) If the reason for decision rule is incorrect beliefs on the part of the employer or incorrect information, the solution is to educate the employer: he must be shown that his decision rule is not in his best interest. If the problem is a matter of taste, then preferences must be changed, which may be a long-term project.

SEX DISCRIMINATION: PROFIT VERSUS NON-PROFIT INSTITUTIONS

Should we expect profit maximizing firms to discriminate more than non-profit, say, governmental organization? On the surface, one could argue that public, non-profit organizations are set up for the purpose of operating in the "public interest," which may mean in part that the people who work in such institutions are more public spirited and are more tuned to social needs. One might expect them to be more "fair" when it comes to employment policies. As we will discuss in more detail in a later chapter, this idealized picture of the "public servant" is probably inappropriate. As a group, it may be more appropriate to describe public servants as rational, utility maximizing human beings who, as a group, are not distinctly different from everyone else in the private sector. Indeed, it may be a little inconsistent to view public bureaucrats as private utility maximizers when it comes to their non-working lives and as social utility maximizers when it comes to their work. Public servants do have their own preferences *and* prejudices. (The authors of this book are public bureaucrats—we teach in public universities—and we must confess that we do not believe we are materially different in our motives from the people that work for AT&T.)

In private institutions, profit is not the only incentive for behavior, but it is one of the incentives; and to the degree that the profit incentive is present, people can gain by making and increasing the profit. The objectives of the public institutions are not in general as clearly defined (take a look at the statement of objectives of your university, if you happen to be in school); wages of employees, who can also be employers of other bureaucrats, are more closely associated with years of service or education as is the case in school systems (consider the Civil Service pay scales) and are less closely associated with the profit of the organization. This seems to be a fairly reasonable expectation since profit is generally not an objective. Accordingly, one would expect that a public servant can, if he wishes, more easily express his own preferences with regard to employment practices or any other objective which *he* may consider to be in the "public interest." If pay is fixed with years of work, for example, he can gain very little (or, less as a general rule, than he would if he were in a private institution) by setting his preferences aside. With a profit incentive system a person is in effect paid to do what may not be consistent with his personal preferences. We would, contrary to what may be the general view, expect more sex (and race) discrimination within non-profit, governmental organizations than in profit maximizing firms. This is not to say that profit maximizing firms do not discriminate.

As far as we know, no one has done a study on the sex discrimination in profit and non-profit organizations. There has been at least one study on *race* discrimination in the two types of organizations;[12] and as we would predict, the amount of discrimination within the non-profit firms was significantly greater. This one study, of course, does not confirm our hypothesis regarding sex discrimination, but it is suggestive of what some future study may reveal.

EQUAL PAY LEGISLATION

Laws requiring equal pay for men and women doing the same jobs may appear on the surface to be an unambiguous solution to the achievement of greater social justice. However, as is often true in economics, appear-

---

[12] William J. Haley and John Paul Combs, "The Profit Motive and Labor Market Discrimination," Ann Arbor: Michigan State University, Econometrics Workshop Papers, September 1973.

ances can be deceiving. The purpose of this section is to use supply and demand curves to demonstrate that, contrary to the good intentions of those who favor equal pay legislation, effective enforcement of the law can reduce the employment opportunities of women and expand the opportunities of men. The analysis suggests that achievement of social justice for some will be at the expense of an injustice to others.

In demonstrating the above conclusion, we assume that men and women produce a homogeneous product, and for this women are paid less than men. We further assume that men and women are substitutes in employment, although not perfect substitutes,[13] and that the demand for both men and women has the normal negative slope. It is also assumed that the supply curves of men and women are upward sloping and, for simplicity, are equal and that the labor market is purely competitive.[14]

If the markets are competitive, the explanation for the higher wages of men must lie in the fact that the demand for men is greater (relative to the supply) than the demand for women. In Figure 7-4A the demand and

FIGURE 7-4

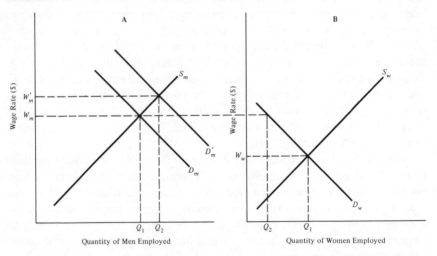

Quantity of Men Employed   Quantity of Women Employed

supply for men are respectively D_m and S_m; the demand and supply for women are similarly labeled in Figure 7-4B. The wage established in the market for women is W_w which is below the wage for men, W_m.

If the demand for men is greater relative to the supply, it must be due to one of two conditions: either the men are actually more productive (in

---

[13] If men and women were perfect substitutes in the eyes of employers, it would be difficult indeed to explain why wage rates differ between the sexes.

[14] Given the relatively large number of employers in most labor markets, the assumption of competitive markets is reasonable.

some tangible or intangible sense) or the employers have been misguided and *believe*, although incorrectly, that men are more productive than women. (We will avoid engaging in the debate on which explanation is relatively more important.) In either case, the demand for men will still be greater and the predicted wage differential holds. Furthermore, any discriminatory "taste" factor for men employees can be fully accommodated in this analysis and does not alter the conclusions drawn. (If it is argued that women are crowded into female occupation, then the same model can be used since there will still be some wage differential.)

Assume now that the Justice Department requires (through effective enforcement) that the men and women in the two markets be paid the same and that the requirement is implemented by raising the wage of women to W_m.[15] The results are that, assuming the employers' attitudes toward the sexes are unaffected, the quantity of women employed falls from Q_1 to Q_2 in Figure 7–4B. As indicated in Figure 7–4B, there are women who will benefit from the legislation; these are the ones who retain their jobs and who receive the higher wage. However, this may be small solace to those women who lose their jobs and are forced on to the unemployment roles or to seek employment in jobs that do not come under the scrutiny and enforcement of the law. In fact, economic theory would predict that if the equal-pay-equal-work law is enforced, more women than at present would be forced to accept employment where their large numbers now determine the wage rate, such as cleaning, teaching, clerical and secretarial work, and cooking. Isabell Sawhill, in a study mentioned earlier, draws this conclusion from her empirical work.[16]

At the same time, just as an increase in the price of one good will increase the demand for its substitutes, *ceteris paribus*, the increase in the wage of women will increase the demand for their substitutes, for example, men; and if permitted, not only will the quantity of men employed rise (to Q_2 in Figure 7–4A), but their wage rate will also rise to W_m').[17] Pursuit of equality of pay scales for the sexes may only lead to an ever-shrinking market for women.

The policy implication is that if the economic status (that is, the wage) of women is to be improved, the basic market conditions (supply and demand) for women's labor must be changed, not just the price. If the supply is left unchanged, the way to narrow (or eliminate) the wage differential between the sexes is to increase the demand for women relative

---

[15] It is highly unlikely that Congress would force the wages of men down to the level of women.

[16] Isabell V. Sawhill, "The Economics of Discrimination against Women: Some New Findings," *Journal of Human Resources*, 8 (Summer 1973), 383–396.

[17] If the wage rate of men is not allowed to rise, all of the traditional problems associated with price controls would develop, and the wage differential between men and women may be merely disguised.

to men. Assuming that employers are in fact prejudiced against women or mistakenly believe women are less competent than men, employers must be re-educated or proven wrong and/or have their preferences changed. (Accomplishing this is a major thrust of the women's liberation movement.) In addition, the productivity of women can be up-graded by a change in women's skills and, perhaps, in their socially derived attitudes toward work, careers, and the family.[18] These changes mean, in essence, that in the eyes of the employers women must become indistinguishable from men, which, in the final analysis, may be impossible. These changes will take time, and this may explain why so many have opted for the apparently simple solution of immediately raising the wage. In any event, the analysis suggests that if women are not to lose ground in employment opportunities, equal pay laws may have to be accompanied by quantity controls.[19]

There are three major criticisms that may be leveled against the foregoing analysis. First, it may be argued that there are labor markets that are not competitive and that under monopsonistic conditions an increase in the wage for women will not reduce their level of employment. More sophisticated theories of market structures supports this last inference, and it may be conceded that there are markets which are monopsonistic. However, the general conclusion—that an increase in the wage of women will result in a *marginal* reduction in their employment—will remain valid as long as there are labor markets that are competitive. To assume all labor markets are monopsonistic is indeed an extreme assumption. Besides, no one seems to be arguing that sex discrimination is the result of monopsonistic labor markets.

Second, the analysis does not consider the dynamic effects equal-pay-for-equal-work laws will have on employer attitudes: by paying women the same as men, employers will realize that women are every bit as valuable as men; and, therefore, the demand for women will rise in the long run. It may be argued that the observed effects of other similar laws demonstrate the importance of the dynamic effects and that the analysis is probably wrong. These arguments are often voiced, but the mechanism through which the change in attitude occurs is left unclear. Statements such as the law will have a psychological effect are not very satisfying. Why would an increase in the wage paid to women change the employer's assessment of the laborers' value? An answer is needed because the issue raised goes to the heart of economic theory: Does the employer look to the

---

[18] A frequently heard complaint from feminists is that women are culturally bound to low paying jobs.

[19] One solution, which may not be politically practical, is to impose a legal minimum wage for men above their current wage level. This would increase the demand for women.

wage paid to determine what the value of a laborer is, or does he look to what the laborer produces to determine what the laborer's wage should be? Which provides the sounder basis for theorizing? Because of the experience economists have had with the latter approach, we as economists, have a strong bias for it. Besides, if there is a short-run negative response to the increase in the wage of women, it would appear that since there will be fewer women employed, there will be less opportunity for the employers to "learn" that women are indeed as productive as men; there will be fewer opportunities for women to demonstrate their capabilities.[20]

The empirical evidence relating to the effects of legal wage floors tend to support our conclusions. Clearly, the equal pay laws are a form of minimum wage legislation: women must be paid no less than men. And, the weight of the evidence supports the conclusion that minimum wage laws do have an adverse effect on the employment opportunities of those who are covered by the laws. Since John Peterson and Charles Stewart have made an extensive review of past studies of the effects of minimum wage laws, several of their conclusions may be noted:

> The impression created in most government studies that federal minimum wage policy has produced no adverse employment effects is erroneous.
>
> The general model of economic theory (that is, the competitive model) most clearly corresponds to the observed results of statutory minimums, whereas the alternative models used to be non-predictive in theory and in fact.
>
> Minimum wage rates produce gains for some groups of workers at the expense of others. . . .[21]

A recent study by Kosters and Welch[22] found that in addition to reducing the level of employment, minimum wage rates increased the instability of those who have been covered by the laws, particularly nonwhites and the young. Is there any reason to believe that equal pay laws for women will have any different consequence than the more conventional minimum wage laws? In support of minimum wage rates, many advocates have argued forcefully that those who are covered would otherwise be the victims of discrimination and would, once covered, demonstrate that they deserve the higher wage.

---

[20] Furthermore, not all dynamic effects are likely to be in favor of women. Because of the equal pay laws, the employer may substitute capital, as well as men, for women and by doing so may discover that the capital equipment is more productive than he had originally thought. A greater effort may be made to develop new nonhuman substitutes for labor.

[21] John M. Peterson and Charles T. Stewart, *Employment Effects of Minimum Wage Rates*, Washington: American Enterprise Institute for Public Policy Research, 1969.

[22] Marvin Kosters and Finis Welch, "The Effects of Minimum Wages on the Distribution of Changes in Aggregate Employment," *American Economic Review* 62, (June 1972), 323–331.

Third, it may be contended that the adverse effects of the law may be inconsequential and that the benefits to the many far exceed the harm done to the few. Such a position would not, as noted above, be very comforting to those women who are made worse off because of the law. The fact that there will probably be many more women whose wages are raised than there will be women who are adversely affected by the legislation probably goes a long way toward explaining why Congressmen are prone to support such laws.

The whole argument does suggest a strategy for women leaders: equal pay laws should be coupled with quantitative controls to insure against adverse employment effects. In addition, by requiring employers to hire more women than they otherwise would (for example, through "affirmative action" programs), the result can be an increase in the demand for women *and* an increase in their wage rates. This, of course, brings into focus the problems associated with controls and the prospects of "reverse discrimination." Currently, because of the pressure being placed on departments of economics in universities to hire more women economists and because of the relatively few women economists, the starting salary of a new and inexperienced female economist is approximately 10 to 25 percent above her male counterparts.

part three

The Family

8

Marriage, Divorce, and the Family

The family is generally considered to be the basic building block on which social order is founded. However, even with all the attention that social scientists and others have given it, the family remains perhaps one of the least understood institutions. The purpose of this chapter is to develop insights into the marriage and family processes. Our approach is somewhat unusual. Certainly we recognize the importance of "love" in marriage and the family. However, we also recognize that in considering the establishment of a family, individuals are driven by a variety of motives. Some of these are not fundamentally different from those that lead people to buy a car or new clothes.

In addition, we will treat the family in its function as a producing unit. It is a "firm" that takes resources, including labor from within the family and the goods that are purchased, and produces things desired by family members. We want to look inside the family unit and analyze its behavior in terms of the behavior of its members. In the process we are able to make observations regarding the importance of the marriage contract, the difficulty of divorce, the economic implications of "love," and organizational principles underlying the family structure.[1]

---

[1] Because of his pioneering efforts, we are indebted to Gary Becker for his work in the area. Gary S. Becker, "A Theory of Marriage: Part I," *Journal of Political Economy*, 81 (July/August 1973), 813–46, and "A Theory of Marriage: Part II," *Journal of Political Economy*, 82, supplement (March/April 1974), s11–s26.

THE MARRIAGE CONTRACT AND DIVORCE

Marriage can be defined in many different ways,[2] but for our purposes we view it as a contract between a man and woman (or between two parties of the same sex if homosexual marriages are ever legalized). Each party explicitly or implicitly makes certain commitments as to his or her responsibilities within the family. He and she agree to recognize certain rights and privileges of the other, and both agree, again explicitly or implicitly, to a set of rules by which household decisions and changes in the contract are to be made. This last provision is necessary because not all issues concerning the relationship are ever likely to be settled before the vows are said and because conditions do change.

Such provisions of the contract may only be vaguely understood and recognized as such; but nevertheless, they are generally present in one fashion or another. The couple may simply have an understanding that they will "work things out together," tacitly realizing from their knowledge of the other's behavior what this means. The "process of marriage" may be compared with the development of a constitution and bylaws for any firm or organization; and as in the case of any one organization, the rules of the game can be as restrictive or as flexible as the people involved desire. In fact, the central purpose of dating and engagement may be to give the couple a chance to work out such provisions and to develop the contract by which both agree to live. (All couples do not, however, avail themselves of this chance to the same degree.) The contract, for example, may incorporate a provision on whether or not and how many children will be included, who will do the housework and mow the lawn, and which decisions will be democratically determined by the whole family and which decisions will be administratively determined. Although we might like to think that everything regarding the marriage *should* hinge on love, the division of the responsibilities and rewards may be greatly influenced by and relative bargaining power of the two involved.

Without the opportunity to develop such provisions, or if they are left undetermined, considerable disagreement can arise in the future, resulting in divorce. Because people have different views on what a marriage should be, the marriage may never take place, and very often does not. This is because the couple involved cannot agree on what the contract should be. In this sense the dating process screens out some of those marriages that will otherwise fold. Resources are used in dating, but at the same time the process saves resources from being tied-up (albeit temporary) in an unsatisfactory marriage.

---

[2] Webster's defines marriage as "the institution whereby men and women are joined in a special kind of social and legal dependence for the purpose of founding and maintaining a family" (*Webster's Seventh New Collegiate Dictionary.* Springfield, Mass.: G&C Merriam Company, 1967).

Divorce can often be the result of insufficient resources (time, energy, and emotional hassle) being invested by the couple in developing the marriage contract. This may be because the two misjudged how many resources are required; it may also be that either or both of the parties calculate that the expected gain from spending more time and energy on the contract will not be worth the cost.

Except in the cast of divorce, most provisions of the marriage contract generally do not have the force of law. Occasionally, there are cases in which a wife or husband takes her or his spouse to court (e.g., for lack of support) but these are indeed relatively rare events. One reason is that the mutually agreed upon contract is vague and rarely written down. Another is that the cost of one spouse taking the other to court can be considerable in terms of time and lawyer's fees and can be easily greater than any benefits that may be achieved. So many of the violations of the contract are of a trivial nature, such as one party's refusal to take out the garbage, to spend time with the children, or to refrain from flirting with other men or women. The potential benefits are just not that great, even if the court will consider the case. In addition, the court fight itself, which may generate a great deal of antagonism, can represent considerable cost.

If the provisions have any meaning, it is mainly because of the moral obligation such agreement engenders, the pressures that can be brought to bare on the parties involved by either party or by friends and others, and the threat of one party retaliating by shirking his/her responsibilities. The main role of the court has generally been one of refereeing the division of the family assets (children included) between the husband and wife at the time of divorce. On occasion the court does attempt to bring about reconciliation.

This role of the court in the divorce process is one that is not unimportant and without economic implications. The reason is that the court's intrusion insures that the husband and wife each has *some* property rights in the family assets, both tangible and intangible. To this extent, the husband and wife have a greater incentive to "invest" their time and other resources in the development of family assets and building a strong marital relationship. The family is an investment project in the sense that returns can be received over the span of years.

An analogy of an investment in a business is useful here. Suppose an entrepreneur is considering an investment in an office building. Will he be willing to make the investment if he knows that after doing so he has no property rights to the building—that is, someone else can take it over without any objection from the courts? Although he may be willing to make some investment in the enterprise and to protect it, he will probably be more willing to do so and to invest a larger amount if he has some rights that are protected by the state. The whole investment project will be less costly to him. The same can be applied to the willingness of the partners in a marriage to invest in the union. To the extent that the stability and durability of the marriage is favorably affected by such investments, the legal status of the marriage yields benefits to all parties in the family.

There is one problem here. That is, by giving each partner property rights over the family assets and to some extent over the other and by making the dissolution of the marriage costly, the husband or wife *can*, if she or he desires, abuse the other. Since there is a cost involved in divorce, one may allow himself or herself to be "exploited" because he may then be better off than if he/she incurs the cost. If the abuse is greater than the cost of going through with divorce, it goes without saying that the marriage will be dissolved. If the parties are single and living together, any one party can walk away without legal constraints. This may force the other party to be more considerate.

THE COSTS AND BENEFITS OF
MARRIAGE AND THE FAMILY

In the sense that all behavior is *rational*, people's behavior with regard to marriage must also be rational. (Can you think of any reason we should assume differently?) This, of course, means that in choosing a spouse, both sexes are out to maximize their utility. It also means that in the process of becoming married, each individual must address two very fundamental questions:

1. What are the costs and benefits in general of being married as opposed to remaining single?
2. Given these benefits and costs, how long and hard should he or she search for an appropriate mate?

The Costs of Marriage

In assessing the pros and cons of marriage, the individual must reckon with several major cost considerations. One of the most important for some but by no means all persons is the loss (cost) of independence. An individual is never completely free to do exactly what he pleases; he must consider the effects his actions have on others. However, in the close proximity of the family, the possible effects which any one person's action can have on another in the family are more numerous and direct than for the person who lives alone. The result can be that everyone may willingly agree to restrict their own behavior to a much greater extent than would be necessary if they all lived alone. They may, and very likely will, also agree to make many decisions by democratic or collective action. In taking this step, the members of the household essentially agree to incur future decision costs, which include the time and trouble of reaching a decision. This is because it is generally more costly to make decisions with a larger number of people involved.

For example, it is more costly for one of the authors, McKenzie, who is married, to purchase a new car than Tullock who is single. All Tullock has to do in buying a car is consider his own preferences. McKenzie, on the other hand, must not only consider his own preference, but also those of his wife and children. The result can be and almost always is that buying a car is a long drawn out process for the McKenzies. Note that if McKenzie and his wife had identical preferences, which to be sure is never the case in marriages, their decision cost would be the same as Tullock's. In such event, McKenzie would not have to bring his wife in on the decision to buy the car or anything else, and she would not care that he did not. Because of identical preferences, they both could be assured that whatever he bought, each would like it as well as the other. We have used just one example of the numerous times in which decision costs are incurred in a family. (If the reader thinks that such costs are unimportant, he should try marriage for a convincing empirical study!)

It is because of such decision costs that husbands and wives often agree to have many decisions made administratively by one party or the other. One party can be allowed, without consulting the other, to make decisions with respect to, say, the family meals, except under unusual circumstances. The other party can determine what clothes will be purchased for the children and what types of flowers to plant in the yard. Each party may make decisions not agreeable with the other; however, the savings in decision costs can yield benefits that more than offset the effects of "wrong" decisions.

Wives often have the responsibility of making decisions with respect to meals and the interior of the house in general and husbands make decisions with respect to the yard and the exterior of the house, and this fact has been attributed to inculturated values; that is, spouses are merely role playing. Although there may be some truth in the statements, we suggest that such argument does not explain why the responsibilities for decisions are divided in the first place. Our analysis indicates that the division of decision-making power within the home can be added efficiency to the operation of the household and that if roles are not assumed to begin with, they would tend to evolve. The division of powers may not end up in the same way that we now observe them, but given what they are there may then be the criticism that inculturated roles are being assumed.

As suggested above, the family is involved to a considerable extent in the production of goods and services shared by all members of the family. These are basically of one type and available in one quantity and quality. Such a good—take for example the car considered above—may not be perfectly suitable for any one individual's tastes, but it is the good everyone agrees to buy. In this instance, and there are many of them, each individual must bare the cost of not getting the good in the amount and quality that is most suitable to his preferences.

This type of cost is not only incurred because of the goods produced by the family—such as cars, television programs, recreation, and "family life" (which tends to defy definition)—but is also applicable to relationships with other people. Both spouses may agree to associate with certain people, not because either finds the people to be *best* suited to what they find desirable in friends, but because the selected friends represent compromises for them both. This is not to say that each person will not have several friends of his/her own, but only that they are likely to agree on "mutual friends." To the extent that they associate with their mutual friends, there is less time for them to be with their individual friends. We submit that this can be a legitimate cost calculation in marriage.

To the extent that household decisions are democratically determined, members of the household have a say on how the burden of the production of the household goods is to be distributed. In this way they can determine who pays, either in terms of contribution of money income or time, and effort. The family can effectively "tax" family members in a way that is similar to any other collective, governmental unity. Any family member can, like any citizen, be forced to pay for collective goods and projects with which they may not be in perfect agreement. This can be considered a potential cost to a family member. This is evident from the complaints that one may hear in a home when the decision is made to go on a picnic and the burden of preparation is distributed or when one is asked to take out the garbage or mow the lawn.

Other costs associated with marriage and the family in general include the risk cost of developing strong emotional ties with one specific group of individuals and the forgoing of the opportunity to date and in other ways associate with other people. These factors may be of no consequence to some, and may in fact be an advantage to others. Further, the cost of marrying one particular person can be the loss of the opportunity to have married someone else who is not known at the time of marriage but who, if he/she were sought out, would be a more desirable spouse. The list of cost provided can, of course, be extended.

The Benefits of Marriage and Family

The benefits of marriage and the family are derived mainly from the ability of the family to produce goods and services wanted. First, the spouses have the opportunity to produce things not readily duplicated in non-marriage situations. Such a list may include children (at least ones that cannot legitimately be called bastards), prestige and status that can affect employment and the realm of friends, companionship that is solid and always there, a "family-styled sex life" that may be more desirable than sexual associations with which the individual may disapprove, and "family life" in general, which we indicated above defies definition. Granted, many of these goods can be had in certain quantities and qualities outside of the family; we are only suggesting that they take on special characteristics within the family and for that reason are valuable to people. (We recognize that to some these are costs.)

Secondly, the family operating as a single household—that is, more than one individual—can produce many goods and services more efficiently than can several single-person households. This is because there are economics of scale in household production. Take for example, the problem of cleaning the household rug. Although there may be some selection in size and power of vacuum cleaners, generally speaking, the machines available are capable of handling the dirt of several people. However, *one* cleaner must be *purchased*. If more people are added to the house, the household need not increase the number, size, or power of the vacuum cleaner proportionally. The same can be said of many of the resources that go into the production of a garden, meals, and other household goods such as washing machines, rakes, mixers, brooms, electric toothbrushes, etc.

Indeed, many of the goods and services provided by individuals in the home are *public goods:* they benefit everyone involved and do not diminish in quantity or quality if additional people are added to the household. For example, many things done to beautify the house are this kind of good. If a picture that all like is hung on the wall, one person's enjoyment of it does not detract in any significant way from the enjoyment by others. Because they all live under the same roof, they each do not have to provide such goods for themselves individually, meaning that they can raise the quality of the goods that are had or they can divert resources to other purposes. Such goods may not be enjoyed or appreciated by a very large group of people and because of the decision costs involved, as explained, there is some point at which the collective group would be too large. Therefore, we would expect some unit in society to develop that would be small enough that people of similar tastes can be together to have them and large enough that they can be provided efficiently. The family, in our view, is that unit. It is large enough to provide such goods as these efficiently yet small enough that the decision costs incurred are minimized. By having provision for numerous such family units, individuals are given considerable choice over the type, amount, and quality of these goods.

The efficiency of household production can also be greater because of the opportunities for the parties to specialize and effectively trade with one another. In this way the parties can take advantage of their comparative efficiency in production. Suppose that, for simplicity sake only, there are only two things for the household to do, clean a given size house and mow its lawn which is of a given size. Suppose also that we are given the following information about the abilities of a husband and wife in doing these two things:

	Cleaning the House	Mowing the Lawn
Wife	60 minutes	100 minutes
Husband	100 minutes	300 minutes

What this table shows is that the wife can clean the house in 60 minutes and can mow the lawn in 100 minutes. It takes the husband 100 minutes for the house and 300 minutes for the lawn. If they both live separately and have lawns to mow and houses to clean, it would take them a total of 560 minutes. If they lived together and each cleaned half the house and mowed half of the lawn, it would take them a total of 280 minutes (80 minutes for the house cleaning and 200 minutes for the lawn). However, there is a possibility here for the two to specialize, one cleaning the house and one mowing the lawn. Since each will be doing something for the other, we can, in a sense, say they are trading.

To see this prospect, recognize that every time the wife cleans the house she gives up 3/5 of the lawn being mowed. If she spends 60 minutes on the house, those are minutes she cannot be mowing the lawn. Since it takes her 100 minutes to mow the lawn, we can assume that she could have mowed 3/5 of the lawn. On the other hand, each time the husband cleans the house, he gives up 1/3 of the lawn being mowed. (Why?) We can thereby argue that it is more costly (in terms of the portion of the lawn not mowed) for the wife to clean the house.

If we want the cost of production to be minimized, we would then argue that the wife should mow the lawn, the husband clean the house. If they do this, the total time spent by both of them would be 200 minutes. If the wife cleans the house and the husband mowed, the total time would be 360 minutes.

Notice what we have demonstrated here: by being under one common roof, the cost of the goods demanded by the members can be minimized by the husband and wife specializing and effectively trading. Notice also that we have made this demonstration even though one spouse, the wife, is actually more efficient in the production of both the mowed lawn and the cleaned house. By specializing, the wife and husband can also avoid many of the costs associated with developing the same skills. Each can concentrate his/her attention on a more limited number of household tasks, improving the efficiency with which they can be done.

This demonstration is important because it indicates that if husband and wife are interested in maximizing household production or minimizing the cost of household production, which amounts to the same thing, then they will specialize to some degree in the functions of the households. They will have what many derrogatively call *roles*. However, *these roles need not be what they presently are.* Further, it indicates that certain roles may be assumed by, say, the wife not because she is necessarily less efficient than the husband in the production of those things which the husband does, but rather because her comparatively greater efficiency lies in what she does.[3] The same is true for the husband. To acquire the efficiency benefits described here, the husband and wife need to have the appropriate preferences for the assigned tasks.

Furthermore, if the decision facing the family is the allocation of members' time between work internal to the home and work external to the home and if the family is interested in minimizing the cost of goods produced in the home, then it should use that labor with the lowest value outside of the home. The cost of cleaning the house is equal to the cost of the materials and supplies and the value of the individual's time outside the home who does the cleaning. Assume that it takes two hours to clean the house, that the wage the wife can earn outside the home is $3 per hour, and that the wage of the husband is $5 per hour. (Here, we are only attempting to use a realistic example; it is a fact, which is the subject of considerable complaint by women, that husbands do tend to earn more than their wives.) It follows that it would be cheaper for the wife to do the cleaning. If the man did the cleaning it would cost an additional $4 since his wage is $2 per hour higher.[4]

Many sociologists and psychologists contend that roles are assumed within the house, such as child care, because of socially determined values. We are unwilling to argue that such forces have *no* effect on the organization of many households. All we wish to add is that much of what we observe in household relationships may very often be the result of a conscious, rational choice on the part of the couples. Clearly, women do tend to earn less than men in the market, a point made above and in Chapter 6, either because they are the victims of discrimination or because they are less productive. Given this, which is not something individual households can do much about, it is reasonable to expect households to delegate many responsibilities, such as child care, to wives. In this way,

---

[3] If the wife takes as much as 180 minutes to mow the lawn and everything else about the example above is the same, it would still be most efficient for the wife to mow the lawn and the husband to cook the meals.

[4] The same allocation of wife- and husband-time would result if the wife is substantially more efficient in the production of household goods. Consider the case of the wife being able to earn $5 per hour and the husband earning $3 per hour. Suppose that it takes the wife an hour to do some household task and it takes the husband two hours. If the husband stayed at home to do it, it would cost the family $6 (two hours at $3 per hour). However, it would only cost them $5 (one hour at $5 per hour) for the wife to do it. In such case the family would choose to have the wife stay at home if it were interested in minimizing production costs. Inculturated values would perhaps come into play as an explanatory factor if the couple did not obey rules for time allocation that have been developed.

the cost of the child care is minimized and the output of the family is maximized. If the household production is greater by the wife staying at home, then one can suggest that the output of the wife is actually greater than what is indicated by her work in the home; she should get some credit for the greater output of the household.

If discrimination which women face outside of the home is reduced and/or they are able to raise their productivity relative to men, we should expect their wages to rise relative to their husbands'. We should then expect to see more and more wives working outside the home and *relatively* more time being spent by husbands in housework. It is clear that the labor force participation rate of women has been on the rise over the decades. There are many reasons for this, including changes in attitudes of men and women toward women working in jobs; the greater wages of women can be another explanatory factor.

There are other possible benefits to marriage and the family, like the benefit of making communication less expensive. Communication is an important aspect of any production process. (Can you name other benefits?)

SPOUSE SELECTION

The rational individual, in search of a spouse, will attempt to maximize his utility as he does in all other endeavors. He will not pretend to seek the "perfect mate," but only that one individual among those whom he knows and are willing to marry him that *best* (not perfectly) suits his preferences. (Whom do you know that has married the *perfect person?*) This means that he will seek to minimize the cost incurred through marriage and the family.[5] If he/she marries someone who agrees with him/her, the cost associated with arriving at the marriage contract is less than otherwise. There is not as great a need for (implicit) bargaining. If he/she marries someone who agrees with him/her as to what the family should do, what kinds of recreation they should have, and the number and way in which children should be reared, then the cost of having to give up friends and goods that suit his/her preferences better will be minimized. In other words, we would expect rational individuals to tend to marry persons who have similar values and preferences and are in other ways like themselves. Interestingly enough, this is generally what researchers have found.[6]

Rational behavior has other implications with regard to search for a

---

[5] In searching for a mate, he will extend his search until the marginal cost extending the search is equal to the marginal benefits.

[6] See, for example, R. F. Winch, *Mate Selection*, New York: Harper and Row, 1958. This conclusion, of course, does not apply to the situation in which one party prefers a mate who will dominate him/her.

mate. It implies that the greater the benefits from marriage, the greater the costs that a person will be willing to incur in searching for the spouse. This means that the greater the efficiency benefits that are to be achieved in family production or the greater the esteem people give those who marry, the more costs, in terms of time and effort, that a person will apply in looking. Greater costs may take the form of later marriages and a smaller fraction of the population married. Also, the longer the individual expects the marriage to last and the more stable he expects it to be, the more careful he will be in his search. This does not mean that mistakes will not be made; it only means that greater costs will be incurred in trying to avoid mistakes.

It also follows that the difficulty (cost) of divorce should affect the extent to which people search for a spouse.[7] It may affect the extent to which people marry, the extent of more informal arrangements, and the availability and economic well-being of prostitution as an institution. If a divorce is made impossible, a person knows that if he chooses the "right" person then there are more benefits to be had than if divorce were easier to come by. The impossibility of divorce will assure him/her that his/her spouse cannot freely marry someone else whom he/she may later prefer. If, on the other hand, he/she chooses the "wrong" person, the impossibility of divorce will mean that the decision would carry with it greater cost than if the marriage could be easily dissolved by divorce. Therefore, as Gary Becker has argued, we would expect the resources applied to search for a mate, to be directly correlated with the difficulty of obtaining a divorce, and he writes that "Search may take the form of trial living together, consensual unions, or simply prolonged dating. Consequently, when divorce becomes easier, the fractions of the persons legally married may actually *increase* because of the effect on the age at marriage."[8] Alan Freiden has in part corroborated this hypothesis by demonstrating in a study of the effects of different state divorce laws. He found that the more costly the divorce process, the smaller was the fraction of women married.[9]

If divorce is made easier, this line of analysis indicates that people will tend to incur fewer search costs, perhaps reflected in a declining age at which people marry; and aside from the experience of the last few years, the age at which men and women marry has generally been on the decline. One might reasonably assume that the durability of marriages in general is positively related to the extent to which people search the "marriage market" before they choose *the* one. If this can be accepted, and it might be a poor assumption, then making divorce easier, can result in more

---

[7] Becker, "A Theory of Marriage: Part II," s22–s23.

[8] Becker, "A Theory of Marriage: Part II," s22.

[9] Alan Freiden, "The United States Marriage Market," *Journal of Political Economy*, 82 supplement (March/April 1974), s34–s54.

divorces because they are less costly and also because people are expending fewer resources in search of a spouse and, therefore, making more wrong choices.

THE IMPLICATIONS OF LOVE

For our purposes we say that a person "loves" another if his or her level of satisfaction is in part dependent upon the satisfaction level of the other person.[10] In this sense one person genuinely "cares" for the other person and cares what happens to him (or her). This is because he (or she) will have greater utility if it is known that the other person is in some sense better off. He will, therefore, be motivated to help improve the situation of the person who is loved. The more intense the "love" the stronger is this motivation.

As we have explained, responsibilities are typically delegated to family members, and each member is dependent upon the others fulfilling their end of the bargain. In this way the welfare of the family members will diminish if any one member shirks his responsibilities.[11] Because shirking hurts others, the person who loves the others will be less inclined to shirk than the person who does not. It is for this reason that a person, if given the choice, would naturally want to marry someone who loves him. He would also naturally want to marry someone whom he loves because what he does for the family will also give him satisfaction to the extent that it makes everyone better off.

Where love does not exist, we will be more likely to find individuals shirking family responsibilities.[12] This in turn means that family resources will have to be diverted into the "policing" of family members. In this way love has an economic dimension. This does not mean that a person will not marry someone he does not love or who does not love him. Because of the benefits of being in a family situation, the person may prefer that to the single life. Many people do marry for money as well as other benefits.

All of this adds up to one interesting conclusion and that is that the *efficient* marriage is one in which the two are in love and are, in terms of values and preferences, alike. Oddly enough, this is what most people would readily argue. The interesting thing about this conclusion is that it is derived from the perspective of economics and the family as a producing unit. The greater the "love" and the closer the preferences of the couple, the closer will the marriage approximate what may be considered

---

[10] Here we are following Gary Becker in defining "love." The central point we make is also his. See "A Theory of Marriage: Part II," s12–s17.

[11] A person can "shirk" by failing to carry out any part of the contract or by making it more difficult (costly) for the other person to see that the contract is obeyed.

[12] In the jargon of economics, love can be said to internalize the externalities generated from family living.

the ideal. However, in the realistic world in which we live, it is clear that the maximizing individual does not always have the opportunity to choose a spouse who both loves him and has similar preferences, or at least to any great degree. He must often choose between a person who may love him very little, but who may be in many ways like himself, and the person who loves him, but who is very unlike himself. All the individual can do is maximize over the range of opportunities he has.

The discussion suggests that love adds to the efficiency of the household; we also argued earlier that differences in preferences can detract from the efficiency with which the household is operated. If this is the case and the individual is seeking to maximize the output from being in a family, then we must conclude that love is not all that is necessary for a successful family and marriage. Marriages have been known to break up in which the parties professed to love each other dearly; the problem was that they violently disagreed over what the marriage should be and do and the roles that each was to play. The gulf in preferences could have been so wide that the love, as intense as it was, could not bridge it. This seems to be fairly descriptive of the marriage and breakup of Cher and Sonny Bono, who during the 1973–74 television season had one of the top ten programs. They broke up telling reporters that they still loved each other but that they both had such markedly different interests that they had to go their own ways. In the same way we might expect that many marriages are held together with little love, but because their preferences are so much alike, they still find their relationship very beneficial, at least given their next best opportunities.

CONCLUDING COMMENT

Marriage and the family are terribly complex subjects to discuss, and the readers probably detect there is a lot that has been left unsaid. We definitely agree. We believe that the field is wide open for future research. This has only been a sample of what economists are beginning to say about such basic social institutions, and we think that the economic approach shows great promise of contributing much to our understanding of the subject.

9

Child Production

Children may be "little darlings" in their parents' eyes, but they are also economic goods. They can provide considerable benefits to their parents and relatives, and they are the result of a continuously evolving production process. This process involves resource expenditures like everything else that is produced in the home.[1]

CHILDREN AS ECONOMIC GOODS

From children parents obtain a good deal of companionship, resulting in benefits not unlike those received from other goods, such as a new car or a good martini. Children can be someone to talk to or go on a walk with, and they can be ready-made partners for a game of ping pong or checkers (if one can bear the hassle of getting them to do it). Their existence gives parents some hope that they will not be left alone later in life. Children also provide parents with the pleasure that comes from being respected and needed and, at least at some stages of a child's development, adored by someone else. There are very few parents who are not touched when their small children run to them when they return from work or a trip. Rightly or wrongly, children are used to fulfill parents' goals and to extend themselves beyond their own physical limitations. By having children parents are able to negate the unspoken criticism of relatives and

---

[1] We are again indebted to Gary Becker for his work in the economics of fertility, which underpins the discussion in this chapter and the work of many other economists. Gary S. Becker, "An Economic Analysis of Fertility," in *Demographic and Economic Change Developed Countries.* Princeton, N.J.: Princeton University Press, 1960, 209–240. For a critical evaluation of this literature, see Harvey Leibenstein, "An Interpretation of the Economic Theory of Fertility: Promising Path or Blind Alley?" *Journal of Economic Literature,* 12 (June 1974), 457–470.

friends that they are incapable of having or in some way loving them. The motivation for having children may include a means of fulfilling a sincerely felt need to make a contribution to society, to explore the unknown, or to test the hypothesis that they can do a better job in rearing children than others.

Children at one time in our history, and this is still true in many undeveloped areas of the world, were a means by which parents could develop their own old-age pension plan. As the children grew up, parents paid into the plan by feeding and clothing their children; in later years, the children took care of their parents when they were unable to provide for themselves. This, incidentally, was at a time when security markets and insurance companies were not very well developed, particularly in newly opened territories. This kind of arrangement has not completely dissipated; however, for the most part today people in the industrialized countries rely much more heavily on the impersonal, financially based retirement plans for old-age income. The reason may be in part due to the fact that the market has provided alternative retirement schemes that are cheaper than those incorporated in children. As we will see, children can be extremely expensive. Further, the benefits in the financially based plans are contractural and to that degree are more certain or less risky. Another reason may be that the government has forced people to become a part of the social security system which may have contributed to reduced reliance on children for retirement maintenance.

Last but not least, children can be an important source of labor, particularly for families living on farms and where child labor is less expensive than mechanization. The parents in the beginning stages of the children's lives "invest" resources in their growth and development in order that they can become workers. When the child is old enough to work, they reap the returns from their investment.

Granted, parents in general may not have children for the sole purpose of seeing them become good and loyal workers or for the purpose of gaining a sense of immortality. All of the benefits that can be listed are fused in the typical decision to have a child. But, this is true in the decision to buy a new car or house; there are a multiplicity of reasons for buying or producing almost anything. All of the benefits of having children that can be enumerated add up to one total level of parental satisfaction and, to that degree, to the parents' demand for children. This demand for children —or, perhaps more properly, "child services"—can be reflected in the total *number* of children that are had or in the *quality* of the children born and reared. The one thing that can be said at this point is that the greater the benefits reaped from children, the greater the number and/or quality of children that will be had. This assumes, of course, that the cost of the children is held constant and that parents, or at least some of them, look upon the decision to have children in the same rational way that they do everything else. Because some readers will doubt the reasonableness of this latter assumption, we will return to it later.

The cost of rearing a child includes the family expenditures on giving birth, food, clothing, shelter, education, entertainment, medical expenses, insurance, transportation, etc. Other major cost items, which are often overlooked, are the emotional drain and the value of the parents' time spent on rearing the child. Estimating the cost of children is a difficult problem at best. The actual cost of a child will depend on exactly how much the parents want to spend, and all costs will vary with the economic status and location of the parents. Given these problems, however, Ritchie Reed and Susan McIntosh have made estimates of a child reared on a "modest-cost" budget in an urban setting.[2] A summary of their estimates, by the education level of the mother, is included in Table 9–1. The cost of giving birth, which includes prenatal and hospital care and the maternity wardrobe of the mother, is estimated at $1,534 in 1969. The expenses associated with rearing the child until the age of 18 are estimated at $32,830. Reed and McIntosh made the simplifying assumptions that the parents' incomes and the prices of the things that go into determining these figures are held constant throughout the 18 years. The cost of four years of college education for the child is estimated at being $5,560 in a public institution. The total of these costs (referred to as "Total Direct Costs" in the Table) is $39,924, and they are held constant for all education levels of the mother. The reason for this is that Reed and McIntosh wanted to focus on the impact of the different educational levels of the mother.

The opportunity cost of the mother's time is dependent upon the wage she could have earned and the number of weeks she would have worked had she not had children. In the case of the mother who has an elementary school education, the estimated opportunity cost is $44,121. For the mother who had a four-year college education, the opportunity cost is estimated at $82,467.[3] This means that the total calculated cost for the first child is a whopping $84,045 for the mother with the elementary school education, and $122,391 for the mother with four years of college.[4] The marginal cost for each additional child is $46,497 and $52,644 for the mothers with the elementary school education and college education, respectively. The reason the cost for the second and following child is lower

---

[2] Ritchie H. Reed and Susan McIntosh, "Costs of Children," *Economic Aspects of Population Change: The Commission on Population Growth and the American Future*, eds. Elliot R. Morss and Ritchie H. Reed, Washington, D.C.: Government Printing Office, 1972, 330–50. The authors in their report provide more detailed information than can be given here.

[3] For a description of how these figures were determined see Reed and McIntosh, "Costs of Children," 341–44.

[4] Note that we have not included an estimate for the opportunity cost of the father's time, the emotional drain, risk cost, or the cost which may be associated with the depreciation of the mother's market skills.

TABLE 9–1
Total Cost of a Child by Educational Level of Mother, 1969

Type of cost	All Women	Elementary	High School	College, 4 years or less	College, 5 years or more
Undiscounted					
Cost of giving birth	1,534	1,534	1,534	1,534	1,534
Cost of raising a child	32,830	32,830	32,830	32,830	32,830
Cost of a college education	5,560	5,560	5,560	5,560	5,560
Total direct costs*	39,924	39,924	39,924	39,924	39,924
Opportunity costs	58,437	44,121	58,904	58,904	103,023
Total costs of first child	98,361	84,045†	98,828	98,828	143,947
Marginal cost of each additional child spaced two years apart‡	48,793	46,497	48,867	48,867	55,939
Discounted					
Cost of giving birth	1,534	1,534	1,534	1,534	1,534
Cost of raising a child	17,576	17,576	17,576	17,576	17,576
Cost of a college education	1,244	1,244	1,244	1,244	1,244
Total direct costs*	20,354	20,354	20,354	20,354	20,354
Opportunity costs	39,273	29,647	39,583	55,419	69,001
Total costs of first child	59,627	50,001†	59,937	75,773	89,355
Marginal cost of each additional child spaced two years apart‡	28,924	26,701	28,995	32,652	35,841

* These costs may be somewhat overestimated because of possible duplication occurring when the cost of giving birth as calculated by perspective is added to the USDA figures on the cost of raising a child to age 18.

† For a woman with only an elementary school education, a low income figure for the cost of raising a child may be more appropriate. This would reduce the total discounted cost to $44,181 and the total undiscounted cost to $72,845.

‡ Differs from cost of first child in that the opportunity cost and the cost of giving birth are less. For additional children, the $500 cost of nursery supplies is subtracted from the cost of giving birth to the first child.

Source: Richie H. Reed and Susan McIntosh, "Costs of Children," *Economic Aspects of Population Change: The Commission on Population Growth and the American Future*, eds., Elliot R. Morss and Ritchie H. Reed, Washington, D.C.: Government Printing Office, 1972, p. 345.

than the cost for the first is mainly due to the fact that if the children are spaced closely together, the opportunity cost of the mother's time is not duplicated with additional children. Since 1969, prices have risen considerably, and if the same study were redone today, the figure would be substantially inflated. Clearly, the cost of a child is by most standards substantial.

The costs given above are the result of the simple summation of the expenditures made and the earnings forgone during the rearing phase of the child's life. However, $1,000 spent today is worth more than $1,000 spent several years in the future. The reason is that the $1,000 spent today can earn interest during the course of years if it is deposited in a savings account or invested in interest bearing securities. Therefore, to determine the *present value* of the expenditures made on the child and the earnings foregone in the future, Reed and McIntosh discounted the yearly costs by eight percent and the new cost figures are recorded in the lower half of Table 9–1. The result is that the *discounted* total cost is $50,001 for the mother who has an elementary school education and $75,773 for the mother with four years of college. The marginal cost of each additional child is reduced to $26,701 and $32,652, respectively. Certainly, for most people the first child is the biggest single "good" they are likely to buy during their life!

THE DEMAND AND SUPPLY OF CHILDREN

By pointing out the costs and benefits of children, the authors do not mean to imply that children are just like every other good a family purchases. There is substantially more risk and uncertainty in having a child than in buying a new house or almost anything else. Parents are not able to see the good (i.e., child) before they buy it; in fact, their task is to produce it from scratch. The child comes with a will of his own from birth, which adds an element of surprise, which is not a feature of a new house. In the case of the house, the buyers can sell if they decide later that it is not what they want, perhaps recouping their investment and then some. In modern American society, to do the same with a child is frowned upon.

All of this means that the decision to have a child is more difficult than other decisions a family confronts and that there is more room for error in child production than in the production of other things. It does not follow that some parents will not attempt to approach the problem with the same rational *intentions* that they approach everything else.

Parents may conceive a child they did not plan to have because the momentary importance of sex was so great that they forgot to take the necessary precautions. This seems to be very likely if it is recognized that based on a study in 1965 there are approximately two billion acts of sexual intercourse between married couples in the United States each year.[5] One could add a substantial number of acts between those who are unmarried. It is simply a matter of probability that some "goofs" will occur; no contraceptive is fool-proof. To the degree that accidents occur, there will be children born and reared who are not the result of the conscious consideration of the expected costs and benefits. However, to the extent that there are parents who consider the costs and benefits in child-bearing decisions, the demand curve for children will be downward sloping. The cost of a child will influence the fertility level; more children will be had the lower the cost or price. Parents will, in addition, rationally balance off the numbers of children conceived with the quality.

In Figure 9–1 we have illustrated the total market demand for children

FIGURE 9–1

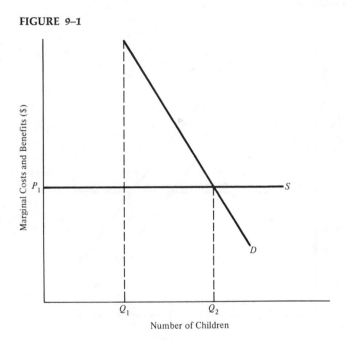

Number of Children

(D). In our example Q_1 children will be born and reared because of impulsive or in other ways non-rational behavior on the part of parents. However, how many children will be had in total will depend also on the supply, which means cost, of children. If, for simplification, the supply

---

[5] Leslie Aldridge Westoff and Charles F. Westoff, *From Now to Zero: Fertility, Contraception, and Abortion in America.* Boston: Little, Brown, and Company, 1971, p. 24. The estimate is based on a coital frequency of 6.7 times per month for all couples.

of children is assumed to be horizontal *(S)*, that is, the marginal cost is constant at P_1, the total number of children had will be Q_2. Of this total, Q_1 will be the result of "accidents" and Q_2-Q_1 will be the result of cost-benefit calculations.[6] If the reader is inclined to doubt our assumption that many child-bearing decisions are conscious, rational acts, he should reflect on the number of times he has heard someone, or himself, say, "Not me! I can't afford to have another child. There is just not enough time in the day to handle the two that I've got." This is just another way of saying that the cost of the additional child is too great for the expected benefits. We might expect the people who make such statements often go to great extents trying to avoid conceiving again.

FIGURE 9–2

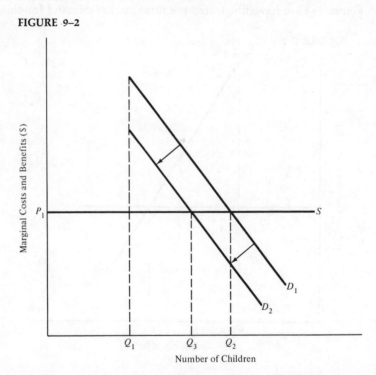

If the demand for children falls, the economist would predict that the number of children had will fall. This situation is described in Figure 9–2 by a shift in the demand curve from D_1 to D_2. The number of children drops from Q_2 to Q_3. The number of accidentally conceived children re-

---

[6] It is quite likely that many of the births that are unplanned take the place of births that were planned for a later date. If this is the case, the demand curve will move in to the left to account for it. This does not affect the analysis.

mains at Q_1; however, the number of "rationally determined" children falls, causing the drop in the total.[7]

This change in demand can result from an exogenous drop in people's "taste" for children. It can also result from a decrease in the relative prices of other goods produced and consumed in the home. If the latter happened, rational couples would tend to reallocate their resources toward the cheaper goods and away from children. It may be that one explanation for the declining birth rate has been the growing relative cheapness of goods, such as cars and all forms of entertainment, which may be substitutes for children.

In general, the location of the demand curve is dependent upon the *relative* benefits attributable to children and upon the family resources. Children who grow up on farms have many more opportunities to contribute to the family's income than the children who grow up in an urban setting. One explanation for this is the child labor laws which do not restrict children from working on farms but do restrict them from working in industry. For this reason alone economists would expect the benefits attributable to children and their parents' demand for children to be greater for farm families than for families living in the cities. In other words, the farm family's demand for children (D_1 in Figure 9–2) will be greater than the demand of urban families (D_2). The result is a tendency for farm families to be larger. If there is a migration of people from the farms to the cities, as there has been over the decades, one would expect birth rates to fall and the population growth rates to taper off somewhat. Interestingly, this is precisely what demographers and economists who have tested these hypotheses have found.[8]

Over time, if there is a reduction in the price of mechanized equipment, *ceteris paribus*, there may be a decrease in the size of farm families if the equipment can take the place of child labor. Cheaper farm equipment would encourage families to buy more equipment and use less labor, i.e., have fewer children.

The leftward shift in demand can also be the effect of the availability of cheaper and better contraceptives. Because they are cheaper we may anticipate more extensive use of them and fewer accidental births; the summation of the accidental plus rationally determined births would fall. Also, people's preferences for children may turn away from *numbers* to *quality*, causing the demand curve based on the number of children to shift in.

---

[7] The change causing the drop in the demand may make unwanted children *more* undesirable and may induce parents to take greater precautions in their coital relations.

[8] John D. Kasarda, "Economic Structure and Fertility: A Comparative Analysis," *Demography*, 8 (August 1971), 307–317; Stanley Kupinsky, "Non-Familial Activity and Socio-Economic Differentials in Fertility," *Demography*, 8 (August 1971), 353–67.

The reader should understand that for parents there is the ever-present decision between using their resources for the purpose of having more children and using them for the purpose of giving the number they have more attention: this can be reflected in what the parents consider a quality improvement.

We have concentrated in this section on a drop in demand for children because that appears to us the current trend. The reader may want to extend the discussion himself by considering possible causes for an increase in demand and the consequences of such developments.

Given our model, anything that reduces the cost of children, *ceteris paribus*, will shift the supply curve downward and increase the number of children had. In the case of Figure 9–3, the supply goes from S_1 to S_2 and

FIGURE 9–3

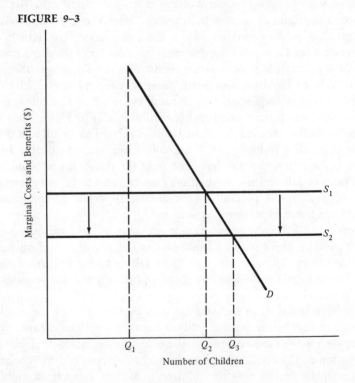

the number of children demanded goes from Q_2 to Q_3. The reason for the expansion is that prior to the cost reduction, the cost of the additional children, Q_3–Q_2, exceeds the benefits indicated by the demand curve between Q_2 and Q_3. Once the supply curve shifts down, the benefits of the additional children become greater than the cost. It is therefore rational for the couple to divert more resources into child production.

Such a change may have been the consequence of an increase in efficiency of rearing children, making the whole process less costly. It may have also been attributable to a decrease in the prices of those resources purchased from the market that are peculiar to the production of children or it may be attributable to changes in such exogenous forces as government policy.

As an example of a proposed change in government policy that can affect fertility rates, take the proposal of Senator Vance Hartke who in 1974 introduced a bill to increase the personal exemption for federal income tax purposes. Senator Hartke argued that the allowable personal exemption of $750 is too low to accommodate the high cost of rearing a child today and that it should be raised to $1,000. Clearly, such a policy effectively lowers the cost of having children. If a person were in a tax rate bracket of 30 percent, Hartke's proposal reduces a person's tax liability by $75 ($250 × 30 percent) per year. In this way, the proposal reduces the cost of having a child by $1,350 (undiscounted) over the first 18 years of the child's life. This may not seem like much of a saving since the undiscounted cost of an additional child can be upwards of $50,000.

Even though such a change in the tax structure is not likely to have an effect on everyone's decision to have a child, it can affect those marginal couples whose estimated costs and benefits of having an additional child are very close or who are more or less indifferent to the idea of having a child but are inclined to hold off. For illustration, suppose a couple figures that with the $750 exemption per child the undiscounted marginal cost of the additional child is $50,000 and the marginal benefits are $49,500. Since the marginal cost is greater than the marginal benefit, the couple would not have the child. However, if the Hartke proposal is adopted the marginal cost will be lowered to $48,650, an amount less than the marginal benefits of $49,500. The passage of the higher exemption will give the green light to this couple and to others in a similar position. Such a change in the tax laws will tend to make slightly more difficult, the problem of population control. Welfare payments tied to the number of children, including payments to unborn fetuses (an issue in the courts at the time of this writing, 1974), and public provision of education and day care centers can, in a similar manner, encourage population growth. In a similar way, high rates of inflation like those experienced in the United States in recent years reduce the *real* value of exemptions, thus increasing the total real costs of having children. (The above analysis actually applies to increases in the real value of personal exemptions.)

As seen in Table 9–1, the major cost in the rearing of a child is the opportunity cost of the parents' time. The higher the potential wage of the parents' time outside the home the higher is this component of the cost. The effect of greater cost can be to reduce the number of children had. This is illustrated in Figure 9–4 by the upward shift in the supply curve and the accompanying reduction in the desired children. On the other

FIGURE 9-4

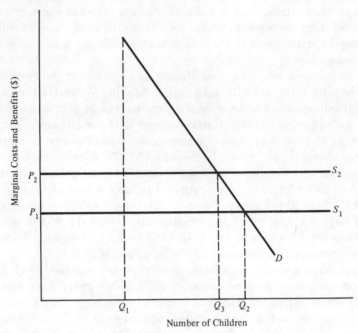

Number of Children

hand, the higher wage gives the couple added income to allocate to family purchases, including children. This "income effect" can have a positive influence on the production of children.[9] If this is the case, the net effect of the higher wage depends upon the relative strengths of the negative cost effect and the possible positive income effect. The empirical studies that have been done on the subject tend to find a negative correlation between family income and number of children.[10] This suggests, but does not confirm, that the negative cost effect is stronger. As opposed to being reflected in the number of children, the income effect can be realized in the *quality* of children demanded by people with higher incomes.[11]

---

[9] We recognize the possibility that children can be "inferior goods," meaning the income effect can be negative.

[10] Bruce Gardner, "Economics of the Size of North Carolina Rural Families," *Journal of Political Economy*, 81, supplement (March/April 1973), s99–s122; Dennis N. DeTray, "Child Quality and the Demand for Children," *Journal of Political Economy*, 81, supplement (March/April 1973), s70–s95.

[11] Testing the relationship between income and child quality is a difficult task because of the problems associated with defining and obtaining data on *quality*. Nevertheless, Dennis N. DeTray has made an effort by defining child quality as the extent of the child's education. He finds that the education of the mother, which can be mirrored in her opportunity wage, does have an effect on the "efficiency with which child

The discussion of the impact of higher wages on birth rates is interesting and important because it has implications regarding population growth rate trends in developing countries. If the negative cost effect is stronger than the positive income effect, as empirical studies indicate, and this relationship holds for underdeveloped countries, then the "population explosion," which has been the concern of many in recent years, may fade *to some degree if the underdeveloped countries are ever able to develop.* The higher opportunity wage, coupled with the greater dependence on industry, could lead to a lower birth rate. All we have argued here, however, is the probable direction of the effect of development on population growth and not how strong the effect is.

EDUCATION AND CHILD PRODUCTION

The education level of parents can influence the child production process in several ways. First, it can change the parents relative preferences for children by introducing them to things they find more valuable. Second, education can increase the opportunity wage rate of the parents and have the positive income effect and negative cost effect mentioned above. One of the more firmly established relationships in fertility literature is the negative correlation between the amount of education of the wife and the number of children she has; that is, as the wife's education level rises, the number of children tends to fall.[12] There is some evidence that shows that the relationship between the husband's education level and the number of children is positive.[13] One possible explanation for these findings is that, as many studies have found, the wife's time is relatively more important in child production than is the time of the husband, and the cost of her time will accordingly be more influential in the child production decisions. In the case of the husband, whose responsibilities have traditionally included earning the money income, his education has had little cost effect, since the amount of his time involved may not be very great, but has had a positive income effect.

Third, education can increase the efficiency with which the "quality" of children can be reared. At least one empirical study tends to support this.[14] Even with a higher opportunity wage rate, greater efficiency can make a unit of "child quality," however defined by the parent, cheaper to

---

quality is produced" (p. s93). Because of the data that was used, he considers his conclusions to be weak and tentative. ("Child Quality and the Demand for Children," *Journal of Political Economy,* 81, supplement (March/April 1973), s70–s95.)

[12] Gardner, "Economics of the Size of North Carolina Rural Families."

[13] Masanori Hashimoto, "Economics of Postwar Fertility in Japan: Differentials and Trends," *Journal of Political Economy,* 82, supplement (March/April 1974), s170–s194.

[14] Ibid.

the more educated person. For example, suppose it takes the parent with an elementary education two hours to teach his child a certain task which contributes to the child's quality. The parent's market wage rate is $2 per hour. The total cost is $4. On the other hand, if it takes the more educated parent, who earns $5 per hour, one-half hour to accomplish the same thing with his child, the cost is only $2.50. Everything else being equal, we would expect the more educated person to demand more units of child quality.

Fourth, the effects of education can show up in the parent's knowledge and use of contraceptives and in the number of unwanted children. A number of studies have found a direct relationship between parents' education and knowledge and use of contraceptives.[15] More educated parents tend to use the more effective contraceptive methods and use them to a much greater extent. Robert Michael gives three possible explanations for this: (1) Education makes the technical literature on contraception more easily understood and to that extent lowers contraception costs; (2) it raises the value of the couples' time and thereby makes more effective methods, which may be more expensive but less time consuming, more economical (the time expenditure for a couple does vary somewhat from the pill to the use of diaphragms and foam tablets); and (3) education raises the cost of children by raising the cost of parents' time and, thereby, increases the cost of an unwanted child. This makes knowledge and use of contraceptives more valuable.[16] In the process of developing his argument, Michael makes an interesting point regarding the efficiency of contraceptive devices. He writes, "If a couple used a contraceptive technique that was "only" 90 percent effective, in a 15-year period their expected fertility outcome would be 2.7 births. . . . Or, if a couple used a contraceptive technique that was "only" 99 percent effective, the chance of a conception in a five-year interval exceeds ten percent. "Good" (but not perfect) contraception does not provide the long-run protection one might think."[17] He also estimated that if a fertile couple does not use any method of contraception for five years, the probability of conception is 100 percent.

CHILD PRODUCTION AND OVERPOPULATION

Economists are in general agreement that the optimum quantity produced of anything is that quantity at which the marginal cost of the last

---

15 Robert T. Michael, "Education and the Derived Demand for Children," *Journal of Political Economy*, 81, supplement (March/April 1973), s128–s164. The author of this article refers to a number of studies connected with this point on page s140.

16 Michael, "Derived Demand for Children," p. s159.

17 Michael, "Derived Demand for Children," p. s141.

unit is equal to the marginal benefits of it. This will be the case if all costs and benefits are actually considered by the individual making the decision on the output, and this rule of thumb holds for the production of children. However, if the person making the decision does not consider all costs in the production of, say, children, that is, someone else bears a portion of the cost, the perceived marginal cost will be lower than it really is. Using Figure 9-4, because not all costs are considered by the person making the child production decision, the couple will perceive that the cost of children is represented by supply curve S_1, whereas in fact the true supply curve, considering all costs, is at S_2. Couples, will rationally choose to produce Q_2 children. Note that the true marginal cost (P_2), when all costs are included, between Q_2 and Q_3 is actually greater that the demand curve. This indicates that the marginal cost of the children is greater than the marginal benefits, and as a result, too many children are produced.

In our present society there are two basic ways in which couples deciding to bear children can underestimate the cost of their children. They may not consider the added congestion their children can create. This may mean that there are simply more people taking up the same limited area, reducing the freedom all persons have to move about without affecting others, or it may mean that more people are competing for resources, other than space, causing another form of congestion. This cost of an additional child is incurred in general by people not involved in the decision to have the child.

The other basic way by which the private decisions of parents can impose costs on others is through the tax system. Presently, there are many public facilities, such as schools, that are provided with tax money. If the facilities are not free to the user, they are most often subsidized. To this extent, a portion of the total cost of a child is borne by the general taxpayer. The private decision of one couple to have a child can, therefore, increase the tax bill for the rest of the community. Because these costs may not, and to a substantial degree are not, considered by the child bearing couple, the costs they consider will be understated, resulting in overproduction of children. (It is indeed an interesting thought that the tax burden of the general public is partly dependent upon the coital frequency of couples!) One way to turn this around is to have the child-bearing couples pay the cost by imposing a tax on them for each birth. This, to put it mildly, is not likely to be a popular proposal with those who want children. They no doubt would prefer that the rest of us continue to pay the bill for their fortune or misfortune as the case may be.

CHILD PRODUCTION AND THE FUTURE

Thomas Ireland in a paper on "The Political Economy of Child Production" has suggested some interesting, but to some, we are sure, disturbing prospects for the future course of child rearing.[18] If it were not for the rather dramatic change over the past ten years in the public's acceptance of abortions, we would indeed consider his ideas to be futuristic. But, as it is, Ireland's paper may indicate what is "just around the corner."

His paper is based on two main propositions: First, scientists now have the capability to transplant an animal fetus from its mother to a "host mother" with the birth following in due course. There is every reason to believe that if medical science is not able to do it now, the know-how will be developed in the future to accomplish the same thing in humans. Second, the problems associated with pregnancies cause some women pain and inconvenience and make many unable to work in the market for several months.

The prospects of fetus transplant provides a potential solution to the dwindling number of adoptable babies and the moral problems surrounding abortions. Because adoptable babies are becoming very expensive, the mother who would like to bear a child but who cannot because of the sterility of the husband, would have some incentive to pay to have an aborted fetus transplanted into herself.[19] This may not sound so crazy if it is remembered that women now pay handsomely for artificial insemination and for the rights to adopt a child. In fact, a public interest group interested in the rights of the fetus' life may be willing to pay another mother to accept the transplant and carry the child to term. Such a solution may be disgusting to some readers who are concerned about the life of the fetus. Granted, this may be a less than ideal solution, but it may be a better solution than one of standing around discussing the question of when life begins while many fetuses are being destroyed.

In addition, there are possibilities for payment arrangements whereby the true mother and host mother gain by a fetus transplant. Suppose that there is a mother who earns $20,000 per year, who wants to have a child of her own, but who is not willing to endure the pain and loss of income associated with pregnancy. If there is another woman who earns $8,000 per year, then the mother can possibly agree through some institution, which is not yet established, to pay a host mother to carry the baby to term at which time the baby would be transferred back to the original mother. If the disability associated with the pregnancy is three months, the real mother could be willing to pay (ignoring taxes) as much or more than $5,000 to the host mother. By making the payment, it will be the host mother who will lose the time at work, which will cost her $2,000. She can receive from the real mother, say, $4,000, and her income will rise to

---

[18] Thomas R. Ireland, "The Political Economy of Child Production," paper presented at the Public Choice Society meeting, University of Maryland, March 1973.

[19] Adoptable babies of minority groups are still relatively easy to obtain but with the legalization of abortions this supply is dwindling.

$10,000. Furthermore, the total output of the economy can be $3,000 greater than what it would have been if the real mother had lost the time from work.[20] All of this may sound a little cold-hearted, but we really do not mean for it to be taken that way. These are, however, solutions which may be more than just attention getters in the relatively near future.

CONCLUDING COMMENTS

In recent years it has been the fad to project the future course of the population trend and accompanying problems. Most of these projections are merely statistical extrapolations of the trends of the recent past. They do not assume that there will be adjustments made in the economy that will alter the course of the trend. We do not wish to understate the importance of getting the world's population growth under control. However, we suspect that the doomsday prophets will be mistaken in their projections because of certain anticipated changes in the child production process. First, we expect that as the population grows larger, putting pressure on resources, the cost of producing children will become relatively greater, reflecting back on the private household decisions. Second, we suspect that as congestion becomes greater, there will be growing pressure on government to change the tax structure and to make abortion and contraceptive devices more readily and inexpensively available to the public. Third, we expect that with the growing cost of children there will be a renewed incentive to find new technology for preventing pregnancies. In fact, we view the recent public concern over population growth to be a part of the self-correcting changes we see. Those that are projecting the population are alerting the voting public to the problem and setting the stage for changes in policy.

---

[20] It may be found that transforming a fetus to a host mother will affect the quality of the child.

10

Dying: The Most
Economical Way to Go

It is only human for one to feel sympathetic toward the person who dies with everything going wrong: a malfunctioning liver, arteriosclerosis, a defective kidney, ulcers, respiratory problems, and waning eyesight. However, such a tumultuous exit may indicate that the individual involved has more thoroughly enjoyed life than the person who dies with only a failing heart and everything else in perfect order. If this is the case, the sympathy may be misplaced. The fact that all of one's organs are malfunctioning at the time of death may indicate that one has fully utilized his organic capital assets in the pursuit of utility; the person who dies with a perfect liver may have foregone a number of drinks during the course of his life that could have contributed significantly to his own welfare: a liver in good order is useless if the heart goes first.

If a person is truly interested in maximizing his wellbeing (which is the natural assumption of economists), he should treat his bodily organs in the same manner he treats his monetary wealth. "You can't take it (them) with you" is just as applicable to organs as it is to a bank account. A person should have a bank balance at death if he intentionally plans to bequeath it to someone (an act, the anticipation of which may give pleasure before death) or if the individual miscalculates the time of his death. The *ideal* exit is to die with a zero bank balance (above that which is planned) and with no surplus capacity in bodily organs (above that which is planned).[1]

---

[1] The planned surplus capacity in bodily organs would be affected by religious values, belief in reincarnation and desire to bequeath one's bodily organs to help others.

Such utility maximizing behavior may go a long way toward explaining why elderly people as a group go to the dentist less frequently than others or why the prisoner on death row may be unmoved by government reports that smoking can cause cancer. Doctors do not, however, seem to fully appreciate this truth about human behavior. Most advice by doctors and most medical research is directed toward maximizing the lifespan of each and every bodily organ. Very little research is directed, it appears, toward ascertaining how a person should treat his organs (in order to maximize his utility during this life), given the life span of the limiting one (whatever it is). In this *vein*, a redirection of much medical research is called for because many medical expenditures (and much abstinence) may be unwarranted.

The economist's advice is that a person should so employ his human and non-human resources that the world ends for him not with a whimper but with a bang.[2]

PROBLEMS

1. Do people behave the way the authors suggest they do? If you believe they do, can you give additional examples of how people attempt to rationally employ their organic capital assets? If you believe they do not, how do they behave? Why do they behave the way that you suggest? Is the problem one of a lack of appropriate information?

2. What effect will religious values have on the behavior of people with regard to their bodily organs? (Before answering the question specify the religious values on which you will base your answer.)

3. Suppose we introduce the possibility of an individual selling his organs before he dies. Will such a system work? What are the problems involved? Will such a system affect people's behavior?

4. Suppose that the amount of suffering one has to endure on his "death bed" is greater when everything goes wrong than it is when only one organ has failed. Will knowledge of this affect a person's behavior? Suppose the opposite were the case. How would a person's behavior be different?

---

[2] In making this statement, the economist is implicitly suggesting that T. S. Eliot was probably misguided when he wrote: "This is the way the world ends/Not with a bang but a whimper."

part four

Crime and Dishonesty

11

The Economic Aspects
of Crime

THE BENEFITS AND COSTS OF CRIME

Costs to the Criminal

Crime is an economic as well as a sociological and psychological problem. There are definite benefits (at least, to the criminal) and costs associated with criminal activity. The criminal can possibly increase his lifetime income even though at times he may be imprisoned. He can reduce the number of hours worked per week and, perhaps, improve his working conditions.[1] In addition, the criminal can within some socio-economic groups raise his status among his peers by commiting crimes and even by serving time.

To obtain these benefits, the criminal must incur the costs of developing the right skills (unless he wants to run the risks of bungling the job),[2] acquiring the necessary tools such as guns and explosives, and making the contacts that may be necessary to pull off the job. In the narcotics business, the criminal must invest in raw materials, storage facilities, and processing and transportation equipment. The criminal may, like other businessmen, have to meet a payroll, which may include salesmen and administra-

---

[1] Remember that even though you may consider the working conditions of the criminals to be bad, they may still be better than the alternative available to him.

[2] As may have been suggested by the discussion in Chapter 2, there is some optimum amount of risk the criminal may rationally decide to assume. How much education, or, for that matter, any other resource input, the criminal is willing to buy depends upon the probabilities of being caught, the extent of the punishment, and the degree to which the criminal is risk averse.

tors. In the business of shylocking, the accumulation of financial assets is important. Prostitutes may have to incur the costs of physical abuse and medical treatment.

If the criminal is a specialist in armed robbery or burglary, he must spend the time required (which implies opportunity cost) to case the site of the crime, to wait for the opportune moment, to pull off the crime itself, to fence the stolen goods, and to stay undercover until things have cooled. If caught, he has the additional costs of legal help (unless a court-appointed lawyer is secured). If convicted, he must forgo the income he could have earned while incarcerated; and because of his record, he can suffer a reduction in his earning ability after being released. There may also be for some the psychic cost of having done something wrong and the loss of respect within his family and community structure. (Consider the cases of former President Richard Nixon and former Vice President Spiro Agnew.)

The cost to the individual of committing his own crimes can be viewed as rising as the general level of criminal activity rises. As the crime rate rises, the public can be reasonably expected (beyond some threshold) to respond by applying more resources to crime prevention, making it more difficult (i.e., more costly) for the criminal to commit crimes. In addition, one might expect all criminals to commit those crimes first that will yield the largest amount of booty per resource expenditure, meaning the lower cost crimes. This implies that to extend the level of criminal activities, criminals will have to seek out higher cost alternatives or less lucrative opportunities. Like all other production processes, one might also expect criminal activity to be subject to the law of diminishing returns. (Why?)

Costs to the Victim

The victim of a robbery or burglary will suffer the loss of the stolen property and, possibly, bodily and mental injury, implying medical bills and loss of income. In the case of rape, the victim may not only be subjected to an extreme amount of violence but also to community gossip; and even though she may be innocent of any wrong-doing, her reputation can be damaged. This may be particularly true if the victim takes the rapist to court. The defense attorney in an effort to make the strongest possible case for his client may parade the victim's past (questionable) relationships before the press and community, distorting them wherever possible. The cost of legal fees and time spent in lawyers' offices and the court can be for her and other victims of other crimes a substantial portion of the total cost borne by victims; and it is because of such cost, no doubt, that many crimes go unreported. In the case of murder, the victims may be, in addition to the one murdered, the family and friends who lose income and friendship.

Costs to Society

The total cost of crime extends far beyond those directly involved in the crime itself. Non-victims must, in an attempt to avoid being victims, incur the costs of locks, burglary alarm systems, outside lights, and the many other devices used to make crime more costly to prospective criminals. The non-victim may also have to incur the cost required to avoid high crime areas. In early January 1974, the *Charlotte Observer* took a survey of approximately 300 persons who had moved from Charlotte, North Carolina, to surrounding suburbs, and they found that a primary reason for over half of the respondents moving out of the city was to get away from the high incidence of crime.[3] Many of the people who had moved then had to commute longer distances to work.

Crime will also impose higher taxes on victims and non-victims alike since police protection and judicial, penal, and (to a limited extent) rehabilitation systems are not likely to be avoided. Society may also experience a loss of social interaction. Because of fear of being sexually molested, children are taught not to speak to strangers and, above all, not to get in their cars. Women may avoid speaking to or walking on the same side of a street with men they do not know. Since policemen are given a considerable amount of discretionary power over whom to stop, search, and arrest, crime can impose on the general population a "liberty tax." Finally, people shopping in stores often go out of their way to insure that they do not give the impression that they are shoplifting.

RATIONALITY AND CRIME

The Rational Criminal

To the degree that crime involves benefits and costs, crime *can* be a rational act, and the amount of crime actually committed can be determined in the same manner as is the amount of any other activity. The only difference may be that crime involves behavior that is against the law. The criminal can weigh-off the benefits and costs and can choose that combination that maximizes his own utility, and he will maximize his utility if he commits those crimes for which the additional benefits exceed the additional costs.

Because of the cost of crime, the amount of crimes committed can fall far short of the amount that can, technically speaking, be committed. This would be true even if we ignore or dismiss the costs of being caught and punished. For example, suppose that the benefits of committing a

---

[3] *Charlotte Observer*, January 6, 1974, p. 1. Charlotte, deservedly or not, has acquired the reputation among many as being the murder capital of the south.

particular crime, such as robbery, for a prospective criminal, are illustrated by the downward sloping demand curve in Figure 11–1. (Why is the demand downward sloping?) (In this graph the quantity of crimes is on the horizontal axis and the marginal costs and benefits are on the vertical axis.) Suppose, also, that we consider only non-punishment costs such as raw materials, labor, and equipment. Further, assume that the supply curve (or marginal cost curve, S_1) in Figure 11–1 is upward sloping.

FIGURE 11–1

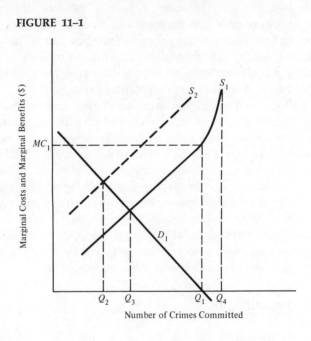

Number of Crimes Committed

As indicated by the graph, there are benefits to committing additional crimes until Q_1 have been committed; beyond Q_1 the additional benefits to further criminal activity become negative. However, at Q_1 the cost of committing the Q_1th crime (MC_1) is far greater than the additional benefits which, at that level of activity, are zero. The criminal, if he is operating at Q_1, can increase his personal satisfaction by reducing the number of crimes committed. If he reduces the number of crimes all the way back to Q_2, the marginal benefits from the Q_2th crime would then exceed the cost in which event it follows that he could improve his utility by increasing the number of crimes. Needless to say by now, the rational criminal can maximize his utility by committing up to Q_3 crimes, at which point the additional benefits are equal to the additional costs. The analysis can be extended to include the total "market" for crime by adding horizontally the individuals' demands and supplies. The total community crime level would then be established at the intersection of the market demand and market supply curves.

There are three important points that should be given particular attention. The first one is that the number of crimes committed by the rational criminal will not be equal to the maximum, which for our purposes can be defined as Q_1, where the demand curve intersects the horizontal axis, or Q_4, where the supply curve becomes essentially vertical. The second point that needs to be emphasized is that, given the demand for crime, the amount of crimes perpetrated is dependent upon the cost. If punishment is introduced into the analysis and the type of punishment employed represents an increase in cost to the criminal, the supply curve will decrease (i.e., move upward and to the left) to say S_2; and as a result, the number of crimes the criminal will *choose* to commit will be lowered. One can also suggest that anything that reduces the cost of crime, such as reduction in the cost of handguns or an increase in the leniency of the courts, can increase the supply of crime and, thereby, the number of crimes actually committed. This would also be the case if society became more tolerant of or sympathetic toward criminals. (Why?)

The third point is that although one can observe that a large number of crimes are committed, such as Q_2 in Figure 11–1, one cannot conclude that the severity of punishment has no effect on criminal activity. If the difference between S_1 and S_2 represents the cost imposed on the criminal by the penal system, then one can deduce that the penal system has deterred Q_3–Q_2 crimes. In other words, the effectiveness of a penal system can be judged by how many crimes are committed; however, a more appropriate indication of the effectiveness of punishment, or any other policy which increases the cost of crime to the criminal, is how many crimes are never committed because of that punishment. This, we believe, is a point policemen readily see, but one which other concerned individuals often overlook.

If the booty from committing crimes increases, while the cost remains constant, one could also predict from our model that the demand for crime would rise to the upper right as in Figure 11–2. The number of crimes committed, we predict, would go up.

The Irrational Criminal

There is a common notion among lay and professional criminologists and sociologists that certain criminals who commit certain types of crime do not behave rationally. They do not weigh-off the benefits and costs of their actions, and we will treat this controversial issue in greater detail in the next chapter. However, at this point we want to insure the reader that we concede the point that there are "sick" criminals just as we would concede the issue if anyone ever suggested that there are sick plumbers, businessmen, and professors.[4]

To the extent that they do not measure the consequences of their actions, the demand curves for sick criminals are vertical. However, this does not mean that the demand for the crime in general is not downward.

FIGURE 11–2

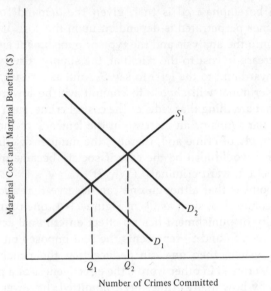

Number of Crimes Committed

The market demand curve will still be downward sloping so long as there are rational criminals in the market. The existence of the irrational criminals just moves the market demand curve for crime out to the right and does not change the slope. The supply of crimes will also increase since there are more criminals. For example, suppose that there are rational and irrational criminals in the market and the market demand for crime by rational criminals is equal to D_1 in Figure 11–3. If, for purposes of illustration there are Q_1 crimes committed by irrational criminals, then the total market demand and supply curves would be at D_2 and S_2. The total number of crimes committed would then be Q_2, Q_1 by irrational criminals and Q_2-Q_1 committed by rational criminals.

The reader should recognize that so long as the market demand for

---

[4] We are also willing to concede the point that "sick" criminals may specialize in certain bizarre types of crimes, rational criminals do not. As we argue in the next chapters, there is presently little evidence that suggests, however, what these areas may be.

crime is downward sloping, the changes in the cost of crime as discussed above should lead to changes in the number of crimes committed *by the rational criminals.* Since the irrational criminals, by definition, do not consider costs in their behavioral decision, one should not expect their level of crime to be affected; therefore, the total market response should be in the same direction as predicted for rational criminals. (The percentage change in the amount of crime would not be as great.)

FIGURE 11–3

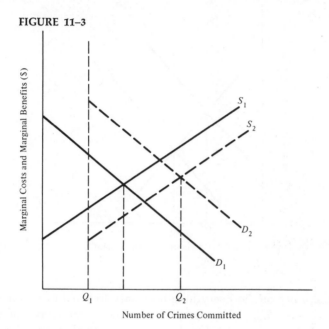

THE ECONOMICS OF BEING A NON-VICTIM

Victims of crimes suffer, and in that sense people can benefit by actively avoiding crimes. For certain types of crimes, such as aggravated assault, the benefits of crime avoidance can be considerable; for other types, such as having a potted petunia plant stolen from one's backyard, the benefits can be very slight, mainly because the value of the stolen property can be very low. In any event, people have a demand for crime avoidance, which implies a demand for locks and other devices and means of thwarting crimes. Furthermore, if non-victims are rational, their demand for crime avoidance is downward sloping, as is the case for everything else they value.

As illustrated in Figure 11–4, this means that a person will avoid more crimes the cheaper it is to do so. If the price (which must be imputed from the cost of equipment and time) of avoiding a particular crime is P_1, the number of crimes avoided will be Q_1. More pointedly, the person will do only so much to reduce the risk of crimes being committed against him.[5]

This means, of course, that he will "permit," in a sense, some crimes to be committed. Granted, if there were no cost involved in crime avoidance, everyone would prefer never being a victim to, at times, being one.

FIGURE 11–4

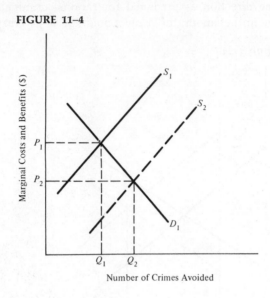

Number of Crimes Avoided

However, if a person did everything necessary to avoid ever being a victim, the cost (including time cost) of avoiding certain types of crimes, such as petty larceny or even burglary, can, over the long-run, be greater than what he would have lost had he been less cautious and at times been a victim. To put the problem in a little different perspective, would you expect someone to spend $100,000 to avoid being robbed of $75,000? This is an extreme example, but do people not address similar questions when they consider taking measures to avoid crimes?

Clearly, people do limit the number and quality of locks on their doors; college professors (the authors included) generally have locks on their doors they know can be picked by any reasonably good thief. In fact, one of the authors is inclined to leave his door wide open when he is out on errands or in class. One reason is that any prospective thief will have to pass by a secretary and can be observed by others who may be close by. Another reason is simply that he calculates that there really is not all that much in his office to steal and that, quite honestly, he generally figures

---

[5] Operationally speaking, reducing the risk of being a victim is the same as increasing the number of crimes he avoids.

the value of his time spent locking, searching for his keys, and unlocking the door can over the long-run far exceed the value of the property likely to be stolen. You can be assured, however, that when he has an expensive calculator in his office, he closes and locks his door upon leaving. (Is his behavior inconsistent?)

People do not put bars on their windows; the major cost here is likely to be the deterioration of the outward appearance of their homes. People are also willing to walk in some areas at some times, well aware that the probability of being mugged is above zero. Admittedly, when the probability is quite high, such as may be the case in New York's Central Park at midnight, they may be willing to forgo their walks. However, just because people may not be willing to walk in Central Park, one cannot conclude that they are unwilling to assume any risk or take any chance of becoming a victim. If individuals tried to avoid *ever* being a victim of crime, we are convinced that they would lead a very dull life! In other words, rational behavior can make the criminal's work a little easier than otherwise.

Given the above discussion and Figure 11–4, it follows that if the cost of avoiding crime falls, the supply of crime avoidance will expand downward and to the right, resulting in an increased number of crimes avoided. That is, a person will buy more locks and/or take more time to avoid being caught in a threatening situation. Again, it should be stressed that given the cost reduction, the rational person will do only so much to avoid crimes.

It also follows that if the benefits from crime avoidance increase, the individual will expend more effort and money in an attempt to avoid crimes. This increase in demand, as illustrated in Figure 11–5, can be the

FIGURE 11–5

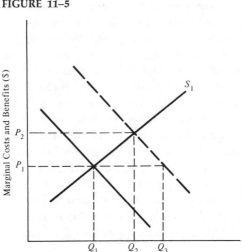

result of an increase in the value of that which could be stolen or, perhaps, an increase in a person's assessment of the worth of his own physical condition and/or life. A person who may be depressed and care very little about living can hardly be expected to divert many resources to avoid being killed. In addition, the increase in demand can result from an increase in the probability of being a victim; in such a circumstance it is reasonable to expect a person to be willing to pay a higher price for crime avoidance. Notice that in all of these cases the increase in the cost of avoiding crimes curtails the number of crimes that the individual will attempt to avoid. In our graph if the price of crime avoidance had remained at P_1 the quantity of crimes avoided would have been Q_3; however, because the price of crime avoidance rises to P_2, the number of crimes avoided is Q_2. This quantity is higher than the original number Q_1, but still it is not as great as it would have been had the price remained at P_1.

POLICE PROTECTION

The individual citizen, not the police, is society's first line of defense against crime. The citizen may be an amateur, undisciplined and untrained in modern police techniques, but he does have one thing going for him and that is his own private interest to protect those things that to him are valuable. If it were not for such motivation, we can be assured that the work of the criminal would be greatly eased. Police can contribute to crime control, but one should understand that in urban areas today there are only about two policemen for every 1,000 residents.

From this perspective, police protection and law enforcement should be viewed as a supplement to the basic protection which people provide for themselves. Generally speaking, but not always, the services of police are provided by local government, and this is done for two basic reasons. First, it may be more efficient to provide the additional protection through some collective organization. As opposed to having every store owner check to insure that his doors are locked after closing hours, the duty can be assigned to a policeman on that beat. A great deal of traveling time can be saved. Such services need not be provided publicly and often are not. Shopping centers, for example, do provide their own security guards; in a sense they are selling police protection along with the floor space.

Second, police protection is not always the type of service that can be bought and sold in the market on a customer-by-customer basis. There are activities for which the police could *conceivably* charge in much the same way as Coca Cola does for its drinks. This might be where the service is specifically intended to benefit one particular individual (or group), and the service can be withheld unless the individual pays the prescribed fee. An example might be a policeman's retrieval of stolen property for a particular individual; if the individual does not pay for the service, the service can be withheld.[6]

On the other hand, the benefits of police activity can be spread quite generally across the community. The presence of the police can provide an additional threat to all criminals operating in the community and the police can contribute to the removal of criminals from the community by making crime less profitable or putting them behind bars. In such cases all members of the community benefit (albeit in varying degrees) since the risk of becoming a victim is lowered. In addition, the community can, because of the police presence, reduce their own private actions intended to thwart crime.

If such generalized benefits are provided, then all members of the community must share in those benefits. The police can deny some benefits to some people by denying them some services, as discussed above, but they cannot deny to anyone those benefits that pervade the entire community. Consequently, it may be extremely difficult (if not impossible) for the police to charge for the generalized benefits. If a resident benefits regardless of whether or not he pays, then it is understandable why he may refuse to pay on a voluntary basis. For one thing, he can figure that he can get the protection free if it is provided. Secondly, he may reason that the amount he would be willing to contribute to the "police fund" may be so small in relation to what is needed that any contribution he makes will neither determine whether or not the police protection is provided or significantly influence the amount of protection he receives. Therefore, police protection must be financed by some extra-market means—that is, by taxation.

The members of the community may gladly consent to *some* additional taxation because they know there are benefits to be reaped from police services; and without the intervention of government, meaning taxation, police protection may not be provided. This can be particularly true in the larger communities where social pressure is impotent. By voting for the additional taxes, not only may the individual acquire the very slight benefits resulting from the taxes he, himself, pays but he can also benefit from the taxes paid by others.

There are limits, however, to amount of police protection acceptable to a voting public, mainly because, as we have seen elsewhere in this chapter, there are costs involved. As the level of protection is increased, taxes must be raised and people will have to give up other things, such

---

[6] We are merely suggesting here that the police could charge for certain types of services. The reader should not interpret our remarks as advocating such a system. Besides, the administration of such a system might be so expensive that other means of collecting may be more desirable.

as ice cream and clothes, which they value.[7] As tax rates are raised, we can reasonably assume that there will be more and more people who will find that the benefits received from the additional protection will be less than the additional costs they must incur in the form of taxes. At some point there will be a sufficient number of votes to defeat any proposal to expand police activities further. The reader should recognize that by restricting the size of the police departments, the voting public is limiting the number of crimes that will be prevented. *They are also allowing, in a sense, some crimes to be committed.* The voting public may not like to have crime in their midst, but at the same time they may not want to see their taxes increased either. We personally see very little chance of the public ever voting to wipe out all crime, even if it were possible.

Having only limited resources with which to prevent and investigate more crimes than they can handle, the police, themselves, must make certain economic decisions. They must decide whether or not their resources should be applied in residential or business areas or whether they should attempt to prevent or investigate burglaries, murders, or rapes. If they apply their resources in preventing burglaries, then they must allow other crimes, such as speeding violations and murders, to occur or go unsolved. In recent times the police have been required to enforce price controls that have been mandated by the federal government. Having used their resources in this way, they cannot use them to solve other crimes. This is one aspect of wage-price controls systems that is not readily appreciated by the public who may favor controls.

CRIME ACTIVITY

We will close this chapter on crime by reviewing the statistics of major crimes in the United States. A note of caution should be made before we proceed. First, it should be understood that we are giving statistics on the *number of crimes reported*; there are, no doubt, many crimes committed each year that for one reason or another go unreported. In fact, the President's Crime Commission found that in three precincts in Washington, D.C., "six times as many crimes were committed against persons and homes as were reported to the police."[8] The number of reported crimes can also change over the years with changes in the number of reporting agencies and the number of police personnel. These two considerations

---

[7] You may feel that police protection is much more important than, say, ice cream. However, remember that is your preference; others may not agree with you at all levels of police protection.

[8] The National Advisory Commission on Civil Disorders, "Crime in Urban Areas," *Problems in Political Economy: An Urban Perspective*, ed. by David M. Gordon, Lexington, Mass.: D. C. Heath and Company, 1971, p. 289.

suggest that the growth in criminal activity reported by the FBI can be exaggerated.

The FBI concentrates its reports on seven types of crime: murder, forcible rape, robbery, aggravated assault, burglary, larceny, and auto theft. The total number of crimes in these categories is referred to as the Crime Index. Table 11–1 reveals the total number of Crime Index offenses per 100,000 people in the country. The table also indicates the growth in offenses during different periods of time. Figure 11–6 depicts the per-

FIGURE 11–6
Crime and Population, 1968–1973 (percent change over 1968)

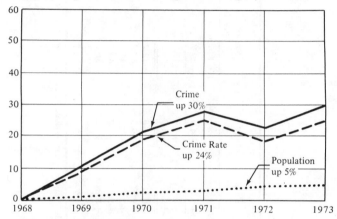

Crime = Crime index offenses.
Crime Rate = Number of offenses per 100,000 inhabitants.
Source: FBI, *Uniform Crime Report, 1973*, p. 3.

centage change in the number of Crime Index offenses and the crime rate over the years from 1967 to 1973. The same type of information is provided for the "crimes of violence" (which includes murder, rape, robbery, and aggravated assault) and "crimes against property" (which includes burglary, larceny, and auto theft) in Figures 11–7 and 11–8.

From the table and figures, several points of interest can be noted. First, the total number of index offenses has risen substantially over the long-run, approximately 30 percent from 1968 to 73. The crime rate has risen almost as much, 24 percent. Second, between 1972 and 1973, the total number of offenses, after falling between 1971 and 72, rose by approximately five percent. However, as vividly revealed in Figures 11–7 and 11–8, the drop in the total number of offenses between 1971 and 1972 was due primarily to the drop in the crimes against property during that period of time. Crimes of violence, in particular have risen continuously during the years covered by the table and charts.

Table 11–2 indicates the crime rate for the United States as a whole, for

TABLE 11-1
National Crime, Rate, and Percent Change

Crime Index Offenses	Estimated Crime 1973		Percent Change over 1972		Percent Change over 1968		Percent Change over 1960	
	Number	Rate per 100,000 Inhabitants	Number	Rate	Number	Rate	Number	Rate
Total	8,638,400	4,116.4	+5.7	+4.9	+29.7	+23.5	+157.6	+120.2
Violent	869,470	414.3	+4.9	+4.1	+47.2	+40.2	+203.8	+159.6
Property	7,768,900	3,702.1	+5.8	+5.0	+28.0	+21.9	+153.3	+116.5
Murder	19,510	9.3	+5.2	+4.5	+42.2	+34.8	+115.6	+86.0
Forcible rape	51,000	24.3	+9.7	+9.0	+62.4	+54.8	+199.2	+155.8
Robbery	382,680	182.4	+2.1	+1.3	+46.2	+39.2	+256.3	+204.5
Aggravated assault	416,270	198.4	+7.0	+6.2	+46.7	+39.7	+172.6	+132.9
Burglary	2,540,900	1,210.8	+8.0	+7.2	+38.0	+31.4	+181.3	+140.3
Larceny-theft	4,304,400	2,051.2	+4.7	+3.9	+24.8	+18.9	+134.3	+100.3
Auto theft	923,600	440.1	+4.7	+3.9	+18.5	+12.9	+183.0	+141.8

Violent crimes include murder, forcible rape, and aggravated assault. Property crimes include burglary, larceny $50 and over, and auto theft.
Source: FBI, *Uniform Crime Report, 1973*, p. 1.

FIGURE 11–7
Crimes of Violence, 1967–1972 (percent change over 1967)

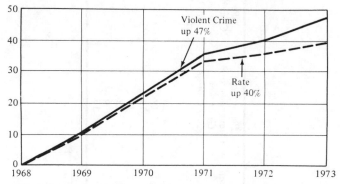

Limited to murder, forcible rape, robbery and aggravated assault.
Source: FBI, *Uniform Crime Report, 1972*, p. 4.

cities with populations over 250,000, for suburban areas, and for rural areas. As most readers may have anticipated the crime rate for all crimes in the larger cities was nearly twice what it was in suburban areas and more than four times what it was in rural areas.

TABLE 11–2
Crime Rate by Area, 1973 (rate per 100,000 inhabitants)

		Area		
Crime Index Offenses	Total U.S.	Cities over 250,000	Suburban	Rural
Total	4,116.4	6,582.8	3,562.6	1,471.8
Violent	141.3	1,003.4	248.5	147.4
Property	3,702.1	5,579.5	3,314.1	1,324.4
Murder	9.3	20.7	5.1	7.5
Forcible rape	24.3	51.4	17.8	12.0
Robbery	182.4	571.5	76.1	17.7
Aggravated assault	198.4	359.9	149.5	110.2
Burglary	1,210.8	1,949.3	1,054.4	564.0
Larceny-theft	2,051.2	2,651.8	1,952.4	677.6
Auto theft	440.0	978.4	307.4	82.8

Source: FBI, *Uniform Crime Reports, 1973*, p. 2.

Table 11–3 provides some information on the disposition of reported crimes. Of all the index crimes committed in 1973, only 21 percent were cleared by the police, meaning the police had identified the offender, had enough information to charge him, and actually took him into custody. Of this small percentage, 89 percent were prosecuted, and 58 percent of those prosecuted were found guilty on the original charge and another 11

TABLE 11-3
Disposition of Reported Crimes for Adults, 1973

	Percent of Index Crimes Cleared by Arrest	Percent of Arrested that Were Prosecuted	Percent of Prosecuted Found Guilty on Original Charge	Percent of Charged Found Guilty on Lesser Charge	Percent of Charged Ending in Acquittal or Dismissal
Total	21	89	58	11	31
Murder	79	66	45	23	32
Forcible rape	51	76	36	17	47
Aggravated assault	63	82	61	17	44
Robberies	27	72	46	16	38
Burglaries	18	82	49	18	33
Larcenies $50 and over	19	N.A.	69	6	25
Auto thefts	16	N.A.	43	15	42

Data does not include the disposition of juvenile crimes.
N.A. denotes data was unavailable.
Source: FBI, *Uniform Crime Report, 1973*, pp. 28–35.

FIGURE 11–8
Crimes Against Property, 1968–1973 (percent change over 1968)

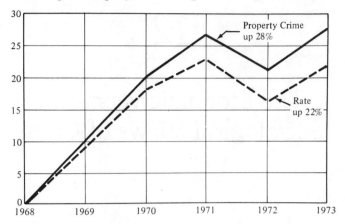

Limited to burglary, larceny-theft and auto theft.
Source: FBI, *Uniform Crime Report, 1973*, p. 5.

percent were found guilty on a lesser charge. Thirty-one percent of the cases ended in acquittal or dismissal.

The police were most effective in apprehending murderers. Seventy-nine percent of all murder cases were cleared, 45 percent ended in conviction on the original charge. Thirty-two percent, however, ended in acquittal or dismissal. The police, on the other hand, were far less successful with burglaries, larcenies, and auto thefts. Not only were the police unable to clear many of the cases, but also many of the cases terminated in dismissal or acquittal. Given this information and the knowledge that many crimes go unreported, it seems reasonably clear that the risk of being caught, convicted, and punished (particularly in certain crime areas) is not as great as most laymen may believe.

12

The Economic versus the
Sociological Views of Crime

TWO HYPOTHESES ON CRIME

The editors of *Washington Post* are against private ownership of guns and devote part of its editorial content to denouncing it. As part of this campaign, they found a professional robber in Washington and interviewed him quite extensively.[1] Under guarantee of anonymity, he was—as far as we can tell—very frank and explained fairly accurately his motives and *modus operandi*. His special field was armed robbery and he was apparently making a very good income from it. He was vaguely unhappy about his occupation because he realized it was risky, but as he said, "I want to go to barber school, but I know there's not that kind of money in barbering." In general, he calculated the risks with care: "Now I know if I's gonna rob somethin' it ought to be big, because I'm gonna get the same time. "I stay in the District where the police is too busy. . . . It's too risky in Prince Georges." He read the papers daily, "for crime." "I want to know how much people out there are gittin' and who's gettin' what kind of time."

Thus, this young criminal explains his own behavior largely in terms of calculations of profits and risk of cost. It is notable that the *Washington Post* reporter seemed to pay little attention to this aspect of the matter, although he reported verbatim lengthy statements made by the criminal. The crimes in the article are blamed on the environment. The article begins by pointing out that the criminal came from a poor family background, but it devotes far more attention to the simple fact that guns are readily

---

[1] "Dodge City on the Potomac," *Washington Post*, May 11, 1969, p. D–1.

available in Washington, D.C., than to any other aspect of the environment. Further, there seems to be no evidence that the reporter thought of the ready availability of guns in Washington as merely a reduction in the cost of criminal activity. He regards these environmental factors as direct causes of crime, rather than as changes in technological conditions that may conceivably lead profit-seeking individuals to choose a life of crime. We get the impression reading the article—albeit we must read between the lines for this—that the reporter feels that the statements the criminal makes about the risks and profits are evidence of the fact that he has had a bad environment, rather than statements about the cost-benefit calculations that lead him to continue his life of crime.

It is possible we are misrepresenting the reporter's attitude by imputing to him values and positions we find in the *Washington Post* and, indeed, in a very large part of all modern discussions of crime. The conventional wisdom in this field holds that criminals are either sick persons who require treatment or are the result of environmental deprivation (which seems to amount to much the same thing operationally), and that the possibility of punishment—which plays such a large part in this criminal's calculation—actually is unimportant in determining whether a person does or does not commit any crime. It is argued that people commit crimes not because they see an opportunity for profit, but because they are somehow socially deformed. Further, it is thought that the way to deal with this problem is to change the basic environment so that no person is deformed by the environment, or to "rehabilitate" the criminal once captured. This is one of two dominant hypotheses in the criminal activity. The other hypothesis, the one that immediately occurs to any economist, is that criminals are simply people who take opportunities for profit by violating the law. Under this hypothesis, changing the costs of crime—i.e. increasing the likelihood of being put in prison, lengthening the period of imprisonment, or making prisons less pleasant—would tend to reduce the amount of crime. As discussed in the preceding chapter, the reasoning is simply that the criminals' demand for crime, like their demands for other more normal goods and activities, is downward sloping; the greater the cost or price, the lower the quantity demanded. Rehabilitation for such criminals would be relatively pointless, since the individual is not "sick."[2] He is simply behaving rationally. This point of view is held by very few professional students of crime, although it does seem to be growing in popularity.

People with economic training are apt to take the latter of these two

---

[2] Our prisons, in point of fact, devote practically no effort to "rehabilitation." This is probably wise since those experiments in rehabilitation that have been undertaken seem to show that we do not know how to do it. See Robert Martinson, "What Works? —Questions and Answers About Prison Reform," *The Public Interest*, XXXV (Spring 1974), 22–54.

hypotheses as true, and those with sociological training, the former. Sociologist are inclined, as does Paul Horton in the following quote, to dismiss the economic view of crime:

> This misplaced faith in punishment may rest upon the unrealistic assumption that people consciously decide whether to be criminal—that they consider a criminal career, rationally balance its dangers against its rewards, and arrive at a decision based upon such pleasure-pain calculations. It supposedly follows that if the pain element is increased by severe punishment, people will turn from crime to righteousness. A little reflection reveals the absurdity of this notion.[3]

The problem, however, is basically one for empirical research. Before turning to a discussion of what empirical research has been done in the field, we should like to clarify the two hypotheses a little bit to explain the difficulties of testing the difference between them. The economic hypothesis holds that crime would tend to occur whenever the cost fell below the receipts. The costs, in a very straightforward and simple way, would be the energy and equipment put into the actual crime—which is usually quite small—plus the probability of punishment, which in our society is apt to be imprisonment. From the sociological standpoint, these two variables would appear to be largely irrelevant. Indeed, we have never been able to understand how people who believe in the conventional wisdom favor imprisonment at all.[4]

The costs and benefits, however, are to some extent affected by the type of variable in which the sociologists are interested. First, a poor man is probably less injured by being put in jail than the wealthy man. Thus, one would anticipate that a poor man would count the cost of imprisonment as being lower than would the wealthy man, and hence—other things being equal—opportunities for crime that would attract the poor man would appear to be unprofitable from the standpoint of the wealthy man. Second, the size of the booty would be of interest. Large concentrations of wealth would attract potential criminals who would not be interested in small quantities.

These two factors, taken together, would indicate that wide disparity in income might increase crime. A wide disparity of income means that there are some people in the community for whom imprisonment is of relatively light weight, and some targets for crime in the community that would pay off very well. Both poverty and disparity of income might increase

---

[3] P. B. Horton and G. R. Leslie, *The Sociology of Social Problems*, New York: Appleton-Century-Crofts, 1960, p. 155.

[4] Indeed, some of them have drawn the logical conclusion from their reasoning and are opposed to imprisonment. This opinion, however, is more apt to turn up in private conversation than in print. For one example in print, see *The Nation*, September 27, 1971, 258–59.

the crime rate under *either* the sociological or the economic explanation. Lastly, life in the larger city may reduce the cost of crime as opposed to life in a smaller city. The reasons may be that crime targets are located more closely together and the lower degree of social interaction (implying lower social costs). Ethnic groups may be more willing to protect their own and, in general, it is harder for the police to catch criminals in large cities.

It will be observed that we have listed a number of variables—which the sociologist might consider as causes of crime—as factors that affect the cost and benefit, and hence somewhat indirectly the cause of crime. This might appear to make the test of the two hypotheses difficult, and indeed it would, were it not for the fact that there are some remaining variables. If we believe that criminals are sick and are not deterred by threat of punishment, then we would predict that changes in the rate of punishment would have no effect on the crime rate. From the economic viewpoint, we would predict that such changes *would* have an effect on the crime rate. Both the sociologist and the economist would expect the same outcome if statistical tests were made of these factors; but when it came to the effect of imprisonment upon the crime rate, there would be a clear difference.

It should be noted that, although the significance or non-significance of the effect of punishment distinguishes between these two hypotheses, it cannot strictly speaking prove the economic hypothesis. A much weaker hypothesis that people respond to costs whether sick or well would lead to the same result as what we have referred to as the economic hypothesis. Indeed, Gary Becker (an economist) and his students have always used this simpler hypothesis quite explicitly. Most of the research we shall discuss below, then, goes to the question of whether or not punishment deters crime, but does not directly relate to the rationality or "sickness" of the criminal. This is, however, enough. If punishment deters crime, then the sociological approach falls to the ground, and much of the advice given to governments by sociologists over the past 50 years is clearly wrong. Indeed, such advice might well be one of the major reasons for the rising crime rate.

Before going on to the question of whether punishment deters crime, it is necessary to make a brief digression on the type of punishment to be used. At the moment, there are only two forms of punishment in general use in the United States, fines and imprisonment. Of these two, fines are clearly superior because of the immense dead-weight loss involved in imprisonment. Not only is output largely lost because very little useful work is performed by prisoners, but the cost of imprisonment, which must be borne by society, is very substantial. Unfortunately, a large percentage of all criminals cannot pay fines large enough so that we would be able to regard them as having the same deterrent effect of, let us say, 10 years in prison. Under the circumstances, we are driven back on imprisonment; but we should be more than willing to explore other possible alternatives.

Prevention of crime by such things as better locks, more careful police patrols, etc., is one way of reducing the crime rate; and to some degree, in any event, it is cheaper than the imprisonment threat. Rehabilitation of criminals would be a desirable alternative.[5] Going back a little bit in time, there is, of course, the death penalty, which will be discussed below; and going back several hundred years, the use of torture and other physical punishments. The latter, of course, are constitutionally prohibited in the United States. Various African and Arab countries, however, are returning to public floggings as a basic deterrent mechanism.

DOES PUNISHMENT DETER CRIME?

Sociologists sometimes say that empirical tests indicate that there is no deterrent effect from imprisonment, etc. In practice, however, little or no investigation has been undertaken by sociologists on this point. Further, the small number of tests that have been undertaken deal with the death penalty and/or are radically defective methodologically. It is not necessarily true, of course, that if the death penalty did not deter murder, then imprisonment would not deter burglary. Indeed, in our opinion, the "research" done on the death penalty largely rationalizes the moral feelings of some groups (sociologists included) without much effort to find the real truth.[6]

Testing the deterrent effect of the death penalty on murder is rather difficult because, in the United States where most of the research has been done, death sentences have always been quite rare; even in the 1930s a murder had only about one chance in a 100 of being executed, whereas his chance of going to prison for a long period of time was 20 to 30 times as great. Under the circumstances, changes of the frequency of the death penalty would tend to be less significant by a wide margin than other variants in punishment policy. There is a modern statistical technique, multiple regression, which is suited to deal with this type of problem; but so far as we can discover, no sociologist or criminologist used this technique until the last few years. Further, they have not concerned themselves with the frequency of the death penalty in any efficient way. When they have considered the death penalty, they have mainly simply pointed out that the rank ordering of states by number of murders is

---

[5] For a careful and exhaustive study of the published reports on rehabilitation, see Martinson, "What Works?" Although some of the techniques he discusses showed some signs of promise for future development, none has yet shown a valid statistical ability to "rehabilitate" the criminal.

[6] For a survey of the conventional sociological research, see, Hugo Adam Bedau, *The Death Penalty in America*, rev. ed., Garden City, N.Y.: Doubleday & Co., 1967.

highly correlated with rank ordering of states by number of executions. This brings in the size of the state as a hidden explanatory variable, and obscures the actual relationship. If you are contemplating committing a murder, you should not be concerned particularly with how many other murders or how many executions have taken place in your state, but with the probability that you will be executed.

In a way, however, we are being unkind to the sociologists. Data in crime are almost incredibly bad, even for murder. Still, we can see little evidence that the sociologists have tried to apply really suitable methods to the problem. These inadequate tests of the deterrent effect of the death penalty were, however, until recently the *only* empirical investigations that had been undertaken on the deterrent effect of punishment. In spite of the fact that this evidence was extremely weak, sociologists and criminologists continued to say that it had been demonstrated that punishment had no deterrent effect.

The widely popular view that criminals are sick is based not on a few poor empirical studies, but on zero empirical studies. Some criminals are indeed, mentally ill and they are customarily segregated from the other criminals during the trial process. Thus, most states maintain facilities for the criminally insane, as well as for ordinary criminals. There seems to be, however, absolutely *no* evidence that criminals who are in the ordinary prisons are more likely to be insane than people outside, or that what neuroses they do have, have much to do with their crimes.[7] In addition, if investigations deal exclusively with criminals who are in prisons and who are by definition "failures" at their jobs, one can easily get a distorted picture of the criminal population. We would obtain the same type of distorted picture if we attempted to judge the intelligence and sanity of the business community as a whole by primarily observing those businessmen who go bankrupt.

What, then, have the criminologist and sociologist investigated? The answer is the environmental background of the criminal. As we have pointed out, people from poor backgrounds are apt to have a lower cost of crime, and hence, even under the economic explanation, we would anticipate that they would commit more crimes. Studies of this sort, then, do not differentiate between the two basic hypotheses, and such studies have dominated the work on the determinants of crime by sociologists and criminologists. Indeed, until very recently, those economists who turned their attention to crime simply accepted the dominant opinion of sociology and criminology, and repeated the sociologists' studies, albeit with somewhat different methodology.[8] Thus, until really very recently, most

---

[7] One of our ways to investigate this subject has been to ask people if they can refer us to such empirical research. We repeat the question here.

[8] See, for example, Belton M. Fleisher, *The Economics of Delinquency*, Chicago: Quadrangle Books, 1966.

"experts" on crime believed that punishment did not deter crime. This belief indicated that we were wrong to put people in prison, although this conclusion was seldom drawn. Further, it was based on an extraordinarily small quantity of very inferior work, which in turn was mostly addressed to one very special case.

Once economists began working on crime, however, it was inevitable that they would begin to investigate the possibility that crimes—like everything else—are affected by price. The deterrence theory of punishment is, after all, simply a special version of the general economic principle that raising the price of something will reduce the amount purchased.[9] Further, the first serious empirical research to test this proposition was undertaken by a master's candidate under Becker's direction. Presumably the basic research design was his, and it set the standard and style for the bulk of the empirical research that we shall discuss.

For certain types of crime, Arleen Leibowitz ran a multiple regression routine in which the crime rate by state was a dependent variable, and the punishment the independent variable(s).[10] Leibowitz used three different specifications of the equation in which the likelihood of conviction and the average sentence were treated in different ways, with the objective of attempting to determine which of these was more important. For reasons that will be discussed below, she was unable to cast a great deal of light upon this subject. She did, however, find a pronounced deterrent effect.

Unfortunately, in the traditional literature, there has been some discussion as to whether the certainty of punishment is more important than the severity of punishment. Like most of the other scholars we will be citing, Leibowitz attempts to solve this problem by taking these two terms separately. Theoretically, this is unwise, since it is not obvious that individuals would have very much choice between, say, a 50–50 chance of two years in prison or a 1–4 chance of four years in prison. Further, any difference would be the effect of either risk aversion or time discounting. Both of these are apt to be small compared with the effect of the present value of the punishment.

---

[9] For earlier and more rigorous discussions of the economic approach to crime, see Gary S. Becker, "Crime and Punishment: An Economic Approach," *Journal of Political Economy* 76 (March/April 1968), 169–217, and Gordon Tullock. "The Welfare Costs of Tarriffs, Monopolies, and Theft," *Western Economic Journal* 5 (1967), 224–232. The latter refers to the deterrent effects of punishment only in passing.

[10] Arleen Smigel Leibowitz, "Does Crime Pay: An Economic Analysis," Unpublished M.A. thesis, Columbia University, New York, 1965. In not being published it is typical of the research in this area. Many of the papers we will discuss have not been formally published, presumably because journals regard their conclusions as beyond the pale. We have obtained copies of these, mainly in mimeographed form, through the "invisible college." It seems likely that we do not have all of them. We would appreciate being informed of further examples.

The next study discussed was by a sociologist, Jack P. Gibbs, who apparently had not been at all influenced by Becker and who had used a somewhat different research design.[11] Gibbs took the homicide rate for each state in 1960 from the Federal Bureau of Investigation statistics and correlated it against two other variables. The first was the average time in prison for each person now in prison for homicide in each state, and the second was the likelihood of being sent to prison for homicide by state, calculated by dividing the number of people who had been imprisoned for this crime in each state by the number of homicides committed in that state (as shown in the *FBI Uniform Crime Report*). His tests also unambiguously showed the deterrent effect of punishment upon homicide.

Unfortunately, Gibbs also attempted to determine whether certainty or severity of sentence was more important. Gibbs' article set off quite a flurry of further research in the same area and a good deal of it was devoted to this essentially irrelevant question. It should be said, however, that all of this work showed the deterrent effect for punishment. Louis Gray and David Martin reexamined Gibbs' statistics, using a different technique and, uniquely, came to the conclusion that efforts to untangle the effects of severity and certainty were a waste of time.[12] Once again, they showed the deterrent effect. Frank Bean and Robert Cushing also reexamined Gibbs' work, using still a third statistical technique and, once again, turned up deterrence effect.[13] Lastly, Charles Tittle published an expansive attack upon the severity versus certainty aspect of Gibbs' article.[14] In this study, he used basically the same sort of data but a different statistical technique than that used by Gibbs and took it for *many* crimes rather than just homicide. Once again, it clearly shows that punishment has a deterrent effect.

We now turn to a most interesting paper by Michael Block.[15] In this study, Block used Los Angeles Police districts as his observations, which meant that his data are quite different from most of the studies that use entire states as the observations. It also raises some fairly difficult problems having to do with the variables. Nevertheless, Block succeeded in

---

[11] Jack P. Gibbs, "Crime, Punishment, and Deterrence," *Southwestern Social Science Quarterly* 48 (March 1968), 515–530.

[12] Louis N. Gray and J. David Martin, "Punishment and Deterrence: Another Analysis of Gibbs' Data," *Social Science Quarterly* 50 (September 1969), 389–395.

[13] Frank D. Bean and Robert G. Cushing, "Criminal Homicide, Punishment, and Deterrence: Methodological and Substantive Reconsiderations," *Social Science Quarterly* 52 (September 1971), 277–89.

[14] Charles R. Tittle, "Crime Rates and Legal Sanctions," *Social Problems* 16 (Spring 1969), 409–23. It would appear to us that Tittle started out intending to demonstrate that Gibbs was totally wrong, but had to settle for bickering about this essentially irrelevant issue.

[15] Michael Block, "An Econometric Approach to Theft," Stanford University, mimeographed.

making use of these data for a very elaborate series of regression operations in which the offense rate per district for each offense considered
is negatively correlated with the clearance rate in that district, and positively correlated with the loot gained. It would be hard to find a more
perfect expression of the economic hypothesis. Although there are some
problems of a technical nature in this study, it seems to us that it offers a
most intriguing opportunity for further research of the same sort in other
cities. In a sense, the state-wide observation data have been largely exhausted. All we can do now is try different years. Block's methods, however, can be tested in a number of different areas with completely independent data.

More recent work, in what we may call the Becker-Gibbs tradition, has
been more ambitious. Phillips, Votey, and Howell, for example, produced
a paper aimed basically at providing optimal enforcement recipes for the
crime control system.[16] This goes far beyond our concern in this chapter,
but it should be noted that in the process of obtaining their results, they
ran a complex regression in which the deterrent effect of punishment
showed up quite clearly. This study used a time-series for the nation in
general as its basic data, and hence it is independent of any of the previous
studies. A time-series study, taken by and of itself, would not be very
convincing, since various things other than deterrence change over time.
Nevertheless, evidence that the time-series study leads to the same conclusion as the cross-section studies does add an element of confirmation.

Morgan Reynolds also had a good deal more ambitious goal than those
we have reported so far.[17] Once again, however, his study involved—
among other things—a multiple regression routine in which the deterrent
effect of punishment is implicitly tested. It is a cross-section study, differing from the others only in that the other variables used in the regression
were somewhat different, because it has somewhat different objectives.
The deterrent effect showed up as usual. Isaac Ehrlich—once again under
the supervision of Gary Becker—prepared a doctoral dissertation for
a Ph.D. in economics at Columbia University.[18] The dissertation, available to us only in preliminary form, is the most ambitious study that has
been attempted in this area and shows a very clear deterrent effect of
punishment.

There is a very good study by R. A. Carr-Hill and N. H. Stern, "An

---

[16] Llad Phillips, Harold L. Votey, Jr., and John Howell, "Apprehension, Deterrence,
Guns and Violence: The Control of Homicide," paper presented at the 46th meeting of
the Western Economic Association, Vancouver, British Columbia, August 1971.

[17] Morgan Reynolds, "Crimes for Profit: The Economics of Theft," unpublished
Ph.D. dissertation, University of Wisconsin, 1971. We have seen only a paper he read
at the Western Economic Association meeting entitled "The Economics of Theft."

[18] A condensed version of this dissertation has been published; see Isaac Ehrlich,
"Participation in Illegitimate Activities: A Theoretical and Empirical Investigation,"
Journal of Political Economy, LXXXI (May/June 1973), 521–65.

Econometric Model of the Supply and Control of Recorded Offenses in England and Wales." We have this only as a Xerox copy of the first draft. Due to different types of statistics, the Carr-Hill/Stern research design is not identical with the ones we have discussed before, but the basic principles are the same. They show a very clear deterrent effect of imprisonment and, indeed, the coefficients they get for imprisonment appear to be markedly higher than those in the United States. Let us hope that with time further studies in other foreign countries will become available. A good deal of further work has been done with the American data, and there is indeed room for more, but it does not seem necessary to discuss it in detail here.[19] Isaac Ehrlich returned to the problem of the death penalty in a recent article, and finds that each execution prevents somewhere between 8 and 20 murders.[20] The data problems he faced were formidable and it is not certain in this case that his conclusions are correct, but this suggests that the repeal of the death penalty is a costly business.

There is another line of research that can be said to be indirectly related to the deterrent hypothesis. Under a grant from the National Science Foundation, a number of graduate students at Virginia Polytechnic Institute and State University have been conducting cost-benefit analyses of various types of crime in order to find out whether crime pays. As can well be imagined, the data problems are appalling. Further, it would be quite possible for deterrence to have an effect on crime, even if the criminals were so irrational that they went into the activity when the costs were greater than the benefits. Nevertheless, the general finding of this study is consistent with the deterrence hypothesis. We do find, on the whole, that professional criminals seem to have made sensible career choices. In other words, crime pays.[21] This implies but does not prove that if the cost of crime were raised, they would pick other occupations.

---

[19] See Harold L. Votey, Jr. and Llad Phillips, *Economic Crimes: Their Generation, Deterrence, and Control*, Springfield, Va.: U.S. Clearinghouse for Federal Scientific and Technical Information, 1969; ———, "The Law Enforcement Production Function," *Journal of Legal Studies*, I (June 1972); ———, "An Economic Analysis of the Deterrent Effect of Law Enforcement on Criminal Activity," *Journal of Criminal Law, Criminology, and Police Science*, LXIII (September 1972); ———, "The Control of Criminal Activity: An Economic Analysis," in *Handbook of Criminology*, ed. by Daniel Glaser, Chicago: Rand McNally & Co., forthcoming); Joseph P. Magaddino and Gregory C. Krohm (untitled paper, in progress); David L. Sjoquist, "Property Crime and Economic Behavior: Some Empirical Results," *American Economic Review*, LXXXIII, No. 3 (1973); Llad Phillips, Harold L. Votey, Jr., and Donald Maxwell, "Crime, Youth, and the Labor Market," *Journal of Political Economy*, LXXX (May/June 1972); and Maynard L. Erickson and Jack P. Gibbs, "The Deterrence Question: Some Alternative Methods of Analysis," *Social Science Quarterly*, LIII (December 1973), 534–51.

[20] Isaac Ehrlich, "The Deterrent Effect of Capital Punishment: A Question of Life and Death," *American Economic Review* (in press).

[21] William E. Cobb, "Theft and the Two Hypotheses," and Gregory C. Krohm, "The Pecuniary Incentives of Property Crimes," in *The Economics of Crime and Punishment*, ed. by Simon Rottenberg, Washington: American Enterprise Institute, 1973.

A FINAL COMMENT

Ideas influence the real world. The fact that most specialists in the study of crime have believed, written, and taught that punishment does not deter crime has had an effect upon public policy. Legislatures have been more reluctant to appropriate money for prisons than they otherwise would have been; judges have tended to feel that imprisonment had little effect on crime, and hence at the intellectual level, in any event, were less willing to put people in jail for long periods of time. Further, the shortage of prisons so induced has made it impossible to keep people in jail for long periods of time for serious crimes. As a result, halfway houses (which are very inexpensive), parole, and probation have been resorted to on a very large scale, and this has sharply reduced the cost of crime. This in turn leads to a rise in the crime rate that leads to further clogging of facilities, and hence further reduction in the cost of crime. The rising crime rate in the United States to a very considerable extent can be blamed upon our intellectual community.

We began this chapter with quotations from a juvenile delinquent in Washington, D.C. We suspect that he may be illiterate, or close to illiterate, and certainly has none of the academic credentials we normally require for research into the origins of crime. Nevertheless, we cannot escape the feeling that he is far better qualified to advise our government on matters of crime prevention than most professors of criminology.

13

Traffic Violations

In the preceding chapters, we discussed in general terms the economic approach to crime. The purposes of this and the following chapter are to further demonstrate the utility of the economic perspective and to present some simple computational tools in two areas of the law with which the reader is likely to have fairly extensive personal experience: motor vehicle code violations and tax evasion. In the case of the former, we are not only fully experienced, but we also have a very good and clear idea in our own minds of the consequences of the violation. While our knowledge and experience in regard to tax evasion are rather less than those concerning violations of the traffic code, most of us have at least contemplated padding our expenses on the income tax form, and we find very little difficulty in understanding why other people actually do it fairly regularly.

In addition to reader knowledge based on experience, there is a further advantage to discussing motor vehicle offenses and tax evasion. The customary element in such laws is extremely small. Most of our laws on crime came down from great antiquity and hence contain all sorts of quaint nooks and corners. The motor vehicle law is almost entirely a creation of the 20th century and is periodically changed quite drastically. Similarly, the income tax code is largely a recent development, and in this case is being continuously changed by both legislative enactment and the actions of various administrative bodies. Thus, we do not have to deal with the weight of immemorial tradition when we turn to these problems.

ILLEGAL PARKING

To begin, let us consider the most common and simplest of all violations of the law: illegal parking. This is a new problem. In the days of yore, there were not enough idle vehicles to require special parking laws;

when, however, common men began to buy automobiles, the number of vehicles was such that simply permitting people to park where they wished along the side of the street led to very serious congestion. The number of spaces was limited, and rationing on a first come, first served basis seems to have been felt to be unsatisfactory. In any event, the proper governmental bodies decided that there should be a "fairer" distribution of parking space, and it was decided that individuals should vacate spaces at some specified time, frequently an hour, after they occupied them.

The question then arose as to how to assure compliance. The method chosen was to fine noncompliance. The police were instructed to "ticket" cars which parked beyond the time limit, and the owners of the ticketed cars were then fined a small sum, say $10. Thus, the individual could choose between removing his car within the prescribed period or leaving it and running some chance of being forced to pay $10. Obviously, the size of the fine and the likelihood that any given car owner would be caught would largely determine how much overparking was done. The individual would, in effect, be confronted with a "price list" to overpark, and would normally do so only if the inconvenience of moving his car was greater than the properly discounted cost of the fine.

Not all overparking is the result of a deliberate decision, however. Clearly a good deal of it comes from absentmindedness, and part is the result of factors not very thoroughly under control of the car owner. Nevertheless, we do not in general feel that the fine should be remitted. The absence of a criminal intent, or indeed of any intent at all, is not regarded as an excuse. When one of the authors was working for the Department of State in Washington, he served under a man who got several parking tickets a week, and all of these violations occurred without any conscious intent on his part. He would get involved in some project and forget to move his car. The District of Columbia was levying what amounted to a tax on him for being absentminded.

As far as could be told, the police force of Washington, D.C. was not particularly annoyed with the man. Apparently, they thought the revenue derived paid for the inconvenience of issuing tickets and occasionally towing away his car. Suppose, however, they had wanted to make him stop violating the parking laws. It seems highly probably that a drastic increase in the fines would have been sufficient. Absentmindedness about $10 does not necessarily imply absentmindedness about $100 or even $1,000. With higher fines he would have felt more pressure to train himself to remember, to avoid parking on the public streets as much as possible, and to arrange for his secretary to remind him. Thus, the fact that he was not engaging in any calculations at all when he committed these "crimes" does not indicate that he would not respond to higher penalties by ceasing to commit them.

So far, however, we have simply assumed that the objective is to enforce a particular law against parking. The question of whether this law is sensible, or how much effort should be put into enforcing it, has not been discussed. To deal with this problem, let us turn to a more modern tech- nology and discuss a metered parking area. In such areas the government in essence is simply renting out space to people who want to use it. It may not be using a market-clearing price because it may have some objectives other than simply providing the service at a profit, but this does not seriously alter the problem. For simplicity, let us assume that it is charging market-clearing prices. It would then attempt to maximize total revenue, including the revenue from fines and the revenue from the coins inserted in the parking meters minus the cost of the enforcement system. We need not here produce an equation or attempt to solve this problem, but clearly it is a perfectly ordinary problem in operations research, and there is no reason why we should anticipate any great difficulty with it.

OTHER MOTOR VEHICLE LAWS

However, parking is clearly a very minor problem; in fact, it was chosen for discussion simply because it is so easy. In essence, there is very little here except calculation of exactly the same sort that is undertaken every day by businessmen. For a slightly more complicated problem, let us con- sider another traffic offense: speeding. Presumably, the number of deaths from auto accidents, the extent of personal injuries and the material dam- age are all functions of the speed at which cars travel.[1] By enforcing a legal maximum on such speed, we can reduce all of them. On the other hand, a legal maximum speed will surely inconvenience at least some people, and may inconvenience a great many. The strictly material cost of lower- ing speeds is easily approximated by computing the additional time spent in traveling and multiplying this by the hourly earning power of an aver- age member of the population. This is, of course, only an approximation, leaving out of account such factors as the pleasure some people get from speed and the diversion of economic activity which would result from the slowing of traffic. Nevertheless, we could use this approximation and the number of deaths, injuries and the cost of material damage from auto accidents to work out the optimal speed limit.[2] The computation would be made in "social" terms because the data would be collected for the whole

---

[1] This relationship has been somewhat obscured by the publication of Ralph Nader's *Unsafe at Any Speed.* It is undoubtedly true that cars can be designed to reduce fatalities in accidents and, for that matter, that highways can be designed to reduce accidents. Recent discoveries of methods of reducing skidding by improved highway surfaces probably indicate that there is more potential in highway improve- ment than in car redesign. Nevertheless, for a given car and highway, speed kills.

[2] For those who object to approximation, more elaborate research, taking into account much more of the costs of slowing down traffic, could be undertaken.

population. Individuals, however, could regard these figures as actuarial approximations for their personal situation.

To the best of our knowledge, no one has ever performed these calculations in a reasonably direct and precise way. Presumably the reason for the omission is an unwillingness to consciously and openly put a value on deaths and injuries, which can then be compared with the strictly material costs of delay. When we point out to people that the death toll from highway accidents could be reduced by simply lowering the speed limit (and improving enforcement), they normally show great reluctance to give any consideration to the subject.[3] They sometimes try to convince themselves that the reduction would not have the predicted effect, but more commonly they simply shift quickly to another subject. They are unwilling, for reasons of convenience, to approve a substantial lowering of the speed limit, but they do not like to consciously balance their convenience against deaths (including, possibly, their own). Nevertheless, this is the real reasoning behind the speed limits. We count the costs of being forced to drive slowly and the costs of accidents, and choose the speed limit that gives us the best outcome. Since we are unwilling to do this consciously, we probably do a bad job of computing.

As an example of this reluctance to think about the valuation we are willing to put upon deaths and injury in terms of our own convenience, a colleague of ours undertook a study of the methods used by the Virginia Highway Commission in deciding how to improve the roads. He found that they were under orders to consider speed, beauty, and safety in presenting projects for future work. The beauty was taken care of by simply earmarking a fixed part of the appropriations for roadside parks, etc. For speed they engaged in elaborate research on highway use and had statistical techniques for predicting the net savings in time from various possible changes. It was the possibility of improving these techniques that led them to invite our colleague to make his study. For safety, on the other hand, they had no system at all.

It was clear that they did take safety into account in designing roads, and spent quite a bit of money on various methods of reducing the likelihood of accidents. They did not, however, have any formula or rule for deciding either how much should be spent on safety or in what specific projects is should be invested. They must have had some trade-off rule that they applied. This rule, however, remained buried in their subconscious even though they used fairly elaborate and advanced techniques for other problems. This is particularly remarkable when it is remembered

---

[3] In the fall of 1973, states began passing laws reducing the speed limit to 55 miles per hour. The results were a dramatic reduction in the number of accidents and deaths on the highway. It is interesting to note that the overriding reason for the speed limit reduction was to conserve gasoline consumption and not to reduce the number of deaths. (Why were the speed limits not lowered below 55?)

that, given any exchange value, the computations of the amount to be spent on safety would be fairly easy.

Methods of determining the value of human life have not yet been worked out, and we have nothing to contribute to that area. We do note, however, that since the highway engineers clearly make some kind of decision on how much they will spend on reducing the death rate, we could compute the average implicit price the engineers put on death and injury from their previous decisions as to how much money they will put into various safety measures. This number would not be scientific in the sense that it is clearly the correct amount, but it would be the amount now being used. Since the engineers do not think of it consciously, they probably are doing a bad job of applying it. Its systematic use in the form of mathematical calculations would probably permit more lives to be saved at the same expense, because the present "subconscious" method must lead to overinvestment in some cases and underinvestment in others.

If, for example, it is decided that we will count one fatal accident as "worth" $500,000 in inconvenience to drivers (measured in increased travel time), then, with statistics on accidents and volume of traffic, it would be possible to work out how much should be spent on safety and how much on speed. Since the Highway Commission did not spend all of its money on safety, some such "price" for accidents must have taken some part of its reasoning, but rather sophisticated engineers were unwilling to admit, probably even to themselves, that this was so. Perhaps more surprising, our colleague fully approved of their attitude. Basically a "scientific" type, with a great interest in statistical decision theory, he felt that here was one place where careful reasoning was undesirable. He did not want to consider ratios between deaths and convenience himself, did not want the people who designed the highways on which he drove to consciously consider them, and did not want to discuss the subject with us.

But even if we do not like to examine critically our decision process, clearly the decision as to the speed limit is made by balancing the inconveniences of a low limit against the deaths and injuries to be expected from a high one. The fact that we are not willing to engage in conscious thought on the problem is doubly unfortunate, because it is difficult enough so that it is unlikely that we can reach optimal decisions by any but the most careful and scientific procedures. The problem is stochastic on both sides, since driving at a given speed does not certainly cause an accident; it only creates a probability of an accident. Similarly, our convenience is not always best served by exceeding the speed limit, so we have only a stochastic probability of being inconvenienced. There will also be some problems of gathering data we do not now have (mainly because we have not thought clearly about the problem) and making reasonable estimates of certain parameters. To solve the problem, we need a table of probabilities rather like Table 13–1. Obviously, with this table and one more thing—a conversion factor for deaths and delay, we could readily calculate the speed limit that would minimize the "cost" of using the road.[4]

TABLE 13–1
Effects of Speed Limits

Speed Limit (mph)	Deaths per 100 Thousand Miles	Costs of Delay
10	1	$50,000,000,000
20	2	35,000,000,000
30	4	22,500,000,000
40	8	15,500,000,000
50	16	5,000,000,000
60	32	2,000,000,000
70	64	500,000,000

Equally obviously, no direct calculation of this sort is now undertaken, but our speed limits are set by a sort of weighing of accident prevention against inconvenience. The only difference between our present methods and the ones we have outlined is that we are frightened of having to admit that we use a conversion ratio in which lives are counted as worth only some finite amount of inconvenience, and we refuse to make the computations at a conscious level and hence are denied the use of modern statistical methods.

Having set a speed limit, we now turn to its enforcement. If, for example, the limit is 50 miles per hour, then it does not follow that the people who drive over that speed will automatically have accidents. Nor does it follow that driving at 51 miles per hour is very much more likely to lead to an accident than driving at 50 miles per hour. The use of a simple limit law is dictated by the problems of enforcement rather than the nature of the control problem itself. If we had some way of simply charging people for the use of the streets, with the amount per mile varying with the speed,[5] this would permit a better adjustment than a simple speed limit. In practice, the police and courts do do something rather like this by charging much higher fines for people who greatly exceed the speed limit. Let us,

---

[4] Note that we are ignoring all consequences of accidents except deaths and that it is assumed that the speed limit is the only variable. These are, of course, simplifying assumptions introduced in order to make Table 13–1 simple and the explanation easy. If any attempt were made to utilize explicitly the methods we suggest, much more complex data would be needed. The figures are, of course, assumed for illustrative purposes only.

[5] Needless to say, the cost of driving 50 miles per hour in a built-up area would be higher than in the open countryside.

however, confine ourselves to the simple case where we have a single speed limit, with no higher fines for exceeding it by a sizable amount.

Our method of enforcing this law is in some ways most peculiar. In the first place, if a citizen sees someone violating this law and reports it, the police will refuse to do anything about it. With one specific exception, which we will footnote in a moment, you cannot be penalized for speeding unless a police officer sees you do it. Think what burglars would give for a similar police practice in their field of endeavor!

A second peculiarity is that the penalty assessed is unconnected with the attitude of mind of the person who violates the speed limit.[6] Driving at 70 miles per hour may get you a fine of $100 or a ten-year prison sentence, depending upon the occurrence of events over which you have no control. Suppose, for example, two drivers each take a curve in the highway at 70. The first finds a police car on the other side, gets a ticket, and pays a fine. The second encounters a tractor driving down his side of the road and a column of cars on the other side. In the resulting crash, the tractor driver is killed and the outcome may be a ten-year prison sentence for the driver of the car.[7] We can assume both men exceeded the speed limit for the same motives, but the second had bad luck. Normally we like to have penalties depend upon what the defendant did, not on external circumstances beyond his control. (The only other situation in which this kind of thing is done involves the rule that makes a death caused while committing a felony murder regardless of the intent.)

The peculiarity of this procedure is emphasized when it is remembered that the man who risks being sent up for ten years for killing someone in an accident almost certainly had no intent to do so. He was driving at high speed to get somewhere in a hurry, an act that normally leads to a moderate fine when detected. The heavy sentence comes not from the wickedness of his act, but from the fact that he drew an unlucky number in a lottery. The case is even clearer in those not terribly rare cases where the accident arises not from conscious violation of the law but from incompetence or emotional stress (losing one's head). In ordinary driving we frequently encounter situations where a small error in judgment can cause deaths. A man who has no intent to drive carelessly may simply be a bad judge of distance and try to pass a truck where there is insufficient room. An excitable person may "freeze" when some emergency arises,

---

[6] There is a partial and imperfect exception to this for certain special cases. The man who speeds to get his wife to the hospital before the birth of their child is perhaps the one who gets the most newspaper attention.

[7] Note that the rule that a traffic offense is prosecuted only if seen by a police officer is not followed in the event of a serious accident. A third driver may be imagined who took the curve at the same speed and met neither the police nor the tractor. He would, of course, go off scot free even if his offense were reported to the police.

with the result that there is an accident which could easily have been prevented. Both of these cases might well lead to prison terms in spite of the complete lack of "criminal intent" on the part of the defendant.

> If a driver, in fact, adopts a manner of driving which the jury thinks dangerous to other road users . . . then on the issue of guilt, it matters not whether he was deliberately reckless, careless, momentarily inattentive, or doing his incompetent best.[8]

As anybody who has studied game theory knows, a mixed strategy may pay off better than a pure strategy. It may be, therefore, that the combination of three different treatments is better than a simpler rule providing a single and fairly heavy penalty for speeding regardless of whether you hit anyone or happen to encounter a policeman while engaged in the criminal act. But, although we must admit this possibility, it seems more likely that a single penalty based on the intent of the individual would work better in preventing speeding. The probable reason for the rather peculiar set of rules we have outlined is simply the functioning of the court system. If someone who disliked you alleged that he had seen you speeding and you denied it, the court would have to decide who was lying without much to go on except the expressions on our faces. Since "dishonesty can lie honesty out of countenance any day of the week if there is anything to be gained by it," this is clearly an uncertain guide. Thus, under our current court system, permitting people to initiate prosecutions for speeding by stating that they had seen someone doing so would almost certainly mean that innumerable spite cases would be brought before the courts, and that the courts would make many, many mistakes in dealing with them.

Similarly, the use of two sets of penalties for speeding, depending on factors not under the defendant's control, is probably the result of judicial performance. Charging a very heavy fine or relatively brief imprisonment for every speeding conviction would very likely be resisted by judges who do not really think speeding is very serious unless it kills somebody. That this is the restriction cannot strictly be proven but at least some evidence can be provided for it. In Virginia, as in many states, multiple convictions for traffic offenses can result in removal of the driving license. The state has encountered real difficulty in getting its judges to carry out this provision. Under the conditions of modern life, the deprivation of a driver's license is a real hardship, and judges apparently do not like to impose it for a speeding offense simply because the offender has been convicted twice before. Similarly, if a license is suspended, the courts are unlikely to inflict a very heavy penalty on the man who drives anyhow, provided he avoids killing someone.[9]

---

[8] Hill v. Baxter, 1 QB (1958), p. 277.

[9] Possibly, given the difficulties of enforcement, a restriction of the license rather than a removal might be wise. Restricting the license of a multiple offender to a limited

It is probable that problems of judicial efficiency account for another peculiarity of the motor traffic code; i.e., it is almost impossible for an individual to defend himself against the accusation. Normally the police officer's testimony is accepted regardless of other evidence. Further, in general, the penalty exacted for the average minor violation of the code is small if the defendant pleads guilty, but high if he does not. Parking offenses, for example, may very commonly be settled for $1 or $2 on a guilty plea, but cost $10 to 20 if you choose to plead not guilty. This amounts to paying the defendant to plead guilty. As almost anyone who has had any experience with a traffic court is aware, most of the people who get tickets are indeed guilty, but those who are not guilty normally plead guilty anyway because of this system of enforcement.

Obviously we could apply the same line of reasoning to deal with all other parts of the traffic code. The problem is essentially a technological one. By the use of some type of exchange value and evidence obtained from statistical and other sources, we could compute a complete traffic code which would optimize some objective function. In practice we do not do this because of our reluctance to specify an exchange value for life. Nevertheless, we get much the same result, albeit with less accuracy and precision, by our present methods.

---

area, including his home, a couple of shopping centers, and his place of employment, together with a low speed limit (say 30 miles per hour), might appeal to judges who would be unwilling to remove the license totally. Judges might also be more inclined to give heavy sentences to people who violate such restrictions than to people who continue to drive to work in spite of the lack of a license.

14

Tax Evasion

Turning now to the income tax law, we must begin by noting that apparently almost anybody can get special treatment. The present laws and regulations are a solid mass of special rules for special groups of people. There are innumerable cases where some particularly wealthy man, politician, or large corporation has succeeded in obtaining special tax treatment. Nevertheless, we can consider how the existing tax code should be enforced.

Unfortunately, even the enforcement is full of loopholes. In the first place, there are a great many people (special classes that readily come to mind are doctors, waitresses, and farmers) who have special facilities for evading the income tax. It is also widely believed that certain groups (the farmers in particular) have been able to make use of their political power to see to it that the Internal Revenue Service does not pay as much attention to detecting evasion by them as by other groups. Nevertheless, we can assume that the tax code contains within it both a set of special privileges for individuals and instructions for evasion which apply only to certain classes, and hence that the true tax law is residual after we have knocked all these holes in what was originally a rather simple piece of legislation.

There are further difficulties. The individual presumably is interested in the taxes being collected from other people because he wants the government services that will be purchased by them. He would prefer to be left free of tax himself, but this is unfortunately not possible. He, in a sense, trades the tax on his own income for the benefit he obtains from the purchase of government services by the entire community. It is by no means clear that for everyone the present amount of government services is optimal. If we felt that the total amount of government services being purchased today was excessive (i.e., that lower tax rates and lower levels of service were desirable), presumably we would feel relatively happy about systematic evasion of a tax law on the part of everyone. On the other hand, if we felt that the present level of government services was too low and the taxes should be higher, we might conceivably feel that "overenforcement" is desirable.

Even if we are happy with the present level of government expenditures, it is by no means obvious that we should be terribly much in favor of efficient enforcement of the revenue code. We might favor a revenue code that sets rates relatively high, and an enforcement procedure that permits a great deal of evasion, to lower rates and better enforcement procedures that brought in the same revenue. Surely we would prefer high rates and loose enforcement if we had some reason to believe that we would be particularly able to evade the taxes. But even if we assume that everyone will have about the same ability to evade, we might still prefer the higher rates and higher level of evasion. Nevertheless, it seems to us that most people would prefer the lowest possible level of tax for a given net return. We have been unable to prove that this is optimal,[1] but it does seem to us to be reasonable that this would be the appropriate social goal. In any event, that is the assumption upon which our further calculations are built. It would be relatively easy to adjust these calculations to any other assumption on this particular matter.

Under these circumstances and with these assumptions, the return to the government in taxation from various levels of enforcement is fairly easy to compute. We start with the correct tax on the taxpayer and subtract from that the amount of money the taxpayer refrains from paying to the government because he has made improper deductions. The result is the amount of money that the Internal Revenue Service gets on April 15. It then examines the returns, however, and it has some chance of detecting improper deductions. If it does, it not only assesses the taxpayer for the money but also assesses a fine on him. This fine is, of course, to be added to the net receipts of the government, but we must subtract here the cost of the enforcement apparatus. This gives us the net return on the income tax system.

Ignoring for the moment the taxpayer's attitude toward bearing risk (and there is always a risk when he attempts to evade tax), his decision as to whether or not to evade the tax involves simple profit and loss accounting. If he attempts to reduce his tax by taking, let us say, an improper deduction, then he has some chance of getting away with it and some chance of being caught. If the amount he would have times the probability that he gets away with it is greater than the fine that would have to be paid if he gets caught times the likelihood of getting caught,

---

[1] We sincerely hope that some of our readers may be able to repair this omission.

then he should attempt to evade the tax. It should be noted in all of this discussion that there is an implicit assumption that the individual will be able to pay a fine if he is found to have evaded the tax law. The reason that the individual is normally able to pay a fine is simply that in general those who get into income tax difficulties are well off.

Nevertheless, although this is a very good approximation, it is not entirely accurate. The income tax authorities do sometimes attempt to put people in prison for tax evasion. In general, the Internal Revenue Service has a dual system. If you make a "tax saving" relatively easy for them to detect, they will normally adjust your return and charge you a relatively modest interest payment. If, on the other hand, you do something which is quite hard to detect, which normally means a directly dishonest statement, they assess a much heavier penalty. From their standpoint no doubt this is a sensible way of minimizing enforcement costs.

There is another peculiarity of the income tax policing process. Usually the policeman himself (i.e., the Internal Revenue man) simply assesses a deficiency on the face of the form if he does not suspect what is technically called evasion. This is usually the complete legal proceeding. In small cases the individual normally pays, although he may complain to the person making the assessment. It is highly probable that in this matter, as in other small claims litigation, there is a great deal of inaccuracy on both sides. Since these are small matters, the use of a cheap but relatively inaccurate procedure is reasonable. For major matters, however, very elaborate legal proceedings may be undertaken. These proceed at first through the administrative channels of the Internal Revenue Service and turn to the regular courts only if all administrative methods are exhausted. Here one would anticipate a great deal more care and far fewer errors, and there is no doubt that this is the case.

Returning, however, to our basic analysis, it will be noted that the likelihood of quiet compliance (i.e., the likelihood of the income-tax payer's making no effort to evade) is a function of the likelihood of detection of evasion. The likelihood of detection of evasion in turn is a function of two things: the amount of resources that we put into the revenue service, and the resources that we force the private taxpayer to put into keeping records and filing returns and doing other things that make it easier to enforce the tax revenue code. Thus, our original analysis was incomplete, if we look at the matter from the standpoint of society as a whole. There is another and major cost for enforcement of the income tax, and this cost is the expenditure that individuals must undertake in order to keep approximate records. This is a sort of additional tax, exacted in kind from the taxpayer, to make enforcement of the law easier.

The private cost of enforcement is an interesting and very comprehensive concept. It not only includes the troubles involved in filling out the income tax forms, which we all know may be considerable, but also the necessity of keeping our accounts in such form that the Internal Revenue Service may survey them. It includes the possibility that we will be audited even if we have not violated the law. It does not include any penalty we might incur if we have violated the law but it includes a number of other things that are somewhat less obvious. It includes the inconvenience we might suffer occasionally when the Internal Revenue Service is investigating a potential violation of the internal revenue code by someone other than ourselves; we might, for some reason, have some evidence which the Internal Revenue Service wants and be compelled to furnish it. It also includes the possibility that the Internal Revenue Service will wrongly suspect us and will then assess an incorrect fine upon us. Lastly, of course, it includes legal expenses involved in all of the above. Thus, it is by no means a small figure.

Still, the problem is relatively easy. We can simply maximize the social return on tax. There are some superficially not terribly probable consequences to this apparently simple rule. We could, for example, be in favor of increasing enforcement even though we know it is likely to raise our own payments. It will be noted that there is nowhere in the equation the assumption that we will obey the law and others will not. If we really believe that the government money is being spent for something worthwhile, then we make a net gain of some nature from increasing revenues.

As noted above, we might feel it desirable to include some kind of risk aversion factor. If the penalty for evasion of the tax code is quite large, let us say 25 times the tax that is evaded, and if we feel that there is a fair probability of the Internal Revenue Service going wrong in assessing such penalties, then our "risk cost" could be large. This might still maximize the value of the system, but if we are risk avoiders, we might prefer a lower revenue to avoid the risk of being assessed such a very large penalty.

But these are refinements. Basically we could calculate an optimum tax enforcement policy from a set of considerations such as those here. We think that if the reader considers his own reactions he will realize that his own attitude toward the income tax authorities is based upon something like this form of reasoning. He does, of course, hope that the income tax authorities will give him special treatment and does his best to obtain it. But insofar as this special treatment has already been taken into account, his behavior would be in accord with our model. His behavior with respect to general social policy in this period would then be described more or less by a desire to maximize revenue for a given tax rate. There may be some people who have strong moral feelings about their own payments under the income tax, but we have never run into them. Most of our friends will talk about the desirability of the income tax, but we also find them discussing in great detail what they can get away with. In fact, we suspect that moral considerations are less important in tax enforcement than any other single part of the law.

CONCLUDING COMMENT

In the last two chapters we have discussed two areas of the law with which the reader is likely to have had some personal experience. We have demonstrated in both cases the very simple computational tools defining an "optimum law." Application of these computational tools would, it is true, require the development of certain empirical information we do not now have, but they are nevertheless suitable guides to further work. Further, our computational tools in this respect are simply formalizations of the thought processes now used by most people in dealing with these matters.

15

Cheating and Lying

CHEATING

Cheating is a continual problem in all educational institutions. Exactly how much cheating is likely to go on across a university campus is unclear at this point, but we do have two very interesting studies that have been undertaken recently. Charles Tittle and Alan Rowe, both sociologists, designed a study to determine the influence that moral appeal and threat of sanction had on the amount of cheating that went on in their classes.[1] To do this, they gave weekly quizzes to their students; the instructors took the quizzes, graded them, without marking the papers, and then at the next class meeting, returned them to the students for them to grade. Without any appeal being made to the students that they were on their honor to grade them correctly, the students in one test group took 31 percent of all opportunities to cheat; the other test group took 41 percent of all opportunities. Next, the instructors made an appeal to the students' sense of morality in grading the papers, and the instructors concluded that "emphasizing the moral principle involved in grading the quizzes was also ineffectual. A moral appeal had no effect whatsoever in reducing the incidence of cheating."[2] In fact, in one of the test groups, the amount of cheating went up substantially after the appeal was made. Finally, the instructors threatened to spot check the quizzes for cheating and the amount of cheating fell sharply from the 41 percent range to 13 percent in one class and from 43 percent to 32 percent in the other. They also concluded from the study that the instructor who had a reputation of being

---

[1] Charles R. Tittle and Alan R. Rowe, "Fear and the Student Cheater," *Change*, (April 1974), 47–48.

[2] Ibid., p. 47.

"lovable and understanding" had the greater amount of cheating in his class, and they found that ". . . Those who were most in need of points were willing to take greater risks [that is, cheated more]. This is consistent with the theory that the greater the utility of an act, the greater the potential punishment required to deter it. And perhaps it shows the futility of a moral appeal in a social context where all individuals are not successful."[3]

One of the authors of this book replicated the above study in a somewhat different form and, in this case, for a slightly different purpose. He wanted to see how many students would cheat on a test which the students were told would not be considered in their grades. He gave his classes in Principles of Economics a test on the first day of the term; he had their answer sheets Xeroxed and the Xeroxed copies graded by a graduate student. During the next class session, his secretary gave back the original answer sheets and called out the correct answers. Later, by comparing the Xeroxed copy and the original answer sheet, it was found that 15 percent of the students cheated, and *this was on something that had no bearing on their grades.* As a point of interest, one student was rather ingenious in the way in which he cheated. In taking the test, he had left the last eight answers blank; when he was given a chance to correct his own, he filled in the answers. Because he apparently did not want it to appear too obvious what he had done, he intentionally missed three of them and marked them wrong like all the others that he had missed!

Less dramatically, Nicolaus Tideman, has invented a statistical method of determining how many times a particular type of cheating occurs. This type of cheating, copying the paper from the person sitting next to you on a multiple choice examination, can be detected by computer analysis of the examination papers. Tideman's studies showed the number of cheaters in various classes as low as zero or as high as 20 percent. The problem, then, is a common one; but economically we have to ask two other questions. What is the gain and loss from cheating and who, if anyone, gets hurt?

Consider a student who is worried about his grade in a given course and thinks it would be possible to cheat. The gain if he does cheat is, of course, the improvement in grade he can expect from cheating times the probability that he will get away with it. This is true regardless of how much he learns in the course. How well he has studied is, of course, relevant to how much his grade will improve. If he will get an A anyway, why cheat?

The cost of cheating is, first, the fact that the cheater's conscience may bother him. If he has been ethically indoctrinated with the view that cheating is a bad thing (and it must be remembered that this is not true of everyone), then there is some positive cost to him for violating that

---

[3] Ibid., p. 48.

ethical rule. For some people, this cost is so high that they would never violate the rule against cheating, no matter what the benefits they could expect; and for other people it is so low that they would violate it any time they saw a chance. Senator Edward Kennedy, it may be remembered, was expelled from Harvard for cheating on a Spanish test and being caught. Presumably, at the time he hired a classmate to take the exam for him, he thought the chances of being caught were low; but surely he realized there was some chance and took it into account. (Incidentally, Harvard's decision to readmit him was in no way unusual.)

A student contemplating cheating, then, will compare the benefit with the cost. The moral issue is real, but not the only one. A very immoral student may decide that the risk is too great and a student of more than average morality may be tempted by a very good chance under circumstances where the benefit was very great (suppose that a fellowship turns on the grade in that course) and the chance of being caught is very low.

Who is injured by cheating? Most students tend to think of it as a game with the teacher; but the teacher is, in fact, not hurt particularly by a student cheating. It is true that most teachers rather dislike it and tend to feel that they have been made a fool when the students succeed, but it does not really injure them. The people who are injured are the other students. In saying this, however, it should be kept in mind that the injury caused by any one student cheating is spread over a number of other students, so that the injury to any predictable one of them from a single student cheating is so small as to be almost invisible. Only if a considerable number of students cheat is the injury to any individual student serious.

Suppose a teacher in a class of 100 normally grades on a curve, i.e., he gives the top 20 an A, the next 40 a B, the next 30 a C, and the bottom 10 are flunked. One of the students who normally flunks is successful in cheating and therefore gets an A. This means that one of the non-cheating students who otherwise would have received an A gets a B, one who otherwise would have gotten a B gets a C, and one of the ones who otherwise would have gotten a C flunks. In this case, the injury is concentrated in three specific people; but it is hard to tell in advance which three they will be. Thus, at the time the student contemplated cheating, the potential injury was spread out because no one knew who would be the lowest A, the lowest B or C, etc.

Curve grading of this sort is not, of course, the only way of grading, and many professors use absolute standards. Suppose, for example, that there were 50 questions on the test and the professor intended to give an A to those who got 45 or more correct, B to those who got 37 or more correct, and C to those who got 30 or more correct. The cheater moves himself from 20 correct and a flunking grade to 47 correct and an A. This does not make any other single person flunk, but it does mean that there are more As and fewer Fs than there would be otherwise; hence, in a way this depreciates the value of the As and Bs and makes the pain of flunking somewhat greater than it would be otherwise.

It is an intriguing, indeed paradoxical, characteristic of this reasoning that the cheater injures other people who cheat just as much as those who do not. Let us return to our original example where the teacher is grading on a curve, and suppose that the student has succeeded in raising his grade by cheating so that he is the tenth student in the series and has an A. Another student now cheats and gets a higher grade, with the result that our first student is moved down to a B. Of course, the students who have not cheated are injured by both of these students cheating, so they are doubly injured; but it is still true that any student who cheats is to some extent injured by other students who cheat.

The discussion of cheating has assumed that students are injured by receiving low grades and benefit by receiving high grades. This is not absolutely certain and there are people who maintain that the entire grading system is unimportant. Surely the individual who does not care what grade he receives is not injured by having his grade lowered because other people have cheated. However, the student who hopes that his grades will help him get a fellowship for graduate study or a good job is injured by cheating. Note that he is also injured if the cheating simply increases the number of As rather than moving anybody down in grade, because this means that As are regarded as less valuable by future employers or future graduate schools.

Looked at from the standpoint of society as a whole, cheating reduces the information content of grades. If there is a good deal of cheating, then the grading system does not give very much information as to the quality of students; hence, it is harder to make decisions as to whom to hire, to whom to give graduate fellowships, etc. The size of this cost depends on how good the grades are as a predictor of later success and, unfortunately, we do not have very much data on that issue. Nevertheless, there must be at least some cost.

Rather ironically, we have come to the conclusion that the students should be strongly in favor of rules against cheating, at least insofar as these rules are enforced against other people, and teachers should feel less concern. An unscrupulous student favors a rule that prevents other people from cheating while permitting him to do so. Unfortunately, rules of this sort are not in the cards. In general, we have to choose between institutions that make cheating difficult for everyone or institutions that make cheating easy for everyone. For most students, the former set of institutions will have a net payoff because the gains they may make from cheating, even ignoring the possible conscience problems of cheating, will be less than the loss they will suffer from other people cheating. From the standpoint of teachers, there is little cost either way. It is the students who should be opposed to cheating.

LYING

Let us leave cheating, which is after all a special form of dishonesty, and turn to the more general problem of lying and, a little later, to the law of frauds. Beginning with simple lying, an individual who is thinking of telling a lie once again has the problem of conscience. One of the costs he must face if he is to tell a lie is the moral cost. As we have said before, for some people this is a very large cost and for some people it is a very small cost. In addition to that cost, there is the possibility that he will be caught telling a lie and this must be multiplied by whatever injury he will suffer from being caught. Since we are talking about simple lying and not about fraud at the moment, this injury will be a loss to his reputation. If you are once caught telling a lie, people are likely to think you will tell lies in future statements; hence, you may have difficulty getting them to accept your word, even when you are telling the truth.

For example, a salesman who sells gadgets door-to-door to housewives has little need to concern himself with this type of cost. It is unlikely that he will return to the same housewife again. If she finds out that the gadget she bought is not what he said it was, there will be little cost inflicted on him. On the other hand, a salesman who sells the same people again and again, particularly if what he sells is valuable enough so that they will give careful thought to transactions, can lose immensely from lying. For example, take the vice-president of a large steel company who has the duty of acting as principal sales representative to General Motors, Ford, and Chrysler. The cost to him of losing the confidence of his customers is so great that he would be a fool to lie to them.

This is particularly so since they will be experts and likely to catch him if he does lie. In any event, they will have an opportunity to make a very thorough test of his product if they buy it. In the real world, arrangements of this sort are so honest that the salesman will rarely make an effort to sell a product if one of his competitors has one that is clearly more suitable to the purchasers' needs. Store clerks are trained to suggest a more expensive brand. Our vice-president may frequently suggest a cheaper grade of steel where it would be adequate. Certainly he is very unlikely to make a misstatement on this subject.

Most cases of purchase and sale are intermediate between these two. The manufacturer of canned goods had better have a satisfactory product if he wants to stay in business; but exact truth on the label is not all that important because the housewife probably does not read it.

These are the non-legal costs of telling a lie. We have ignored the costs of possible legal penalties because we want to put off the question of punishment for fraud until after we have dealt with the problem of simple lying. The benefits from lying are a little more complicated. Presumably the reasons for telling a lie are that you want to influence someone to do something they would not do if you told them the truth. The door-to-door salesman, for example, if he accurately described his product might sell very few of them. On the other hand, by a suitably colorful sales pitch, he may make quite a nice living. The benefit from the lie, then, is the profit (whatever it is) from influencing the victim's behavior. For example, suppose that if the salesman correctly describes the object he is selling, he has a 1 in 10 chance of selling it. If he tells a suitable lie about it, he has a 50–50 change of selling it. Assume further that his commission on the sale is $5. If he lies, he moves from a 1 in 10 chance of making $5, which is worth 50¢, to a 50–50 chance, worth $2.50, and the payoff on the lie is then $2.

But this is the gross benefit. Obviously he has to subtract from it the possible cost of the lie. Ignoring possible legal penalties, this cost, as we said above, is the reduction in his credibility. For the door-to-door salesman, this may have substantially zero value; hence, he can say that he has made a $2 profit by telling a lie. For our vice-president in charge of sales for a major steel company, on the other hand, the payoff to him from completing a sale by telling a lie might be $100,000 or so; but the cost to him of being detected in a lie might be $2 or $3 million in reduction of lifetime earnings.

The fact that people may tell lies, of course, has an effect on the behavior, not only of potential liars but of the people who will hear the lie. Most housewives are properly skeptical of door-to-door salesmen selling complicated devices. On the other hand, most purchasing agents who deal in large sums of money are so convinced of the honesty of the sales vice-presidents with whom they talk that they may actually use them as sources of technical information.

All of this, of course, depends on the fact that the people to whom a potential liar might make a dishonest statement try to estimate his truthfulness. The individual who hears a statement by someone else will put resources into determining whether or not it is true. In some cases, he may have great respect for the person making the statement or he may realize that the person making the statement has no particular motive to tell a lie; hence, he would put high credence on the statement and not do a great deal of individual investigation. This is, of course, the reason that having a reputation for truth as opposed to a reputation for lying is valuable to people in business or, indeed, in any walk of life.

Consider, then, the situation that confronts a salesman dealing with a potential customer. If the salesman is known to be honest, the customer will invest fewer resources in checking his statements. In consequence, the cost of the sale will be lower. This honesty on the part of the salesman generates a net and perfectly genuine social gain for the joint society of the two of them: part of this value goes to the salesman and part to the customer. Thus, social institutions that improve the reliability of information can have a positive payoff. Note that this argument has nothing to do with morals, although it is in accord with the received moral code. There are simply economies to be gained if all statements made are truthful. These economies partly have the effect of reduction in resources invested in checking the accuracy of statements, and partly in the reduction of errors made because false statements are believed. No matter how many resources we invest in checking the truth or falsity of someone else's statements, we will be fooled occasionally if he tells enough lies. There is a further saving in the reduction in the "sales effort" of the salesman.

One way of investing resources in preventing lying is simply refusing to believe the word of a man whom you have caught lying in the past. This superficially appears to be costless but it is not, because it means that you disregard many statements which are true; hence, there is the cost of obtaining the same information from someone else or remaining ignorant. The problem is almost a game. The more skeptical we are of things you say, the more resources you will have to invest to convince us and the more resources we will invest in checking what you have to say. Further, the chance exists that we will disbelieve you when you are telling the truth. Under the circumstances, there is a net social loss from our belief that you may be lying.

There is, of course, an optimal amount of resources for us to invest in checking your statements, given that we have some idea of how likely it is that you are lying. Knowing the resources we will invest in checking your statements, there is an appropriate amount of resources you should invest in "improving" your lie. For example, you may generate false data, misinterpret true data, improve the attractiveness of your statements by various means, and generally respond to our skepticism by resource investment. This resource investment, of course, should lead to more resource investment by us in detecting possible lies. It is not sensible, however, for the potential victim of the lie to invest an infinite amount of resources into reducing the likelihood that he will believe an untrue statement. In this case, the cost of further information should be offset against the benefit from the reduction in the likelihood that we will be fooled. Similarly, the potential liar should not invest an infinite amount of resources in making his lie believable, because here again the potential resources do cost something and should only be put in if the potential gain is greater than the cost.

FRAUD

Under these circumstances, with a net social gain by reducing the number of lies or, put differently, by increasing the reliability of the statements, we should search for social institutions that will make lying less common. There is one such social institution that is very widely used:

laws against fraud. Although there are laws against fraud, in most cases not all untruthful statements are covered. Let us consider briefly an optimal law against fraud and why we might permit people to tell lies under some circumstances (in the sense that we may be unwilling to do anything about it).

The problem, of course, is that there are costs to enforcing any law. The first and obvious cost is the necessity of providing police, courts, and prisons. These have been discussed earlier in the discussion of crime and tax evasion. These costs in the laws against fraud do not differ particularly from those in other laws, but there is a special cost in the case of fraud. The probability that the court will go wrong is exceptionally high in cases of fraud. Suppose that we have bought something from you and, for various reasons, it is unsatisfactory. If we simply say that you lied to us when selling it and bring a fraud accusation against you, the possibility exists (and the probability is *not* close to zero) that the court will go wrong—it must, after all, determine which of two people is telling the lie and human beings are not terribly good at doing that. Thus, the prospect of many erroneous decisions in fraud cases is a very significant cost. Most court systems thus attempt to restrict the number of fraud cases that can be brought. In general, they try to get evidence other than the oral statements of the two parties for fraud prosecutions and they restrict them to cases where something of substance is at issue. It is not obvious that real world institutions in this regard are ideal, but they are at least sensible.

A very important situation in which lying occurs in most governments —democracies or dictatorships—is politics. The average man has a very low opinion of the honesty of politicians, and this opinion is completely justified. The basic problem is that the voter has very little motive to check up on the statements of the politician; hence, politicians can get away with a good deal of dishonesty. The reason why the voter has little to gain by checking up on the honesty of a politician comes essentially from the fact that the individual voter has very little effect on the outcome of an election. If we devote a good deal of resources to determining that one of the two candidates is lying and vote against him, in the presidential election this has less than a 1 in 10 millionth chance of having any effect on the outcome. Under the circumstances, we are not even likely to remember very accurately what the politician has promised.

There are complicating factors which make lying in politics even more likely. Most democracies, and the United States government in particular, have governmental structures that disperse power. The arguments for seeing to it that no individual has too much power are very strong, but it does have the characteristic that it is very hard to tell whether a politician has broken his promise. A man running for Congress who promises to do his best to get Blacksburg, Virginia (which is in the Appalachian Mountains), converted into a deep-water port by a massive and expensive government dredging program may in fact do his best, but Blacksburg may never become a port because he is only one congressman. Thus, we cannot tell whether he kept his promise or did not. Further, it is certain that conditions will change between the time the man is elected to office and the time he has an opportunity to act on one of his promises. Whether the change is such that the voters would agree that he should not carry out his promise is, once again, a matter for dispute.

There is one area in which politicians are well advised to keep their promises, but unfortunately this is no great benefit for the functioning of our democratic system. If a congressman makes a promise concerning some matter which is of great moment to a few constituents, then it is likely that they will be very well informed on whether or not he makes a real effort. Since the matter is of great interest to them, they will try to be informed on what he did for them in Washington. In general, they are apt to punish or reward him in the future in terms of whether or not he carries out his promise. Thus, this is the kind of promise politicians try to keep. Unfortunately, this type of special interest activity does not make the political system function well and, indeed, the politician may be simultaneously making public statements against some program and privately telling a small group of people that he will back it. In many cases, this is the optimal course of action for a suitably unscrupulous man. (Do we not observe this kind of special interest legislation?)

Under the circumstances, it is unlikely that people attracted into politics are those who have very strong moral objections to lying. In many cases, of course, they do not consciously think of themselves as lying; they just are not very careful in examining their own motives. It is very easy to convince oneself that whatever is good for oneself is good for the country. Politicians probably do this a great deal, and hence do not consciously feel that they have done anything immoral.

Political lies are one area in which we have great difficulty making use of the government to control lying. The government, by definition, is in control of politicians, and the politicians are more likely to make use of the political process to injure their opponents than to seek absolute truth. In consequence, most democratic societies have very little in the way of controls on lying by politicians. Politicians, of course, take advantage of this. Granted the possibilities for the government in power to use any legal process that punishes telling political lies as a means of punishing political opponents, we can see why there are very strenuous restrictions on this. Unfortunately this means that the politicians are even freer in telling lies than they would be if we changed the institutions.

In the United States at the moment, this is rather compensated for by the fact that it is fairly safe to tell lies about politicians, too. The laws of libel and slander have been adjusted by the Supreme Court recently so that it is almost impossible for a politician to sue a person who has maligned him on the grounds that the statement is both injurious and false. There are special circumstances in which such a suit is possible, but they are extremely narrow and most statements anyone might choose to make, either in print, on TV, or simply in conversation, are perfectly safe, no matter how untrue they are. Unfortunately, although this may even things up with respect to the politicians, it does not mean that public communication on political matters is particularly honest.

This chapter is being written right in the middle of the Watergate scandal. It is clear that the newspapers have uncovered a good deal of dishonesty on the part of a whole pile of politicians. But a careful reading of the *Washington Post*, the newspaper with which we have the most contact, indicates it is not exactly honest itself. To take an example for which the *Washington Post* later half-heartedly apologized, they ran a column on Patrick Buchanan, the President's aide, complete with a picture of him, in which a large number of documents were cited as evidence of his personal unscrupulousness. As a matter of fact, he had had nothing to do with any of them. But this is only an extreme example and, indeed, the *Washington Post* is to be commended for permitting him to publish a letter attacking their handling of this matter and printing a sort of weak apology for the matter. This is, on the whole, above the normal standards with which newspapers handle politics.

CONCLUDING COMMENT

In sum, then, lying and cheating, like most other human behavior, has positive payoffs and it has costs. It also has moral implications and, for many people, these moral implications are more important than the economic calculation. Unfortunately, there are also many people for whom the economic calculation is the controlling one. Any set of social institutions for controlling lying or cheating should be based upon firm recognition of that fact.

part five

Politics, Bureaucracy, and Groups

16

Presidential Elections

In recent years economists have used their tools to investigate political problems. Political scientists, in fact, have begun learning economic tools to apply them in their own discipline. As a result of this movement, there is now a large and very complicated literature in which economics is applied to political problems. As a sort of sampling of this literature, in this chapter we will develop a very simple economic model of presidential election and then use this model to analyze the elections of 1960, 1964, 1968, and 1972. Since the model is very simplified, it will present only a partial picture of these elections; but we think that it will both give the reader an idea of this type of reasoning and improve his understanding of these elections, even if it is not a complete picture.

A SIMPLE MODEL

Our simple model, Figure 16–1A, shows all possible political positions on some issue or some group of issues. Although it will get more complicated later, for the moment you can think of it as being a rather typical liberal–conservative continuum. Any individual voter has some point on this spectrum that corresponds to his own personal preferences. Suppose, for example, it is point B. As he moves away from point B, the voter feels less and less satisfied. For example, he will prefer point C to point D. The bell-shaped distribution line shows the arrangement of voters between conservative and liberal positions. There are more in the middle than at the ends. For our reasoning, the bell-shaped distribution is not necessary, although in our opinion it is realistic. To make this clear, in Figure 16–1B we have drawn in another distribution of voters with some skew and then labeled it in the same way as Figure 16–1A. The student

FIGURE 16–1A

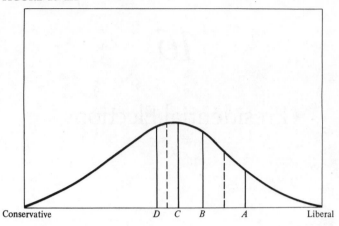

can follow our line of reasoning on either of these two figures or, if he wishes, draw in another of his own.

For a contest between two parties, a simple diagram of this sort is frequently sufficient. For the 1968 election where there were three parties, we will have to use something else and, as a matter of fact, we will find it desirable to use a more complicated diagram for the 1964 election, also. Nevertheless, this very simple diagram is suitable for an astonishing number of political problems in a two-party system.

If one of the candidates for president chooses position A and the other chooses position B, then all of the voters to the right of A will prefer point A and all those to the left of B will prefer point B. The voters between will divide roughly in accordance with the dotted line, and B will win very easily.

FIGURE 16–1B

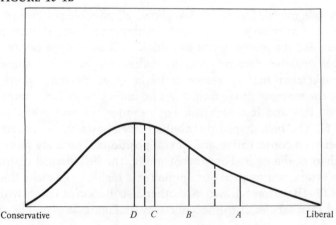

In a two-party system, the intelligent politician attempts to find the middle of the distribution. If he chooses the exact middle, then the other party leader has the choice of choosing exactly the same location (which is not a very good policy) or choosing one which is a little away from the middle, and hence will be thought to be inferior by slightly more than half of the voters; i.e., is certain to be beaten.

In practice it is rather hard to choose the *exact* middle of the distribution because politicians do not have perfect information and, in a way, electoral contests in a two-party system are contests to get as close to the middle as possible. Of course, there are other matters and issues involved in elections—personality, incumbency (which seems to be a big advantage in most elections), past record, etc.; but the positions the party takes should be close to the middle. Assume, then, that the first politician takes position C, which turns out not to be quite in the middle. The other politician obtains a little more information on popular preferences from the reaction to the position of the first candidate; he realizes which direction from the middle the first position is and takes a position at D, a little to the left of C (in this particular case because C was a little to the right of the middle) which is just far enough away so that the voters can tell the two candidates apart. Under the circumstances, if the two candidates have done their jobs with a high degree of skill, they will divide the vote evenly among them. In practice, of course, they are never quite that accurate, and hence one party or the other will have an advantage.

THE 1960 ELECTION

The 1960 election is an example. It is, indeed, so much of an example that it is not at all obvious who actually got the most votes. Not only is there the question of whether or not the Illinois and Texas voters actually cast the majority of their votes for John F. Kennedy,[1] but the situation in Alabama was so confused that it is not very obvious who some 250,000 voters voted for. If they voted for Kennedy, then he had a majority of the popular vote. If it is assumed that they or, let us say, half of them voted instead for Senator Harry Byrd (who received six electoral votes from Alabama), then Richard Nixon had a majority of the popular vote. In any event, it was a very close election, much closer than normal.

In this simple model we see an explanation of one of the outstanding characteristics of two-party democracy as we are familiar with it in the United States. The two parties tend to be very close together and near the middle of the political spectrum. It is often said that this does not give the voters a real choice. To take an early and probably not now

---

[1] In both cases, there was a rather dishonest Democratic machine which might well have generated enough false votes to provide for the margin in the official figures.

popular example, one of the first books urging Senator Barry Goldwater's candidacy called for "a choice, not an echo." More recently, George Wallace in 1968 said, "there isn't a dime's worth of difference" between Nixon and Humphrey. This is the normal rule, and the 1964 and 1972 elections, which will be dealt with later, must be regarded as most unusual in a two-party system. Historically, two parties with very nearly indistinguishable programs, located very near the "middle of the road," is the norm.

It is not clear, however, that this is something we should criticize. The voters have no choice because both parties are trying vigorously to please them. A position in the middle of the distribution, as these two are, minimizes the total loss individual voters receive from not getting their first preference. This, of course, involves comparison of different people's preferences, which economists are not supposed to do, but the numbers are very large and there is no strong reason to believe that intensities are more severe on one side of the middle than on the other; hence, a simple mechanical process of computing the loss an individual suffers from not having his ideal political position win by taking the distance between his position and the position that does win seems not unreasonable. With this calculation, the total loss is minimized by central position.[2]

Politicians are not always perfect in their decisions; they may take a position not near the center, either through mistake or because they are driven by an ideological commitment to some other position. For example, suppose that one of the candidates takes position A. This, by definition, almost guarantees his defeat unless his opponent makes an equally large error by taking a position just as far or farther from the center in the other direction. Under these circumstances, however, it is probably not wise for A's opponent to get as close to A as possible. If one candidate has chosen a highly eccentric position, then it is sensible for his opponent to try to emphasize the difference between the two, which means that he must take a position farther from his opponent's position than he would have had the first politician taken position C. Thus, one would anticipate that if one of the candidates takes a position well away from the center, like A, the other party will take a position on the same side of the center as position A but nevertheless well away from it, as is shown by line B in our diagram.

In essence, this is what happened in the 1972 election, although full discussion of that election will be deferred until later. Senator George McGovern took a position very far from the middle of American politics;

---

[2] Another way of putting it would be that the total gain is maximized. There is an unfortunate tradition, that one of the authors of this book had much to do with starting, under which political activities are largely talked of as ways of reducing losses rather than obtaining gains. This is merely a matter of semantics, but it does give a sort of negative sound to all economic discussions of political matters.

and Nixon, insofar as he took any position at all (it will be remembered that he did absolutely no campaigning), adopted a position clearly distinctive from McGovern's but nevertheless rather in the McGovern direction. It will be recalled that Nixon had already stolen much of the political Left's clothing by introducing price control, visiting Peking, and encouraging détente with Russia. These moves had, of course, been made before McGovern was nominated, but they were parts of the Left's political program.

The need to distinguish one's position from that of the other candidate, which means that it may not be very close to the other candidate's if an eccentric position has been taken, can also occur in one other situation. George Wallace in 1968 was attempting to start a completely new party. Under the circumstances, he could not depend upon any of the existing political capital upon which the two major party candidates could draw. He quite wisely chose a position that was markedly different from that of the primary candidates to attract voters by a differentiated product. Once again, full discussion of this must be postponed until later.

A MORE COMPLICATED MODEL

To discuss the 1964 and 1968 campaigns (and, indeed, to demonstrate why the 1972 campaign was different), it is necessary to complicate our model a bit. Politics is not actually fought along a single dimension but in a many-dimensional issue space. There are many different matters that are considered by politicians and by voters, and for each of these we should really have a separate dimension. This would involve the use of many-dimensional Cartesian algebra and would produce great complications. Fortunately, the single one-dimensional continuum we have been using is suitable for most problems involving two-party politics. When there are three parties, as in 1968, it is necessary to use two dimensions and, for some rather complicated problems in connection with two-party systems, two dimensions are also necessary.

Figure 16–2 shows a two-dimensional model in which parties may differ not on one general issue but two. We have labeled these simply issue 1 and issue 2 because we want to use the same diagram to discuss a number of elections, the earliest of which occurred in 1896 and the last of which occurred in 1972. During this period the issues under discussion changed radically. However, in all of these cases we can analyze the situation with the use of two dimensions, even though what is meant by the dimension differs from election to election.

Each voter is assumed to have some point in this issue space that is his optimum. This means simply that he has some ideal policy on issue 1 and some ideal policy on issue 2. Suppose, for example, it is point Z in the diagram. This means that Z' is optimum on issue 1 and Z'' is optimum on

FIGURE 16–2

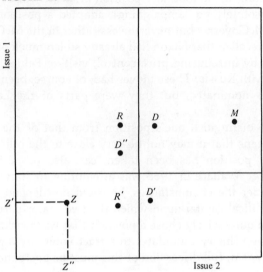

issue 2. He then becomes less and less satisfied as the political outcome moves away from his optimum and, for simplicity, we assume that his lack of satisfaction is equal in all directions, that is, moving an inch away in any direction makes him just as unhappy as in any other direction.

Once again, the voter's optima would be distributed across the issue space in some general form, probably a normal distribution. For simplicity, we are going to assume that there is a normal distribution with its peak near the middle. This assumption is not, of course, necessary. It is possible to duplicate the same line of reasoning using different distributions, but this is rather complicated. Therefore, we will not provide a second diagram for the reader's enlightenment, but merely suggest that if he is curious about this problem, he may turn to Chapter IV of *Toward a Mathematics of Politics.*[3]

In this kind of issue space, there is a very simple rule for determining the division of the voters among the parties. A line halfway between the position of any two parties and vertical to a line connecting the two positions will divide the voters between them. If there are three or more parties, these lines will meet as on Figure 16–3, and the space is thus divided into more than two areas.

If there are only two parties, we normally expect them to be near the middle. Point *R* and point *D*, for example, will divide the voters

[3] Gordon Tullock, *Toward a Mathematics of Politics*, Ann Arbor: University of Michigan Press, 1967.

between themselves according to the vertical line: all points to the left of the vertical line are closer to R, and all points to the right are closer to D. They divide the voters approximately between them, and neither can gain by moving away from the center to some point such as M. Indeed, if the party now located at D moved to M, one could predict electoral disaster.

FIGURE 16-3

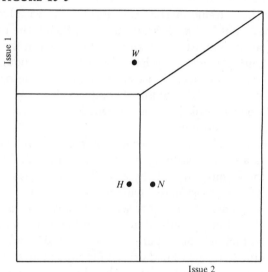

Two parties are once again likely to be found near the middle of this two-dimensional issue space for much the same reasons as they were likely to end up near the middle of the one-dimensional issue space in Figures 16–1A and 16–1B. But with more than one dimension, and of course in the real world there usually is more than one dimension, it is possible for the two parties jointly to make a mistake. Over a series of elections, they can drift off the center down the line dividing them. Thus, if the parties gradually slip from positions R and D to positions R' and D', they will continue dividing the voters about evenly between them; and the managers of the two parties might not realize that they are away from the center. This provides an opening for a political entrepreneur to enter and reorganize politics. There have been two such cases in recent history, William Jennings Bryan and Barry Goldwater. In each case, they came at a point in time where their party had been maneuvered into a position where it actually has somewhat less than a majority of the vote, and its long-run prospects were not very good unless something drastic could be done.

THE 1896 AND 1964 ELECTIONS

Assume that we are considering William Jennings Bryan. The two parties are now (1896) at R' and D' in Figure 16–2, and he restructured politics by moving to D''. This involved deliberately abandoning a number of traditional Democratic voters. Although Bryan himself failed to win, there is no doubt that he set the general outlines of American politics for the next 50 years. The reasons he failed to win the election are probably the extreme inertia built into the system plus the fact that it would appear that he had miscalculated. Although the Republican and Democratic parties had drifted away from the center in the last few years prior to the 1896 election, they had not drifted far enough so that this maneuver gave the Democrats a clear advantage. Indeed, from Bryan's time until the election of Franklin D. Roosevelt, only one Democratic president (Woodrow Wilson) was elected, and that was the result of a split in the Republican party.

Barry Goldwater is a more recent example. He and his backers felt that there was a good possibility of removing the "solid South" permanently from the Democratic side by a similar restructuring. The fact that John Kennedy was assassinated with the result that they found themselves running against a Southerner scuppered any possibility of the tactic winning in 1964; like Bryan's attack, it probably would not have won anyway. Nevertheless, the experience in the 1968 and 1972 elections indicates that the two parties had drifted far enough away from the center so that Goldwater had a better chance than Bryan. The bloc of voters was huge, of course. The Southern whites, whom Goldwater proposed to move from the Democratic to the Republican column, make up 20 percent of the total population of the United States. Today a majority of them are voting Republican, although almost all voted Democratic from the Civil War until very recently.

The repercussions of Watergate may well cancel the tactical advantages of the realignment that Goldwater attempted to make. Certainly, at the moment, both the Republicans and the Democrats are making strenuous efforts to acquire votes among Southern whites. It is hard to predict the future of George Wallace, and he will not find it easy to re-incorporate himself into the Democratic party; but it is certainly true that the Democratic leadership is showing strong signs of wanting to find a détente with him and counter the erosion of the white vote in the South to the Republicans.

In the case of both Bryan and Goldwater, it was necessary for the candidate seeking to restructure politics to move fairly far away from his opponent. This was necessary simply because the information problem was difficult. In 1896 there was little or nothing in the way of traditional attachment to the Democratic party in the upper left-hand square shown in Figure 16–2. The only way of attracting people from that area into the party was to take a very firmly differentiated policy from the Republican policy. Bryan, of course, did so, but it turned out that he was not able to succeed. The same is true with Goldwater, indeed, the Goldwater defeat was much more severe than Bryan's.

THE 1972 ELECTION

This type of thing must be clearly distinguished from Senator George McGovern's campaign. The McGovern campaign took the form of abandoning a number of traditional Democratic voters, but not appealing to any significant bloc of traditional Republican voters. In essence, it was a move away from the center, which made no serious effort to restructure the nature of politics, although the managers of the campaign referred a good deal to the new politics. They moved to M on Figure 16–2.

The explanation for this phenomenon can be seen in a statement made by McGovern early in his campaign. He said that getting nominated was much harder for him than getting elected. We believe this was, indeed, true. If he had taken a more central position, he would have been unable to attract the support within the Democratic party (in particular, within the left half of the Democratic party) which put him over the top in Miami. He may have thought that the policy he backed was highly desirable for ideological reasons or, indeed, that in fact it would appeal to the majority of the population; but it seems more likely that he intended after being nominated to play the campaign by ear. He could, after all, hope that the Republicans would make a series of ghastly errors. Indeed, it should not be forgotten that the newspapers gave more attention to Watergate than any other single issue during that campaign.

McGovern's ability to take advantage of this, of course, was reduced by his own vice-presidential problems. But in fact his loss of the election was largely predetermined by the method he chose to get the nomination. It does not follow from this that he was politically inept. Granting that he was correct that getting the nomination was harder than winning the election, then the course of action he followed was the only one open to him. If he had taken a more central position in the nominating campaign, he would have had the traditional snowball's chance in hell of being nominated. Once nominated, he surely would have had a better chance of becoming president than he would have had he been eliminated in the first round of voting in Miami.

THE 1968 ELECTION

We now turn to the 1968 election, which is both the most complicated and, in many ways, the most interesting because there were three candidates. Two of the candidates, Nixon and Humphrey, were almost plu-perfect examples of the *genus Politician*. As we would expect, they took political positions that were very hard to tell apart. The third candidate, however, was a most extraordinary politician. Before a formal analysis of the election, it is sensible to make a few remarks about Governor George Wallace. There is no effort here to indicate his complete character or political position; but certain statements about him are necessary to apply the model we have developed so far from the 1968 election.

First, Wallace was clearly one of the best political tacticians who has ever lived. In addition, interestingly enough, he was also one of the worst political strategists who has ever lived. His short-range decisions were politically brilliant. His long-range decisions were usually terrible. Indeed, he frequently made decisions that had major long-run effects in terms of very minor short-run considerations, with the result that he had long-run difficulties. He also seemed to be unable to organize anything on the order of an efficient central campaign organization. On occasion, his campaigning was carried on brilliantly, but mainly by a series of local decisions.

No doubt his major single achievement was getting on the ballot in substantially the entire United States in 1968. No other third party had ever succeeded in doing this in such a short period of time, and it should be noted that his own party by 1972 was unable to stay on the ballot in more than about two-thirds of the states. The two major political parties, Republicans and Democrats, have formed what amounts to an implicit cartel to reduce competition from third parties and, on the whole, it is very effective. Nevertheless, Wallace carried out the almost impossible achievement of beating the electoral restrictions in 1968.

Wallace was a poor political strategist and was generally rather badly organized. His approach to politics throughout his national campaign has been a series of short-run improvisations. The fact that he was as suc-cessful as he was turned partly on his brilliance in the short run and his appeal as a speaker to a significant part of the American population, and partly to the fact that the two major American parties had gradually drifted into a position where there was a significant minority—a minority to which Wallace appealed—who were quite dissatisfied with the political system.

This minority, the Wallace group, probably amounts to between 20 and 30 percent of the population. These numbers come from the public opinion polls in the early part of the 1968 campaign and Wallace's as-tonishing performance in the 1972 Democratic primaries. It would appear, however, that his backing, though substantial, is pretty much limited to that group. In other words, he is a candidate who can have a great effect on who wins the presidency but is very unlikely to make it himself. Even if he did get the Democratic nomination, it seems very dubious that he could come even as close to winning as McGovern or Goldwater did.

Another aspect of Wallace's support is that it is almost entirely drawn from traditional Democratic voters. It consists, essentially, of Southern whites and blue-collar workers. Both are groups who have formed in the past part of the Democratic coalition. Indeed, it may well be that his backers are an actual majority of the people who normally vote Democratic, although we would estimate that this is not so. In any event, in 1968 almost all of his backers had the Democratic candidate as their second choice rather than the Republican candidate, probably not so much because their position was closer to Humphrey than Nixon on the issues (indeed, Wallace's statement that there is not a dime's worth of difference between the two was only a modest exaggeration), but because they were accustomed to voting Democratic and had a good deal of emotional involvement with the Democratic party together with antagonism to the Republican party.

Under the circumstances, Wallace's effort to start a third party was doomed from the start; but judging it simply as political theater, it was a brilliant effort. He began by taking a position markedly different from the center of the political spectrum. We have graphed it on Figure 16–3 as being a little closer to Humphrey than to Nixon simply because, as a matter of fact, in 1968 the Wallace voters normally listed Humphrey as their second choice. Indeed, during the campaign a good many people who had originally listed Wallace as their first choice decided to vote for Humphrey, apparently on the grounds that Wallace could not win and they preferred Humphrey to Nixon. This was practically the only shift among voters that occurred during the course of the campaign, but it was large enough to convert Humphrey from an almost hopeless candidate to a man who came to within an ace of beating Nixon.

We have not labeled the two issue dimensions because, in a way, the distinction between Wallace on the one hand and Humphrey and Nixon on the other was more sociological than an issue; but there were certain issues. The most obvious of these, of course, was attitude toward race, which was seldom mentioned during the campaign. There were, however, other issues such as law and order, and during the campaign there was some tendency on the part of Humphrey and Nixon to move toward the Wallace position. Indeed, one comedian summed up the campaign as follows: "Nixon says 'law and order is the issue'; Humphrey says 'law and order is the issue'; Wallace says 'plagiarism is the issue'."

PROSPECTS

The situation provided an opportunity for the Republican party to impose a crisis upon the Democratic party. In general, the people who voted for Wallace, or who took him as their first choice and ended up voting for Humphrey, were people whose attachment to the Democratic party was essentially an emotional attachment to the party rather than a detailed attachment to the issues it represented. Nixon made a play for this particular type of voter, although not nearly as strong a play as a more direct politician might have made. At the same time, the Democratic party was impeded in its efforts to attempt to reintegrate the Wallace voters by the fact that black voters by now represented a very large percentage of Democratic voters and by the fact that, in general, those people who were most antagonistic to Wallace were in the Democratic party. Thus, the traditional Democratic coalition showed signs of coming apart at the seams.

The voters who had favored Wallace and still kept the Democratic party as their second choice began gradually changing so that the Republican party was their second choice. In a way their support for Wallace had cracked their essentially emotional loyalty to the Democratic party, and they tended to move toward the Republicans. In 1972, although the final election was between Nixon and McGovern without Wallace being involved, it seems likely that most of the people for whom Wallace would have been first choice voted for Nixon. This was in a way a result of McGovern's policy, which we have discussed before. To some extent, however, it would have occurred almost with any Democratic candidate. The Democratic party was stuck with a general position on such things as busing which antagonized these voters.

Wallace's astonishing performance in the Democratic primaries, together with his almost complete failure in the caucuses, illustrated both the support he had among certain traditionally Democratic groups and his inability to plan ahead. As of the end of November, 1972, it rather looked as if American politics had been drastically realigned, with the Wallace voters now largely in the Republican camp. Democratic control of the two houses of Congress has normally depended upon their control of almost all of the Southern senators and representatives, and this control was also beginning to erode.

The Watergate scandals have made any long-term prediction very chancy at the moment. Historically, the Harding scandals had substantially no effect on the Republican predominance, largely because Harding himself had the good grace to die at the appropriate moment. In the case of the Nixon scandals, the negative impact on the Republican party in the 1974 election was substantial. It is difficult at this point to say how long the effect will last. What can be said is that politics will never be the same again. The coalitions that will dominate American politics in the future will surely be different from those that dominated it before 1960.

To repeat what we said at the beginning of this chapter, simple models of the sort we have outlined above cannot tell everything about politics. We think, however, that we have demonstrated that they do give an element of insight and information. There are now many other, and much more complex, models, and we hope that the reader will be motivated to look into them.

17

Bureaucratic Entrepreneurs

Presidents come and presidents go, reaping the calumny, but the bureaucrats endure. These soldiers of the swivel chair remain nameless and unnoticed. But now and then, we pause to shine the spotlight briefly upon them in their backrooms.

Jack Anderson

Although elected officials are surely important in our government, they are massively outnumbered by their bureaucratic employees. Further, it is not clear who is actually the employee. Bureaucrats now make up such a large share of the total voting public that it is almost possible to say that the politicians are the employees of the bureaucrats. This is particularly so since bureaucrats are much more likely to vote than the citizens who are not. Bureaucrats, then, constitute a considerably larger share of the voting public than of the actual population. A recent study showed that, although about 19 percent of the employed persons in the United States are bureaucrats, with their families they probably make up approximately 27 percent of all voters.[1] Clearly, this is the kind of voting bloc that no politician can afford to ignore.

However, for purposes of simplicity let us assume that the politicians hire the bureaucrats, rather than the other way around, and proceed on that basis. There is now a small but scientifically respectable literature in which economic concepts are applied to bureaucracy. Once again in this

---

[1] Thomas E. Borcherding, ed., *Budgets and Bureaucrats: Organization of Government Growth*, Durham, N.C.: Duke University Press, forthcoming.

chapter, instead of attempting to cover the entire scope of this rather diffi-cult literature, we will deal with only one aspect of it and use a rather simple model. We hope that this model will be useful in and of itself, and provide an introduction to a much larger literature for those who are interested.

THE BUREAUCRATS

Bureaucrats are not markedly different from other people. Most citi-zens of the United States are to some extent interested in helping their fellow men and in doing things in the public interest. Most citizens of the United States, on the other hand, tend to devote much more time and at-tention to their own personal interests. The same is true of bureaucrats.

In one way the single most important contribution of economics was to make it clear that the market economy converts private desires into public benefits. We can drive our cars not because the automobile workers, the stockholders, and the sales force want us to have good cars, but be-cause the car is generated as a sort of byproduct of the achievement of their own goals, which in this case are income goals. During much of his-tory economics was taught by people who were under the impression that merchants, farmers, etc., were attempting to do what was morally right. Since Adam Smith, we take a different view. Naturally, there is no impli-cation that people in these occupations are particularly immoral; but it is also true that they do not produce their products primarily because they want to benefit their customers, but because they want to benefit them-selves.

The same is true of politicians and of bureaucrats. They are basically in the business to make a living, although, of course, on occasion they sacrifice their own interests to those of others or to charity, just like any-one else. However, most of the time they generate what public good or public benefit they do generate as a byproduct of attempting to maxi-mize their own interests.

The market, *if there are no monopolies present,* is so organized that the individual attempting to benefit himself ends up benefiting others. We should attempt to organize the government in the same way. The govern-ment that organizes itself so that a self-interested and dishonest politi-cian or bureaucrat can benefit himself greatly by injuring the public is subverting its service capabilities. The bureaucrat is like anyone else. He will rarely commit crimes or be consciously dishonest, but most of the time he acts in his own interests and only occasionally sacrifices for others or for the public interest. What we want is a government so designed that people like this will generate benefits for others as they do in the non-monopolistic part of the market. Such a government design is by no means impossible.

The question to which we now turn is how should we organize a bureaucracy in order to achieve this goal. We cannot cover this entire problem in the short space of one chapter and are only going to discuss one particular aspect of it. It is characteristic of most modern governments, although not always true, that each bureau has a monopoly on supplying to the government some particular service. This monopoly is so common that most people think it is a necessary characteristic of government. Indeed, periodically commissions look into government efficiency. Almost uniformly, these commissions object to "duplication," which, in essence, is having competition between two bureaus.

Although the view that you cannot have competition between government bureaus is very widely held, this is primarily merely an unexamined presupposition. It is, of course, true that having two different government agencies doing literally the same thing might cause inconvenience. Their employees would tend to bump into each other all of the time. But we can have competition without that kind of congestion. A more significant possible objection to competition in government would be the existence of significant economies of scale. Such economies may be important with respect to local governments, but there seems to be little evidence that economies of scale would require bureaus of the size we now have in our federal government. Indeed, as far as we can see, these government agencies are far beyond the optimal size from the standpoint of production efficiency.

As an example of competition, most American highways are made by private contractors. They submit bids for constructing certain segments of the highway. Once the bid has been allocated to one of these contractors, naturally the other contractors are not permitted to move their bulldozers, graders, etc., onto the right-of-way and get in his way. On the other hand, most American road repairing is done by a government agency that has a monopoly. Occasionally road repairing is also done by competitive bids and private contractors.

It is not necessary, of course, that the competing units be private companies rather than segments of government. The Department of Defense (DOD) is basically divided into Army, Navy, and Air Force. Many of the missions of the DOD can be accomplished by more than one of these agencies. In areas where this is so, the Secretary of Defense can (and frequently does) solicit programs and plans from both of the services or, in fortunate cases, all three. He can then choose what seems to him the most efficient solution from among two or more competing programs. This method does not work perfectly, heaven knows, but certainly it works better than the DOD does in those areas where the mission is allocated to only one of the services; hence, there is no competition.

As mentioned previously, most people studying government efficiency in recent years have taken the opposite view and have objected vigorously to "duplication." Think of the consequences of such a policy in the private market, where General Motors, Ford, Chrysler, and American Motors not only duplicate each other's services but are also duplicated by a lot of odd foreigners like Toyota, Volkswagen, Fiat, Renault, Mercedes, etc. Clearly, if efficiency means elimination of duplication, we should consider abolishing everything except General Motors and make General Motors stop producing both Chevrolets and Pontiacs.

MONOPOLY AND BUREAUCRATIC BEHAVIOR

Let us turn to a little formal analysis in which we will assume that the government has given one particular bureau a monopoly over performing some particular service. For simplicity, we shall assume that the government is the federal government, the agency is the FBI, and the service it performs is the collection of national police activities. It should be emphasized that there is no implication that the FBI is one whit less efficient or more bureaucratic than any other government agency. In fact, it is the general view of the authors of this book that the FBI is among the more efficient bureaus of the federal government. We do not regard this, however, as very high praise. The choice of the FBI, then, is simply in order to give a concrete example, not an effort to assume the FBI is in any way different from other bureaus.

In Figure 17–1 we have shown the usual demand and cost curves with which you are no doubt familiar from your other texts. The cost and

FIGURE 17–1

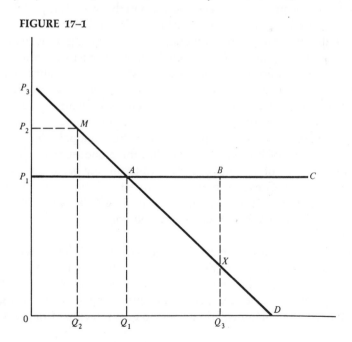

benefit measured in dollars are, as usual, shown on the vertical axis and the quantity, in this case, of police activities is shown on the horizontal axis. We assume that policing is measured in dollar units, therefore the cost line is the horizontal line P_1-C. The downward sloping curve (D) is Congress's demand for such police services from the FBI.

If we could somehow assume that this is a completely competitive market, then Congress would buy from the suppliers the amount Q_1 of police services at price P_1. This is, of course, the optimal quantity (as far as Congress is concerned) in the sense that marginal costs equal marginal benefits. On the other hand, if the FBI were an ordinary monopoly facing a myriad of small purchasers, then they would charge the price P_2 and would sell the quantity Q_2 to the purchasers. This would give them a monopoly profit equivalent to the square whose upper right-hand corner is marked P_2 and lower left-hand corner is at point P_1 on the vertical axis. This monopoly situation is not ideal, of course. The cost of increasing the quantity from Q_2 to Q_1 is less than the benefit as shown by the demand curve.

If we had a perfectly discriminating monopolist, he would sell the police control services in small pieces at different prices to different people, with the result that he would obtain the full triangle above and to the left of A as monopoly profit and would produce the amount Q_1 at a cost P_1. This is usually regarded as socially superior to a simple monopoly. Certainly it is superior from the standpoint of a monopolist who gets as his profit the whole triangle $D-A-Q_1$. In practice it is rarely possible for a monopoly in the private market to perform in this way. It is possible that the government bureaucrat may be able to do so, however.

If the individual bureau has a monopoly on providing a given service, it also faces a monopolistic buyer, called a monopsonist (i.e., one buyer), for that service. Congress has a monopsony status when dealing with the FBI because the FBI can sell its services to no one else. The problem of a monopolist facing a monopsonist is an extremely difficult one, and most economists say that in the general case you cannot tell very much about what the outcome will be. It is possible that the monopolist will be able to get the full gain of his monopoly, or that the monopsonist will be able to get the full gain of his monopsony (which in our particular diagram simply means that Congress buys Q_1 units of police services from the FBI at price P_1). The solution can also be anything in between. Normally, it is said that the actual outcome depends on bargaining tactics and cannot be predicted.

In our particular case, however, it is possible to make a pretty good prediction as to the outcome. We have drawn the cost line in as a horizontal line because it is the easy way of measuring it. Congress, however, will not have any clear idea of the cost of providing services by a given bureau. Indeed, the bureau will do its best to guarantee that Congress does not have a clear idea of the *minimum* cost of providing various services. There are innumerable techniques available to the bureau to make it hard for congressmen to know what the bureau is doing in detail. Further, the bureau does not face a competitor producing the same commodity, so that Congress cannot simply compare its price with that of other people. In most of the negotiations between bureaus and Congress (which take the form primarily of committee hearings) it is clear that Congress never really gets an idea of the minimum cost at which a bureau can perform a given service. Indeed, the congressmen who have many other demands on their time normally do not make any very strong effort.

The bureau, on the other hand, is rather well informed as to the shape of Congress's demand for its services. The reason it is well informed is that Congress's demand for the service of any given bureau is largely a reflection of the views of the voters on the value of that particular service. The bureau has a great many facilities for finding out what the voters think about the need for police services or agricultural subsidies or new parks, etc. It also can take careful note of any speeches that individual congressmen make on those subjects, which gives it further information. Last but by no means least, the bureaus are characteristically very well informed on any lobbying activities that may be going on in Washington with respect to the activities of that particular bureau. Indeed, in many cases the bureaus themselves in essence organize the private lobbies, which push for more of their activities.

Edward Banfield, author of *The Unheavenly City,* in the earlier part of his life was a public relations man for one of the innumerable segments of the Department of Interior. As he is fond of recounting, on one occasion in the pursuance of his duties, he wrote a letter to the Secretary of Interior to be formally signed by the president of a citizens group that the Department of Interior had organized to press for further activities in his particular branch. The letter was sent to the Secretary of Interior and in due· course when the Secretary wanted it answered, it was referred to Banfield for a reply. Thus, he found himself carrying on the entire correspondence on both sides.

Under these circumstances, with the Congress having little idea of the minimum cost the bureau must put out to achieve its service, with the bureau having a very clear idea of Congress's demand for those services, the bargaining between the monopolist (FBI) and the monopsonist (Congress) almost certainly will go in favor of the monopolist. Thus, in this case we can predict the outcome with a fair degree of security, although in the general case it is a very difficult problem.

As the reader will have noticed, we referred to the bureau as being able to keep its minimum cost a secret to a considerable extent; we did not say that it could keep profit a secret. Indeed, those bureaus (and there are some continuously popping up) in which the head has worked out some way of getting a personal profit normally are detected after a period of time; and the man who has pocketed the profit is either fired or, occasionally, jailed. Thus, the bureaucratic monopolist is in a somewhat different position than a private monopolist. He cannot go live on the Riviera on his ill-gotten gains. Indeed, if the comptroller-general and the various other agencies of the government that are directed at making certain that money is not diverted from its appropriated channels into private expenditures do their job, there is no direct way in which bureaucrats can benefit from their monopoly position. Unfortunately, there is an indirect way; and this indirect way probably causes considerably more social harm than would the simple waste of the profit we would anticipate if they could convert it into money to spend on riotous living.

Putting the matter bluntly, the bureaucrat can waste the funds. This waste, of course, is not pure waste in the sense that no one gets any benefit from it, but it is waste in the sense that there are very small benefits and those accrue to the bureaucrats. The obvious case that is always used in talking about this kind of thing (and it can occur in private businesses as well as in government) is the pretty secretary who is a poor typist. Since the busy bureaucrat who has a pretty secretary who cannot type probably also has a significant correspondence, he ends up with two secretaries.

There are innumerable other ways in which the same kind of thing can be done: elaborate offices, a lot of trips to "important conferences" which are held in places like Nice and Las Vegas, or the special dining rooms that are found so much in Washington. Recently the newspapers have talked a good deal about the Presidential Mess.[2] But this is merely froth, if one considers the whole thing. Surely the most expensive set of subsidized restaurants in the world are the restaurants in the capital building for members of Congress.[3] In addition, however, all over Washington there are small dining rooms for cabinet secretaries;[4] and below these establishments are special restaurants for senior officers (called flag officers in the Pentagon).[5]

----

[2] One of the authors was honored by an invitation to have lunch in the Presidential Mess on one occasion. It was by no means the best restaurant in Washington. On the other hand, this visit was in what we might call the "second division." There is a special, very small President's Mess that serves lunch for eight high officials, and then the main President's Mess which serves lunch for about 100 officials at the next rank. The second group of officials is divided into a first division—which has a late lunch—and a second division which has an early lunch. A late lunch is a status symbol among the staff of the White House.

[3] Once again, one of the authors has eaten in these *august purlieus* and can testify that the food was better than in the President's Mess. It was also a good deal cheaper, which implies that the subsidy was larger.

[4] The only one in which either of the authors has eaten is the Attorney General's dining room, and the food there is highly varying.

[5] The flag officers' mess, in which again one of the authors has eaten, is clearly subsidized, granted the prices they charge; but it is not really a very good restaurant.

Regarding the elaborate offices of bureaucrats, Jack Anderson was able to collect the following information on how tax dollars are spent:

> It is . . . a matter of solemn protocol that no bureaucrat with any status can move into a predecessor's lair without refurbishing it. Offices must be done over to fit the personality of the new personage.
>
> To determine whether this sacred rule is still in effect, we checked on several bigwigs who have been appointed recently. There is Alexander Butterfield, for instance, who was put in command of the Federal Aviation Administration after departing the White House. He was the man, it will be remembered, who broke the electrifying news that President Nixon was bugging himself.
>
> Sure enough, Butterfield has redone his chambers. New drapes and furniture were installed at a cost to the taxpayers of $5,400. . . .
>
> We also checked with the Secret Service to see if the new director, H. Stuart Knight, had been able to manage with the luxurious suite the previous chief left behind. . . . Knight has somehow managed to spend $11,200 to do over his digs. Some $3,500 went for a new paint job alone.
>
> At the Bureau of Standards, Director Richard Roberts splurged over $55,000 to remodel his office layout. He magnificently extended the job to redo his secretary's office and adjoining conference room.
>
> Social and Rehabilitation Administrator James S. Dwight, a stern critic of welfare cheats, didn't mind lavishing $120,000 upon his own welfare. The money was expended for plush carpets, tinted glass, sliding doors, a floor-to-ceiling bookcase, and other fancy fixtures in his domain. . . .
>
> In recent years, the bureaucrats have become smitten with campaigns to trim the waistline bulges, which are an occupational hazard of too much time in the swivel chair. As a result, almost every large government agency has constructed recreational facilities where barrel-bellied bureaucrats can shed their flab—usually on government time, of course.
>
> The State Department possesses a fitness room and gym, paid for by an employees' recreation association. A departmental volleyball team takes over the floor for over two hours at a time, much to the consternation of those on the sideline who want exercise when they are supposed to be working. . . .
>
> Under the direction of former Transportation Secretary John Volpe, his department constructed a gym facility complete with the latest in physical fitness equipment, a soothing suana, and a Tartan track atop the head-quarter building. Cost to the taxpayers: $34,195.[6]

The problem with all of these ways of spending possible monopoly profits is that they are conspicuous and Congress is apt to notice them. Thus, something can be done but not a great deal. There is another very

---

On the other hand, the Pentagon is a long way from any other restaurant. By rumor, the Supreme Court dining room outdoes all of the others in grandeur, cuisine and, of course, subsidy.

[6] Jack Anderson, "Washington Merry-Go-Round," *Raleigh News and Observer*, July 15, 1974.

large area in which money can be spent, which is something we think is best described as "bureaucratic aesthetics." A man who has devoted his life to, let us say, the FBI is apt to develop very strong ideas as to what is a good FBI operation. Thus he might, for example, develop the idea that it is desirable to have an FBI office within 100 miles of any place in the United States, regardless of the density of the population. Congress would never be able to detect this kind of waste. It is omnipresent in government. Congress may notice the elaborate special honor guard unit maintained by the Pentagon, but it is unlikely to realize that carriers are a few knots faster than they really have to be. For the devoted naval officer, those additional knots of speed have a real personal benefit. He thinks the fast carrier is better than a slower carrier, even though the combat capacity is probably not much affected.

There is an immense scope for this kind of waste in government, as indeed there is in private industry; but in private industry, the pressures to get what profit you can get in cash are so strong that this effect is probably rather minor. The federal triangle in Washington is a monument to President Hoover's feelings for this kind of aesthetics. That appalling monstrosity, the former War, Navy, and State Building, is a 19th century edition of the same thing; and anyone familiar with any given segment of the federal government can always find many, many further examples.

THE SIZE AND EXPANSION OF BUREAUCRACY

The most important form of waste is simply making the bureau larger than it needs to be. There are many reasons why a bureaucrat may want his bureau to expand and object to its contraction. First, the prestige of the man at the head of the bureau (and also civil service rank and pay) is very significantly affected by the absolute size of the bureau. Further, such things as the size of his office, whether he has a conference table, the type of chair in which he is permitted to sit, and the type of water cooler near his desk depend on the size of his job. If he can expand his bureau, he can anticipate over time that he will move up in these areas, and they are important to the bureaucrat who is conscious of their effect on his status in Washington. An important consideration from the standpoint of almost everybody in a given bureau is that an expansion will mean that there are more possible promotions.

This list by no means ends the advantages to a chief bureaucrat of increasing the size of his bureau, however. His power obviously goes up as the bureau increases in size, and his ability to control the bureau itself improves if he can hire new people. The reason for this is that under civil service rules it is, to all intents and purposes, impossible to fire anybody. Under the circumstances, the only way in which he can get control over his subordinates is to offer them the reward of promotions or improvements in the size of their staffs. Thus, he has more control over his subordinates if the bureau is known to be expanding. He can dangle before the eyes of a number of junior officers the opportunity of promotion to a new subsection head.

Also, the relationship between the bureaucrat and Congress is advantageously affected by the expansion of the bureau. If the bureaucrat is going to be expending new funds, he usually has a good deal of freedom in deciding how they will be spent. Putting a new building in some particular congressman's district may be a possibility, and he can use this to pay off congressmen for various favors they may do. Note that this also gives the congressman a motive for expanding the bureau.

There is, on the other hand, substantially no motivation for reducing the size of the bureau. Insofar as government agencies are examined for efficiency (and, as a matter of practical fact, in spite of all the noise, there is not very much of this done), this concern for efficiency is concern for how well they do what they are doing. There is little or no attempt to discover whether or not they are doing things that are not worth doing. It is not generally true that government bureaus spend a great deal of energy doing things that are positively harmful to their constituents. *They may, however, do things that are worth a great deal less than their costs.*

In some cases, they actually work harm on society as a whole in order to benefit their constituents. The agricultural support program, which has been in existence now for some 30 years, used tax money for the purpose of making bread and similar agricultural commodities (and at the moment of this writing, beef) more expensive. We could easily find innumerable examples of the same kind. However, these are all cases in which there is a distinct and direct benefit for the constituents of the bureau (i.e., the people who support it) and the cost falls on others. For example, farmers are much richer than they would be without this program, and the rest of us are poorer.

How can a bureau expand to "too large" a size? To return to Figure 17–1, we can see the explanation very easily. For simplicity, assume that the bureau is a monopoly and is able to get the entire monopoly profit of a differentiating monopoly from Congress because Congress does not know its production function. Under those circumstances, it can increase production to point Q_3 on the horizontal axis. Note that all the units of police service provided by the FBI between Q_1 and Q_3 have a positive value, but the value is less than their cost. Congress, on the other hand, is offered an implicit bargain under which the bureau proposes to produce the amount Q_3 of police services, in return for a payment which is the rectangle $P_1–B–Q_3–O$. If we have drawn the diagram properly, the area of this rectangle is the same as the area under the demand curve and to the left of Q_3; i.e., it is the same as the area $O–Q_3–X–P_3$. This is because the triangle $P_1–P_3–A$ and the triangle $A–B–X$ have the same area. The monopoly has exploited its full monopoly profit out of Congress and then has used this monopoly profit to subsidize additional production which, from the standpoint of Congress, is actually not worth its cost. This is the solution that maximizes the size of the bureau and, hence, maximizes the various advantages of a large bureau which we have enumerated above.

Probably few bureaus have actually achieved the goal equivalent to producing at Q_3 in our figure. For one thing, bureaucrats are like the rest of us in that they like leisure, therefore they do not work as hard as they might, even in generating excess capacity. Further, there are, as we have mentioned above, various other things that the bureaucrat can use his power to obtain. Last but not least, perfect adjustment, which would mean expansion to production Q_3, would be unlikely because if the bureaucrat reached this perfect adjustment, Congress would become indifferent between having the bureau continue to exist or not having it at all. Total benefit minus total cost would equal zero.

Nevertheless, it is likely that most bureaus have moved fairly far toward the size that is designated by Q_3 in Figure 17–1. In any event, it is fairly clear that if bureaucratic managers are as interested in their own well being as you and we are in ours, they will generate a bureau that is too large from the standpoint of the desires of the voters, or at least those voters who are not employed in a bureaucracy.

Empirical tests of the hypothesis that bureaucracies are large, indeed roughly twice as large as they should be, are hard to perform. The studies that have been done, however, do seem to indicate that the prediction is borne out. As an example of one study of this nature, there are a certain number of governmental services that are occasionally carried out by private companies on contract under fairly competitive situations. An examination of the costs private companies charge and those of a government bureaucracy seem to indicate that the private companies can generate the same level of service at much less than the cost of generating it by a bureaucracy.[7] Although this might seem to have nothing to do with the absolute size of the bureaucracy, in general the greater efficiency is accomplished by simply using less equipment and personnel.

To take an example, fire protection is normally provided by municipal bureaucracies called fire departments. There are a few companies, primarily in Arizona, that provide fire service on a contract basis. In most cases, these companies have a contract with some city to provide fire protection in the city; but a good many of them also have private contracts with various individuals to provide fire protection in areas where there is no city government.[8]

---

[7] Robert M. Spann, "Public *vs.* Private Provision of Governmental Services," in *Budgets and Bureaucrats*, forthcoming.

[8] The individual contracts are of two types. The customer can pay them a flat

These fire companies have invented a new way of dealing with a fire. They have, in essence, invented a new but simple technique. This technique consists of asking the person who telephones in what kind of fire it is and then sending equipment suitable for that fire, instead of sending two or three large engines for all fire reports. The usual equipment is a simple pick-up truck with two men and a foam unit, which is adequate for most fires. In those cases where it is not, they, of course, send more equipment. Using this very inexpensive technique, they have been able to provide fire service which, judging by fire insurance rates, is just as good as that provided by more conventional fire departments with far more equipment and manpower.

However, this is merely one example. To repeat what we said earlier, empirical work in this field is not very easy and the theoretical proposition that government bureaus will tend to be much larger—perhaps twice as large—as they need to be cannot be said to have been fully validated by empirical work as yet. It is true, however, that so far no empirical study attempted to test the proposition has indicated that the bureaus are less than oversized.

PROPOSED CHANGES IN BUREAUCRACY

What, then, can we do about this matter? The first thing that occurs to most people is simply to hire some experts to go to work to improve efficiency. We have now had a good deal of experience with this particular approach, and it does not seem to do very much good. The problem is that the efficiency experts have no way of measuring the demand for the government service and, although they can improve the efficiency with which the service is delivered, they cannot prevent the bureaucracy from being much larger than it should be and producing service that is not worth its cost. Further, in many cases these efficiency studies seem to be positively perverse.

Almost all efforts to improve efficiency have led to attacks on "duplication" of services. As most economists have noticed, governments frequently organize cartels for private industry. For example, the ICC was organized to reduce, and in fact has reduced, the degree of competition in transportation. The CAB has changed the airways from a highly competitive industry to one of almost complete cartelization. We could go on with this list for quite sometime. It would appear that one of the functions of government efficiency studies is to promote cartelization within the government. Instead of suggesting that there be competition in the government, characteristically intragovernmental competition is strongly

---

amount per year and they will then put out any fire that occurs on his property; or the customer can pay a much, much higher fee by calling them after the fire has broken out.

opposed. As we have said before, they attack "duplication," which is another way of referring to competition.

If we did have competition for the provision of government services, the amount would move back in the general direction of Q_1 in Figure 17–1. This is, of course, the reason that the market, where there is competitive provision, can operate in such an efficient way. There is no obvious reason why the same thing will not occur if we can somehow introduce competition into government.

Under competition, if one bureau was offering quantity Q_3 of service at a price that included the welfare triangle, another bureau could expand its own total size by offering to add on to its present duties quantity Q_1 at a price that reflected its price and gave Congress the welfare triangle above and to the left. Thus, we would anticipate that under competition between bureaus, just as under competition in the private market, there would be a tendency to move toward the optimal quantity and price for the service provided.

The idea of competition between bureaus seems almost a contradiction in terms to many people, probably because of the long continued propaganda against "duplication." In practice, bureaus do make a good many efforts to compete with each other to expand by taking someone else's business away from them. For a particularly striking example, the Department of Transportation does not sound like a very belligerent organization, but it played a major combat role in the war in Vietnam.

In this case, the Navy took the view that there was a minimum size below which combat vessels could not go. Presumably this was a bargaining technique intended to get more money out of Congress. The Department of Transportation, however, has the Coast Guard as one of its subordinate agencies, and the Coast Guard expressed its willingness to provide small combat vessels in Vietnam. The contract went to the Coast Guard and as a result a large number of small speedboats, equipped with machine guns, were run up and down the rivers of Vietnam, operated by Coast Guard personnel on temporary detail from their normal duties of preventing smuggling and rescuing people whose sailboats had overturned.

One can predict that if we have another war of this sort, the Navy will not again try to game Congress into giving them larger vessels than necessary because they will anticipate the loss of part of their budget to the Coast Guard. On the other hand, the Coast Guard, having won on this one, may try to compete with the Navy for some other type of combat mission in any future hostilities. If the Coast Guard continues outmaneuvering the Navy in this way, eventually it will be larger than the Navy.

Any rather careful reading of the appropriation hearings will indicate that this kind of thing happens fairly commonly. Various bureaus propose to do things that are very close to or indeed exactly the same as things other bureaus are already doing or are thinking of doing. Usually these proposals are made with a good sales package claiming lower cost, better service, etc. The bureau whose ground is being trod upon then comes back by (a) cutting the price at which it is making its offer, (b) promising to improve the service, and (c) arguing that permitting the intruder to enter will lead to "duplication." Over time, however, a good deal of this kind of "duplication" always develops.

Unfortunately, at this stage in the normal development of American government a commission is appointed, usually by the President, to look over the government and improve efficiency. It goes through the entire civil service and military with the objective of eliminating "duplication." In other words, it eliminates competition and reintroduces cartels. It has no more likelihood of creating actual efficiency in government than the Interstate Commerce Commission has of generating efficiency in transportation. The simplest remedy to all of this, of course, is to stop having presidential commissions look into efficiency. Since in the historic record they have always attempted to eliminate competition, we can at least stop them from existing.

But why not take a more positive approach? In the private market we do have something called the Sherman Act which prohibits cartels and monopolies. Perhaps it is not well enforced, but at least it exists. Could we not have a somewhat similar approach to our government bureaus? There is no reason why Congress and the President should not encourage individual bureaus to propose the take-over of part or all of the duties of other bureaus at a better price and with better service. The more of this that happens, the more the individual bureau faces a demand curve that is not Congress's demand for, let us say, police services, but Congress's demand for the FBI provision of those police services, as opposed to an expansion of the Secret Service, the Postal Inspectors, various police forces now run by the Pentagon for military purposes, or indeed simply expanding the Washington Metropolitan police. Scotland Yard, which does most of the serious detective work all over England, is, after all, the police force of the city of London.

At the very least, this means that Congressional committees should be willing to listen to substantially any bureaucratic proposal for doing anything. If the Postal Service appears with the astonishing proposition that, although it cannot deliver the mail, it could run aircraft carriers more cheaply than the Navy, it should at least be listened to. It might not be sensible to transfer the carriers from the Navy to the Postal Service, but one could predict that the Navy would be impelled by such an offer to think long and hard about how they can make economies in the operation of their carriers.

Another way of introducing competition takes advantage of the fact that the United States is a rather large country. Various regions of the

United States are much larger in geography, population, and in total income than many nations. Thus, a good many federal government agencies could be broken down into regional agencies responsible for areas larger than France or West Germany. Since there does not seem to be any evidence that our agencies function more efficiently than their French and West German counterparts, there is probably little in the way of economies of scale above that size for most government services. These regional bureaus could then apply to Congress for their budgets. At the end of each year, Congress could compare the service they had received and the cost and perhaps transfer a state or two from the region that did worst to another that did better. Thus, the regional bureaus would be put in a kind of marginal competition with each other and would be motivated to attempt to be efficient.

As the last and most radical proposal, many government activities do not have to be performed by the bureaucracy at all. There is no reason they cannot be contracted out to private people with, of course, precautions to make certain that the market remains competitive. A good deal of government activity is already done this way. Roads, dams, and government buildings are actually built by private contractors. Most military equipment is also produced in this way, although the military service does produce some of its own. We could go a good deal further. The Navy, for example, in addition to maintaining combat vessels, has a large collection of auxiliary and transport vessels. There seems no reason why these could not be contracted out to competitive private operation. The Weather Bureau, to take another case, does not seem to have any particular characteristics which make it necessary to have it operated by a bureaucracy rather than by a series of private companies, each of which gathers weather data and makes predictions in various parts of the country.[9] A good many park services are already contracted out in this way and perhaps more could be. In general, we should take an experimental attitude about this kind of approach toward reducing the power of the bureaucracy; there certainly seems to be no reason to rule out contracting in many areas of government.

But this is only one of a number of possible approaches. Making it easier to fire bureaucrats would be a distinct improvement and perhaps some kind of bonus system under which bureau heads are permitted to keep part of any saving they make without reducing the quality of service would be a good idea. In any event, we now have a bureaucracy that has "jus' growed"; it is not the result of careful planning or thought. Surely we can do better if we try.

---

[9] The predictions could hardly be worse.

18

Riots and Panic

Riots, demonstrations, and indeed behavior of people in large masses have been studied primarily by sociologists or political scientists and little by economists. The purpose of this chapter is to demonstrate that economists have something to contribute, too. In fact we suspect that an economic approach is far more fruitful than the approaches that have been traditionally used.[1] Most discussion of riots, demonstrations, etc., turns on either one of two hypotheses. The first of these is that these riots or demonstrations are set off by generally bad conditions. For example, the blacks rioted all over the United States in the summer of 1967 because they had come to realize how bad their situation was and were taking action to change it. Since their situation was surely better than it had been in previous years, this theory has to turn on a sort of gradual realization on their part that they were not as well off as they could be, with this realization occurring faster than the actual improvement in their conditions. On the other hand, they have done very little rioting since then and, although their conditions have improved, they have not yet achieved full equality; so why they have not continued to riot is hard to determine from this hypothesis.

The second basic hypothesis (and a somewhat older one) for the behavior of demonstrators, rioters, etc., has to do with something called

---

[1] A good deal of this chapter is based on the work of J. Patrick Gunning; although he has published only one article on the subject, he has actually done more work in the area; see J. Patrick Gunning, Jr., "An Economic Approach to Riot Analysis," *Public Choice*, XIII (Fall 1972), 31–46. Since he was a graduate student of one of the authors at the time, this is a clear-cut proof that there is some educational activity carried on in universities. The students may learn nothing from the teachers, but the teachers occasionally learn something from the students.

"mob psychology." It is alleged that people in large groups somehow are different from when they are alone. Since we have never actually fully understood this hypothesis, we are rather at a loss to explain it; but it will be found in the older literature on mob action.

The economist is apt to feel that the easiest way of explaining any change in human action is a change in the cost. Thus, if we observe people who never break windows when they are alone or in small groups but do break windows when they are part of a mob, we are apt to explain this in terms of such things as the fact that the cost of breaking windows is lower (i.e., it is much safer) when you are in a mob than when you are alone and more likely to be caught.

Obviously the difference between these different types of explanations should be subject to empirical investigation. Unfortunately, it is very hard to carry on empirical investigations during a riot. The only study of any sophistication of which we are aware was carried on by Nicos Devletoglou and certain of his friends and students during some riots in London. These riots or demonstrations were carried out by Englishmen who were for one reason or another distressed by political conditions in Greece.[2] Devletoglou's experiment was solely devoted to finding out whether the people engaged in the demonstration/riot were well-informed about Greece and Greek politics. For this purpose he quickly designed a small questionnaire, and he and his assistants went out on the streets and presented the questionnaire to the participants.

Needless to say, this was a difficult task and required a great deal of tact on the part of the pollsters. In spite of the difficulties, they were able to get at least some answers and their results are reported in *Public Opinion Quarterly*.[3] As I suppose no one would be much surprised to learn, it turned out that the demonstrators knew something about Greece but not much. As a sample and politically neutral question, they were able to locate the city of Athens on a map of Greece but not the second largest city in Greece, Salonica. Their knowledge of the political issues about which they were demonstrating was, in Devletoglou's view, equally incomplete, but this is somewhat harder to measure.

Empirical work in which riots are examined after the fact by asking questions of rioters and/or policemen have been done on quite a large scale, but unfortunately most of these experiments have not been designed in such a way that one can use the information to distinguish between the economic approach to rioting and the sociological and political

---

[2] This was before the establishment of the military dictatorship. Indeed, these riots in a somewhat indirect way had much to do with the institution of the Papadopolous regime.

[3] See, Nicos Devletoglou, "Responsibility and Demonstrations: A Case Study," *Public Opinion Quarterly*, XXX (Summer 1966), 285–89.

explanations given above. For example, during some of the 1967 riots referred to above, blacks entered shops and removed TV sets they then took home. An economist would tend to feel that probably the largest single motivating factor that led blacks to go into stores and steal TV sets during a riot, when they did not do it under normal circumstances, was simply that the cost of such theft was much lower. In Detroit, for example, the police were under orders not to interfere.

The questions asked after the riot were unfortunately not designed to discover whether this was true or not. For example, suppose that a black who, during the course of the riot, took a TV set and now has it in his home is asked about his motives by an earnest young assistant professor of sociology. To put it mildly, it is unlikely that he will say that he just wanted the TV set and saw an opportunity to get it without paying. Indeed, the earnest young assistant professor is rather apt to have appeared with a structured question in which the "thief" is asked whether his removal of the TV set was a protest against the establishment, a protest against the white merchants, or simply the enactment of his personal frustration from living in such a corrupt society. This gives him a choice of fairly pleasant-sounding motives and he cannot be blamed if he takes advantage of them. The bulk of the research on the causes of riots has taken this form.

Note that this research simply offers no significant information on whether the economic or the sociopolitical explanation for rioting and demonstrations is correct; it does not disprove the conventional sociological wisdom. We cannot tell from this literature which hypothesis is true of the real world. This is unfortunate and we hope in the future riots and demonstrations will be investigated by people who have the economic hypothesis in mind and therefore design their research in such a way as to tell whether it is true or false.

Meanwhile, however, in the absence of empirical research we will outline in this chapter the theoretical explanation for "mob behavior" which seems sensible from the economic standpoint. It is quite probable that if we had adequate empirical evidence, we would find that some aspects of both the economic and sociopolitical explanation are true; but since this is an economics book, we will present only the economic explanation and leave it to others to present the sociopolitical explanation. We would hope that there are no more riots, and hence there is no way to find out which of these explanations is correct or whether some intermediate point is better than either; but we doubt this will turn out to be true. There have been riots throughout history and we see no reason for them to stop. Thus, future riots may provide the opportunity to test the hypothesis we advance here.

Let us begin by turning to a very special and indeed very minor type of riot the readers may think should not really be called a riot but which does raise somewhat the same issues. This phenomenon is "panic." It is uncommon nowadays for theaters to burn, but at one time they did so quite commonly. When this occurred, very often more people were killed by being trampled to death in or around the exits than were killed in the fire. Further, in general when people were killed by the fire, they were killed because the exits were blocked by dense masses of people who were attempting to get through doors that were too narrow.

The phenomenon occurs in other settings, of course. People on sinking ships may mob lifeboats with the result that they are overturned, an occurrence clearly not in the best interests of the passengers. It is, of course, this phenomenon that leads to fire drills and lifeboat drills. As a general rule, this kind of panic behavior leads to an increased death rate because the effort to put more people through a door than its design will allow or more people in a lifeboat than its normal capacity means that the actual capacity is less than it would be if people behaved in an orderly manner. Thus, a theater that has plenty of doors through which to evacuate the entire audience before the roof collapses during a fire—if they approach the doors in an orderly manner—may in fact find the doors clogged by struggling masses of people. The result may be that a good number of people are not only trampled but are killed in the theater because they are unable to get out.

That this behavior is not inevitable can be seen by using the sinking of the Titanic as an example. Due to the fact that the Titanic was thought to be unsinkable, there were not enough lifeboats on board. The crew and passengers behaved with admirable restraint. Women and children and just enough crewmen to man the lifeboats were loaded in the boats, and no lifeboat was overturned or damaged in the process. The maximum possible number of passengers was saved and the people who were compelled to remain on the Titanic because of inadequate lifeboats were, at least to some extent, consoled by the lack of disturbance on the ship and the ship's orchestra, which was playing "Nearer My God to Thee" when the Titanic rolled over.

Most discussions of the phenomenon of the panic that was so conspicuously absent on the Titanic have put it down to a sort of change of character on the part of the participants. It is alleged that in unexpected periods of great danger people stop acting rationally and crowd around doors or mob lifeboats. There is, however, a perfectly rational explanation. Consider someone in a theater that is on fire and has only a certain number of doors. Every minute that he remains in the theater increases the probability that he will be caught when the roof collapses. On the other hand, if he succeeds in fighting his way to the door, he will delay the exit of other people but not himself. Economically we refer to this as a public good situation. Looked at from the standpoint of the entire collection of people in the theater, they would be better off if they leave in an orderly way, row by row and without any effort on the part of individuals to get in ahead of the others. This will minimize the chance that any of them will be in the auditorium when the roof collapses and, if it does catch some of them, will minimize the number. Further, it reduces to zero the prospect that people will be trampled around the doors.

But this is considering what we might call group rationality—how to get out the group as a whole. Individuals interested in benefiting themselves would realize that if they push toward the door, they reduce the possibility of dying themselves, whereas if they remain in their place and thus prevent congestion around the door (or reduce congestion if there are already people trying to force their way out), they increase the likelihood that they will be killed. Pushing toward the door benefits you and injures others. Remaining where you are and letting other people go out injures you and benefits others. Clearly, the latter type behavior is the nobler and everyone who has considered the sinking of the Titanic has remarked on the courage of those who stayed on the ship, but it is not necessarily the rational thing to do.

Is there any way of telling whether the economic explanation—that each individual is making an individually rational decision—or the sociological explanation, which implies a breakdown of rationality—is correct? Well, there was an experiment run in the early 1950s which, although it does not conclusively settle matters, does cast a great deal of light on it. A professor of sociology tied a knot on one end of a large number of pieces of string. He placed these knots, one by one, in a bottle in such a way that the end of the string stuck out. The neck of the bottle was such that it was easy to pull the strings out including the knot, if only one or two of them were passing through the neck at a time, but that if all of the strings were pulled, the neck of the bottle would clog.

He then gave the other ends of the strings to his students and told them he was running an experiment and that all of the students who pulled their string completely out of the bottle (i.e., pulled the knot out) within 30 seconds would receive a nickel. Clearly there was no cause for panic here—the individuals were not in any way in danger; but, on the other hand, the arguments we have described above as economic would apply. Those individuals who did not pull on the strings and let other people pull theirs out first had less chance of getting a nickel. On the other hand, if everyone pulled on the strings, none of them would get their strings out and no one would get the nickel. As I suppose the reader has already guessed, all of the students pulled on their strings immediately.[4] The neck of the bottle resembled the door of a burning theater when panic had set in.

---

[4] One of the authors has repeated the experiment with students in his class with essentially the same result.

Obviously this experiment does not finally settle the matter, but it does offer some support for the economic point of view. Unfortunately, when we turn to the other kinds of demonstrations and riots, we do not have even this kind of experimental information. We must, therefore, consider them in a theoretical way. Was Edward Banfield correct when he titled one of his chapters in *The Unheavenly City*, "Rioting Mainly for Fun and Profit"?[5]

First, it must be admitted that a great many people do get some enjoyment from participating in riots. This enjoyment is probably greater if they can tell themselves and other people that what they are doing is politically important than if they do not have this rationalization, but there is no doubt that it is fun anyway. Until very recently almost all American children engaged in minor acts of vandalism on Halloween. Clearly, this was a permitted violation of the normal rules much as Saturnalia was in Rome, and once the rules were lifted a certain amount of physical damage to other people's property was in fact carried out by otherwise quite controlled young people for entertainment. They did not as a matter of fact do very much damage, but, on the other hand, the rules were only relaxed for small amounts of damage.

A certain amount of the kind of activity that goes on in riots is surely entertaining and more so if it is a substitute for attending school or working than if it is a substitute for leisure activity. Thus, one of the reasons why there was a good deal of rioting and demonstrations in the latter part of the 1960s was no doubt that the students may have had to go to class if they had not been in the demonstration.

Profits from riot activity tend to be very modest but, at least in the black riots that peaked in 1967, there was a certain element of profit available. Some things were stolen, records of debts were sometimes destroyed in the course of a riot (which benefited the debtors), and there was at least initially a fairly good prospect that as a result of the riot a good deal of government money would be spent in the riot area. In practice the latter "profit" tended to turn out to be rather unimportant. Indeed, in many cases the physical damage to the areas with the consequent difficulty in shopping, etc., was surely of greater importance to the inhabitants as a cost than were the various government programs as a benefit.

But the fact that these benefits existed does not prove that they explain the riots. Indeed, it is not really the intent of this chapter to explain these riots or any others. The problem with which we are concerned is people's behavior during riots. It is an observed fact that during riots, regardless of the basic motive of the rioters (which may be either good or bad), individuals do engage in vandalism, do sometimes start fires, do on

---

[5] Edward C. Banfield, *The Unheavenly City: The Nature and Future of Our Urban Crisis*, Boston: Little, Brown & Company, 1970, ch. 9, 185–209.

occasion attack the police, and very commonly threaten the police even if they do not attack them. Further, there is usually a fairly widespread violation of a large number of minor laws against such things as walking in the streets, littering, and committing noise nuisances. All of this kind of activity is rare outside of the environment of a riot, and what we are interested in in this chapter is the explanation for this activity, not the explanation for the riot itself.

To repeat what we have said before, we will not be able to clearly prove one theory or the other. This requires empirical work that has not yet been done. We will simply present the economic explanation we think is quite convincing and hope that with time the empirical work will be done to determine whether the theory is true or not true. Granting that most people have at least some desire sometimes to commit minor vandalism, acquire property without paying for it, violate the traffic laws, and— although they do not have any particular desire—litter, walk on the grass, or commit noise nuisances, there are some times when avoiding these activities would be inconvenient to some extent. Why do we observe that all of the violations are so much commoner during riots than normally? Can we explain this without assuming that the people have changed at all, but only on the theory that the cost they face has changed?

It is clear that the cost of all of these activities declines sharply during a riot. In the first place, it may be rather hard for the police to tell who in a large collection of rioters is committing the crime or misdemeanor. If, for example, a large number of people are facing a line of policemen and shouting insults or even throwing rocks, the policemen will normally be unable to determine which of the individuals has shouted the insult or thrown the rock, and therefore a direct arrest is difficult. Under the circumstances, what the police normally try to do is "seize the ring-leaders." Since it is not at all obvious the police are able to detect the ringleaders, there is no strong reason to believe they get the right people; but they may perhaps not be completely random in their arrest patterns. In any event, it is clear that this activity is safer under these conditions than it would normally be.

This is particularly true because not only does the mob give some kind of concealment to the person who is, shall we say, throwing rocks at the police, but it also provides him with protection. The police are nor-mally very heavily outnumbered by the rioters and, hence, are not really in a position to push quickly through and arrest any person they want. Unless the individual is in the front ranks or, better yet, actually some-what in front of the mob, the police will find it quite hard to arrest him because of the prospects of physical violence from the rest of the mob. Thus, there is further protection for the individual committing this kind of act. His costs are clearly much lower than they normally would be.

Thus, if we consider that there are at least some people in society who would like to throw rocks at policemen or shout insults at them, then for them the cost of this activity goes down sharply during a riot and one would anticipate that their consumption of these "goods" would rise. This, of course, assumes the kind of mob or riot in which there is no great internal discipline. Mahatma Gandhi, in the early part of the 20th century, organized a number of very large demonstrations in which the demonstrators were subject to extraordinarily tight disciplinary control from the mob itself. The benefits for this discipline were fairly obvious. He was attempting to appeal to the conscience of the English and realized that it was important that his followers do nothing that might offend the English newspaper reader. It is likely that, in general, public order (with the exception of the specific law Gandhi had decided to violate in this particular demonstration) was much better kept in and around one of his demonstrations than it would be elsewhere.

But this is simply a further illustration of the same point. The mobs and demonstrations organized by Gandhi were extremely well behaved because the individual who committed some minor crime while participating in such action would find not only the police but all the people around him would impose costs on him. He would certainly be immediately turned over to the police, together with a group of witnesses, if he violated the rules; and he would find himself permanently barred from membership in the demonstrating political organization. Under the circumstances, these demonstrations were extraordinarily orderly and the proverbial virgin with a bag of gold could have walked through them with much greater safety than she can walk today through Central Park.

A mob, then, changes the environment in which individuals operate. This change can be, as it was in the case of the Gandhi-organized demonstrations, a great reinforcement of the normal police activities in society because the members of the mob will enforce a set of rules and they are far more numerous than are the police. On the other hand, if the mob happens to feel the other way, it can mean a great relaxation of these principles. The ceremonial murder by torture of a considerable number of political figures when the Nuri Pasha regime was overthrown in Iraq was as valid an expression of the change in environment in which the rioters operated as were the Gandhian demonstrations, in general, their opposite.

Once again, however, we have not proved that the economic explanation is the correct one. It is certainly true that when a mob is in the streets, the environment is different. The cost and benefits of various acts are different from the norm. We would therefore anticipate changed behavior and we do observe it. But this is merely one hypothesis. The alternative hypothesis that people somehow change in a riot cannot be ruled out on this evidence. What we need is a further empirical work.

part six

Learning

19

The University Setting

Typically, universities catch hell from their students. Students frequently complain about the quality of food; they deplore "meaningless" general education requirements and criticize professors who are more concerned with their research and professional standing outside the classroom than they are with the quality of their instruction. They do not like being bored to tears while in their classrooms, and some tire easily of humbling themselves before the "lords" of the university, the administrators. Students beef about poor or remote parking facilities or about regulations that prohibit cars on campus altogether. In years gone by they have grumbled about and demonstrated against "petty" rules—such as dress codes, curfew hours, and sign-outs—that restricted their social conduct. More recently, the hot issue on some campuses has been whether or not coed suites within dormitories should be allowed.

On the other side of the desk, professors are not without their complaints. They bemoan what they sense has been a deterioration of academic standards. They are very concerned with what has come to be known as "grade inflation," or the gradual increase in grades given to students. Now, more than ever, there is concern over pay raises not keeping up with the cost of living. As one professor recently complained at a faculty meeting, "I wish the administration would stop talking about 'annual raises'; I haven't had a *real raise* in years."

In this chapter we are not concerned with the legitimacy of student and faculty complaints. Nor will we spend time evaluating the tactics employed by students to get what they want. We prefer to consider the more interesting question of why the university *can* operate the way it does. At the start we readily admit that part of the basis for much student and faculty discontent may simply be an unbridled attempt on their part to get more and more for little or nothing. However, we think a fuller understanding of modern university operations requires some reflection on the instiutional setting of the education process.

UNIVERSITY PRICING

The modern public university has one notable feature and that is, it typically receives part of its funding from state appropriations and/or grants, endowments, and charitable contributions. The rest, generally less than 50 percent, comes from students (or their parents) in the form of tuition and fee payments. Until very recently, there has been a shortage of openings in higher education; more students have wanted to get in than could be admitted. The reason for past shortages, as we will show, can be traced to the way in which education has been financed. Many of the problems students have confronted in their college careers can also be laid at the feet of the subsidies given to education. That may be a mouthful, but we intend to explain in detail. First, we need to lay out the framework for the analysis, which means the market for education.

In Figure 19-1 we have scaled the number of university openings (that is, the number of students that can be admitted) along the horizontal axis, and the price (which amounts to the marginal value of education) along the vertical axis. The *student* demand for education, labeled D_1, is viewed as the horizontal summation of all students' individual de-

FIGURE 19-1

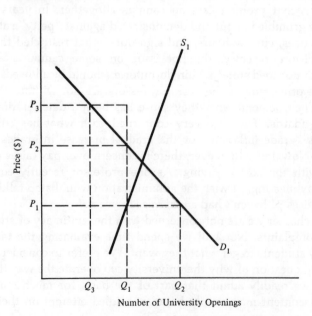

Number of University Openings

mand curves. It is the market demand for education, and it is a function of anything that gives "value" to being an educated person, such as the inherent satisfaction from learning, the additional lifetime income which the educated person can receive, and any change in social status that may be experienced by students and attributable to education. In the discussion, the demand is assumed to have its normal negative slope. (Why?) This means that more people will want to enter college if the price falls.

The supply of education (i.e., how many openings will be offered at each price) is a function primarily of the number of faculty members and/or classroom seats available and of the teaching technology being employed. That is, the greater the number of faculty members employed and/or the greater the number of classrooms and seats, the greater the supply of university openings students can fill. Also, if television or large lecture rooms are used, then more students may be accommodated.

To give some realism to the model, the supply of education, S_1 in Figure 19–1, is assumed to be upward sloping, but highly inelastic with respect to tuition and fee payments from students. We make this assumption recognizing that the number of students universities can admit is determined in large measure by decisions of state legislatures or, in the case of private institutions, charitable organizations. They are the ones who make appropriations for dormitories and classroom buildings. However, it seems reasonable to assume that schools can, and do, respond to a limited degree to changes in the price they can charge their students. Hence, the upward sloping curve.

If education were provided on a free market basis, the market clearing price would be the price at which the supply and demand for education intersect in the graph. On the other hand, assuming that the legislature both subsidizes the students' education and limits the physical size of the university, the price charged students in the form of tuition and fees will be below the market clearing price—for example P_1. (For simplicity, we assume all universities charge the same price.) Note that at P_1 the number of student openings in universities will be Q_1; however, the number of students wanting to enter will be much greater, Q_2. In other words, given the supply and demand and price of education in this illustration, there is a shortage of openings for college students (Q_2–Q_1) and this, we believe, fairly accurately describes the situation of universities and colleges until the late 1960s and early '70s. (If this were not true, one must wonder how else we could have experienced a shortage.)

The existence of the shortage goes a long way toward explaining the behavior of universities. Because of the shortage, the available openings must be distributed among those who want to be admitted in some extra-market manner. Since there are more students knocking at the doors than can be admitted and since the students are not paying the full cost of their education; there is certainly little incentive for the university (when a shortage exists) to pay much attention to the wishes of the students. It is also clear why the criteria for admission has traditionally been on the basis of who the most intelligent students are and who are the best or most efficient learners. Not only do such standards permit the faculty to fashion students after their own idea of what an educated person should be, it may make life in general a little easier for the instructors. It is often much easier to teach an intelligent person than one who may not be so well endowed mentally.

Those students who want to go to college, but who cannot get in, represent a threat to those students who are admitted. If the admitted students do not conform to the requirements (standards) of the university or faculty, they can be replaced by those who would otherwise be a part of the shortage. Therefore, as opposed to accepting a total payment of P_1 from each student, the demands of the optimizing university can be raised. The *effective price*, meaning the money price plus the non-monetary "payments" the university will charge, can, in fact, be raised to P_2 in our illustration. P_1 is paid by the students in the form of tuition and fees and the rest, P_2-P_1, can be extracted from the students in any number of forms. The university can impose general education requirements the student may not appreciate and can impose social regulations that are not liked. The university can also neglect the quality of the accommodations, such as food and dormitory facilities, and it can require students who want to drive cars on campus to park in a remote area. The professor can require more work than students will freely choose, and he can require that they learn material that is of little interest to the student but of considerable interest to the professor. If students do not like the way they are treated in or outside the classroom, they can be replaced or less severely penalized with low grades.

Notice that P_2 is the highest price that can be charged. If the university attempted to extract a higher money and non-monetary price than P_2, for example, P_3, the number of students wanting to go to college would fall to Q_3. Given that Q_1 openings will be available, a surplus of openings (Q_1-Q_3) will exist; universities can anticipate a cut-back in funds from students and state appropriation; and professors will be threatened with a possible loss of jobs and income. In such a situation, what can we expect to happen? Being economists and university professors and recognizing that competition *does* exist among faculty members and universities, we would anticipate that the demands placed on students would fall back to P_2. This means that something would have to give, such as the extensiveness of general education requirements, the "toughness" of courses, the attitude of university personnel,[1] the quality of food, etc.

---

[1] An aloof attitude on the part of professors and administrators is one means of reducing the utility of education to students, and, to that extent, it is one means of extracting a non-monetary price from students.

From this analysis, we may conclude that what professors and universities view as their "standards" may be primarily an expression of their market position and their ability to extract a non-monetary price from students. It also follows that their abilty to lay claim to "standards" and induce compliance from students is dependent in part upon public subsidies; this is revealed in the gap between P_2 and P_1, and their ability must rise and fall with the difference. For example, suppose that the university raised the tuition and fee payment to something above P_1 and there is no offsetting increase in demand. The result would be, barring a change in supply and demand conditions, a reduction in the shortage and, more importantly for our present purposes, a reduction in the gap between P_2 and the price charged for tuition and fees. Here again, if something did not give, the number of students wanting to enter college would drop and we would have the surplus problems discussed above. The anticipated results would be, as above, that the optimizing university would have to concede some of its demands in other areas of university life. Having to make such concessions is one possible constraint on universities' abilities to raise their tuition and fees.

If the university does not concede in areas such as rules governing social conduct and parking, then a reduction in demands may have to be realized in the area of expected academic performance. The reader may think professors have their standards and will maintain them at all costs, and we agree that there are professors who are like that. However, visualize for the moment a professor who may have a family to support and very few employment opportunities outside the university. Consider, also, that he may not have tenure. If there exists a surplus of university openings, such as $Q_3 - Q_1$, then there will be unfilled seats in someone's classroom, portending a possible cutback in the number of faculty members needed. If the university cuts back on faculty, who would you guess would go first? Given the attention administators pay to student credit hours generated by faculty and departments, it is quite likely that if a cut is made, it will be where the number of students in class is low. Recognizing this prospect and remembering that faculty members are not all irrational when it comes to their own welfare, the individual faculty member can attract more students to his classes in two basic ways. He can attempt to change the nature of the course, improve its inherent value to the students, and increase the demand for his courses. This option has the disadvantage of requiring more work on the part of the professor. The other basic way he can attract more students is by cutting back on his demands on students. In other words, he can reduce the price to students of taking his courses by lowering requirements and/or raising the grades students can expect to receive for any given level of achievement.

If one professor, by such methods, attracts more students, then other professors, who may not have originally been caught with an enrollment problem, may now be saddled with unfilled seats and the threat of losing their jobs. The result *can be* a competitive devaluation of "academic standards" and inflation of grades. This is not necessarily bad for the *students* because remember that we originally said that professors may have been imposing what they thought was important on the students, and they may now be catering more to student desires. At the same time, we must recognize the possibility that the public (and parents) may have been subsidizing college education in order that the professors' will (which is thought to be more in the long-run interest of students and society) could be imposed. Because tuition and fee payments can influence the ability of professors to extract work from students, it is understandable why they may side with students in opposing higher tuition payments and in promoting government subsidization of education.

We can complicate the analysis a little by considering the impact of changes in demand and supply conditions. If the demand for college education increases while the supply remains constant, as described in Figure 19–2, the expected result is an increase in the shortage of openings from Q_2-Q_1 to Q_3-Q_1. Note, also, that the effective price universities can charge can go up from P_2 to P_3, meaning the universities can increase their tuition and fee payments and/or increase their demands in other areas of academic life. (Similar conclusion could be drawn if the supply increases,

FIGURE 19–2

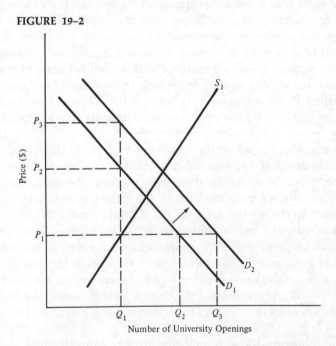

Number of University Openings

but the demand increases by more than supply. Try showing this on a graph of your own.) This situation may be reasonably descriptive of universities in the late 1950s and early 1960s. The value of a college education was definitely on the rise during that period of time. In addition, incomes and the population of potential college students were increasing. The college diploma was generally considered to be a surefire ticket to the "pie-in-the-sky" all young people and parents dream about. All of these factors were increasing the demand for college education faster than openings could be made available.

In the late 1960s the supply and demand conditions in the university education market began to change dramatically. The growth in the number of potential college students began to taper off, the college diploma became much more common and its prestige value began to drop, and surpluses of college graduates, especially in teaching fields and engineering, began to emerge—all of which led to a significant drop in the growth of demand for college education and, in some states or areas, to an absolute drop in the demand. On the supply side, state appropriations for classroom buildings and dormitories gained momentum; community colleges and technical schools began to proliferate. The result was that the supply outstripped the growth in demand; shortages of college openings at first fell and then later evaporated all together.

To illustrate the consequences of these changes, consider Figure 19–3.

FIGURE 19–3

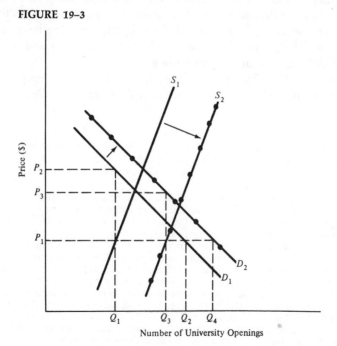

Number of University Openings

The initial supply and demand conditions are depicted by S_1 and D_1. We have increased the demand and supply curves to D_2 and S_2, but notice that the supply has been increased by more than demand (that is, supply has been moved further to the right). For purposes of simplicity only, we assume that tuition and fee charges remain constant.[2] The graph may appear on the surface to be a little confusing; but if you look at it carefully, you may see that the results of the changes are a reduction in the shortage from Q_2-Q_1 to Q_4-Q_3 and a reduction in the *effective price* universities can charge, from P_2 to P_3. Given this latter reduction and the constant tuition price, the university and/or faculty must reduce their demands on students. We would predict that the changes that occurred in the educational market during the late 1960s would be reflected in one or more of the following areas: reduced social regulations, a relaxation of general education requirements and other restrictions on students' college programs, a change in the attitudes of administrators and professors toward students, and, perhaps, lower academic standards, however defined.

Interestingly enough, those of us who have been a part of university systems during the past decade have seen almost all of these changes come about. Colleges and universities have reduced their general education requirements and some have eliminated them altogether. Universities are turning more and more toward student evaluations of faculty and courses as a means of evaluating faculty performance and ensuring that faculty members pay more attention to the desires and feelings of students. Social rules, which used to be very stringent on the activity of women, in particular, have been abolished.[3] Students are being allowed much more freedom in taking independent study courses and in designing their college programs to meet their own needs.

Grades have been going up, so much so that on many campuses more than two-thirds of all grades given are now As and Bs. The Dean's List has

---

2 We realize that tuition charges have gone up dramatically during the period with which we are concerned; however, such changes do not harm our conclusions. In fact, such changes, if introduced would serve to reinforce our conclusions. Can you show why?

3 As a sidenote, one of the authors has been associated with two schools which, when he was there, had very strict dress codes and sign-out requirements for women. For example, at one school women had to be in their dorms by 10:30 pm during the week and could not be gone from campus for more than four hours without signing out again. They also could not wear bermuda shorts on "front" campus. At another campus, women could not date men of another race without written permission from their parents. When students demonstrated against such rules in the early 1960s, the administration would respond by arguing that they were doing what they thought was right and in the best interest of the women students. At both schools when enrollment problems began to appear, the rules were scrapped almost *in toto*. The justification given was that women in the middle and late 1960s were more mature and responsible than were their counterparts in earlier years. Such statements made good press releases, but few in the college communities took them very seriously.

become a joke to those who know what has been happening. *Newsweek* magazine reported the following on grade inflation:

> In 1961, about half of the seniors at Harvard College graduated with honors; this month, when the class of '74 received their diplomas, degrees *cum laude* or better went to an astonishing 82 percent. The average University of Colorado student in 1964 maintained a grade-point average of 2.4 out of a possible 4 points), but his counterpart today has a GPA of 2.82. Between 1962 and 1972, the University of North Carolina doubled the percentage of As it handed out. The average grade at the University of Wisconsin has soared from C-plus to B-plus in just nine years. And the dean's list at the University of Virginia included 53 percent of the student body last year—compared with 21 percent in 1965.[4]

In a survey of over 400 colleges and universities, Roy Burwen found grade inflation to be prevalent during the 1960s, which was a time of considerable expansion in universities and colleges.[5] His findings are reported in the accompanying Figure 19–4.

In addition, one should realize that grades have been going up in face of a downward drift in Student Achievement Test scores of entering freshmen. Employers, graduate schools, and organizations such as Phi Beta Kappa no longer look upon high grades as clear evidence of superior ability. At one time employers looked to colleges and universities as institutions that screened the bad students out and graduated the people who were markedly better than those who failed to make it through. Now, with rising grades and a growing uncertainty over what they mean, more and more employers are turning away from seeking college graduates and are turning toward training their own people. To the extent that this has occurred, the value of the college degree has deteriorated, reducing the demand for education.

Before closing this section, three points need to be stressed. First, we have discussed the problem of education in the context of an environment in which the shortage of openings has been reduced. A more accurate description of current conditions is that a surplus of openings exists among universities. However, this condition does not affect the fundamental nature of our predictions; it may only affect the extent of the affects discussed above.

Second, we recognize that many of the changes that have occurred in education are in part the results of fundamental social changes in attitudes and preferences of people toward what education is and should be. We merely submit that the market has played a significant role in the development of educational policies and attitudes.

---

[4] "Grade Inflation," *Newsweek*, July 1, 1974, p. 49.

[5] Roy Burwen, "Institutional Research Notes," San Francisco: Office of Institutional Research, San Francisco State College, March 1971 (unpublished).

FIGURE 19–4
Grade Point Averages by Year—Total Sample

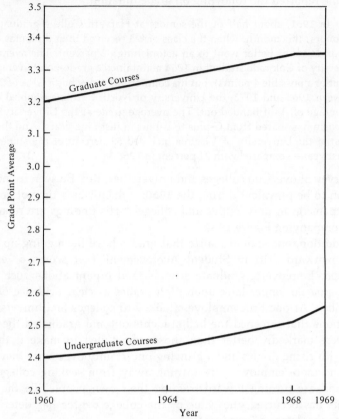

Source: Leroy S. Burwen, "National Grading Survey," San Francisco: Office of Institutional Research, San Francisco State College, 1970, unpublished.

Third, the faculty of any given university could get together and could put restrictions on the grades any given faculty member could distribute to his students. However, such a move is likely to run headlong into the opposition of those who believe that such policy would be a violation of academic freedom. In addition, if one university restricts its grades and others do not, the result can be a movement of students to other universities, jeopardizing jobs in the university that restricts faculty grades.

FACULTY SALARIES

Because of the tremendous growth in universities during the 1950s and '60s, there was a corresponding increase in demand for faculty members. Salaries rose substantially and graduate schools geared up to satisfy the increasing demand for persons with doctorates. Because education appeared at the time to be a sound investment, many persons eagerly sought advanced degrees. The usefulness of the graduate programs that sprung up, however, was predicated on a strong growth in university systems; and when this growth began to level off, graduates continued to be pumped-out. The eventual consequence of a system in which salaries could not be readily adjusted downward was a surplus of prospective faculty members. Many Ph.D.s in the humanities went begging for jobs and ended up selling hotdogs and driving trucks.

Although money wages of existing faculty members could not be easily reduced, salaries of beginning faculty members began to stabilize and, in some areas, to fall. In a situation in which more faculty members abound than can be hired, one might anticipate state legislatures and university administrations to take every opportunity to reduce the *real income* (that is, the purchasing power of money income) of the faculty members. As a result, pay raises have in most states not kept pace with inflation. (If legislatures did not permit this to happen, they would have had a difficult time, perhaps, explaining the rather high salaries of faculty members to their constituencies.) One might also expect universities to reduce the income of faculty members by putting greater demands on them, and so we have had a growing trend toward eight-to-five days for faculty, whereas in the past they have been relatively free to come and go as they pleased. Administrations have imposed standardized student evaluation on faculty and have been able to raise their demands in the areas of research, publications, and community and regional service. In the past, tenure has been offered to prospective faculty as a fringe benefit; now the probationary period before one can receive tenure is being lengthened and many schools are moving to abolish tenure altogether. All of these changes and cutbacks in graduate programs are working to reduce the surplus of Ph.D.s on the market.

In the foregoing paragraphs, we have been generalizing about the broad market for faculty. When the market is segmented by discipline, these generalizations do not always hold. They do appear to hold very well for professors in the humanities and education but not so well for professors of accounting and finance. Herein lies potential pitfalls for university administrators who may attempt to make sweeping rules for all faculty. If the administration dictates that all faculty raises are to be the same, the university may hold on to those faculty whose employment market is glutted, but they may lose, for example, their accountants whose market wage rate may have risen by more than the standardized salary increase. If the university does not pay the market wage to those accountants it has, it will then have to enter that same market they tried to ignore and hire other accountants at the going market wage. If they refuse, their accounting program can suffer.

This is one aspect of market forces many administrators fail to appreciate. As an illustration and as discussed above, universities are putting more reliance on student evaluations in determining salary increments. This may mean that the mean scores received by the different faculty members in different disciplines are ranked and raises are dispensed accordingly. To reveal the inherent problems of such schemes, suppose that all of the accountants are basically "crummy" teachers in the eyes of their students, but they are typical of others in the profession. (Believe it or not, some of our best friends are accountants!) In the College of Business, let's suppose that they score relatively low among other faculty in the College; economists (being inherently superior in all aspects of university life!) score relatively high. The evaluation scheme of allocating raises on the basis of student evaluations would mean that the economists receive more than the accountants. However, suppose that the market for accountants is much tighter than the market for economists; the market wage of accountants would rise comparatively more. The market would dictate that the accountants receive a higher raise. If the university or college employs student evaluations as a criterion for raises, what do you think would happen? You can rest assured that unless the accountants were bound to the school for non-monetary reasons, the College of Business would lose their accountants. The school would then have to enter the market to hire the accountants at the higher wage. The university could avoid all of the expense associated with faculty turnover by simply looking to market as a guide for adjusting salaries.

A WORD OF CAUTION

The reader should understand that the foregoing analysis does not necessarily reflect the way we think university students, administrators, and faculty *should* behave. As has been our goal throughout the book, we have only tried to explain why they have behaved the way they have and how they might be expected to behave, given changes in market conditions.

20

Learning Behavior

Psychologists and educators have been concerned with learning behavior for some time. We now know a good deal about the learning process, particularly among the lower order animals; however, it is abundantly clear from experience that educators have a long way to go before much can be said about how learning among students within a classroom setting can be improved. The federal government and foundations such as Ford and Rockefeller have spent literally billions of dollars over the past decade researching the learning and educational processes. Unfortunately, researchers have frequently concluded that there is no difference between their experimental and control groups—that nothing appears to work in the classroom. For example, Robert Dubin and Thomas Taveggia found this to be the case in their examination of 91 separate studies of experiments which had evaluated different techniques, methods, and classroom conditions,[1] and H. Kiesling concluded that "It is striking to note that such pay-parameter variables [as teacher experience and training] were seldom found to be related to pupil performance."[2] After a decade of actively funding projects to change education in the public schools, the Ford Foundation recently concluded that very little that was done made much difference.

Where there has been a favorable difference between experimental and control groups, researchers have been very reluctant to suggest that

---

[1] Robert Dubin and Thomas Taveggia, *The Teaching-Learning Paradox*, Eugene: University of Oregon, 1968.

[2] H. Kiesling, "Multivariate Analysis of Schools and Educational Policy," Santa Monica: The Rand Corporation, 1971. Darrell Lewis and Charles Orvis drew basically the same conclusions from their review of the literature in economic education, *Research in Economic Education: A Review, Bibliography, and Abstracts*, New York: Joint Council on Economic Education, 1971.

their conclusions be generalized to other similar (but not identical) situations. Policy makers have readily questioned whether or not the marginal benefits achieved were worth the cost incurred.

The inability of educators and psychologists to demonstrate how learning in the classroom can be upgraded stems in part from the terribly complex nature of the classroom environment. In that environment students are being constantly bombarded with thousands of bits of information (i.e., stimuli); and if one assumes that a change in the flow of any one type of information will actually have a material impact on student learning, he may rightfully be guilty of presumption. In addition, we feel that the failure of the educational establishment to explain the educational process may be more fundamental in origin; that is, it may be at least the result of the way in which the learning process is perceived by those who are doing the research. This can mean that the wrong questions have been asked and the evidence has been misinterpreted.

The dominant view of learning among psychologists appears to be a very mechanistic one—and, perhaps, overly so. The subject or student receives stimuli and responds accordingly. The task of the teacher is one of providing the "right" stimuli in order that the "right" response can be imprinted in the behavior of the student. In this way, the student learns by connecting stimulus and response. From the perspective of traditional learning theories, it appears to us that the student does not have *real choice* in the sense that the theories allow him to choose in some rational manner among viable options. This may be because the student is not credited (from a theoretical point of view) with having a preference that is independent of the stimulus-response mechanism and that can operate on or alter that mechanism. He merely responds. Once the imprint, that is the connection between stimulus and response, is made, the student can be likened to a computer. The data cards can be fed in and a print-out is received without any intervening active thought process. The main reason for this approach may be that the admission of choice can muddy the "theoretical waters." One purpose of any social science, such as psychology, is to make predictions regarding human behavior and, more specifically for our purposes, the learning processes. If the choice is admitted to the discussion, then one may suppose that it is impossible to say anything about learning; that is, if choice is to be real choice, then it must be unpredictable. If choice is predictable, then one must wonder how it can be *real choice*. Seeing this roadblock, psychologists tend to avoid the subject.

In these few pages we hope to introduce choice into the discussion of learning.[3] The individual student or instructor is not viewed as an academic robot, responding mechanistically to stimuli from his environment,

---

[3] In this chapter we are at best able to outline certain broad themes in the economics of learning and conventional psychological theories. Robert Staaf deserves consider-

past and present. We accord the individual a "preference" that is to a degree independent of environmental factors. The student or faculty member can, therefore, choose from a range of options or combinations of goods and services, which may include learning or education.

Our approach to learning is different from conventional views in one important respect. Educators, in an attempt to explain the learning process, are inclined to point to genetic and environmental conditions (such as sex, age, race, class size, and method of instruction) as causes of student learning behavior, whereas we, in applying the economic approach to learning, look to the choice calculus of the individuals as a primary explanatory factor and one that tends to be overlooked in more conventional studies. This is not to say that environmental and genetic conditions do not constrain the choice process.

THE RATIONAL STUDENT

We begin by assuming that the student is rational in the conventional economic sense of the term. As discussed in Chapter 1, this means that the student knows what he wants and attempts to maximize his satisfaction by consuming from a range of commodities that are available to him. Perhaps, the reader feels that an assumption of rationality is inappropriate in any discussion of education. A person can only make *rational* decisions among those alternatives which are *known*. By definition, what is to be learned is not known; and, therefore, a person cannot make rational decisions regarding learning he knows little about. The fact is that people make decisions that involve unknowns and uncertainties all the time. The decision to research involves what is yet to be found. People regularly buy cars and appliances (often used ones, at that) they know virtually nothing about. It is certainly questionable whether or not the public knows more about the costs and benefits of the cars they buy than they know about, say, a course in economics before they enter the class. Remember students are not completely in the dark about the classes they sign up for; they do spend a significant amount of time attempting to acquire information about courses and professors they take. People make decisions on the basis of the information they have at hand and can rationally justify acquiring, and this goes for the decision to learn.[4]

---

able credit here for originating and developing the economic approach to learning. For a more detailed and rigorous treatment of the economist's approach, the reader may want to see Richard B. McKenzie and Robert J. Staaf, *An Economic Theory of Learning: Student Sovereignty and Academic Freedom*, Blacksburg, Va.: Center for the Study of Public Choice, 1974. There are actually a number of psychological theories of learning; for a good review of these, see Winfred F. Hill, *Learning: A Survey of Psychological Interpretations*, rev. ed., Scranton, Pa.: Chandler Publishing Co., 1971.

[4] A fruitful departure (but one that cannot be taken) would be the consideration of a question which economists have pondered for years: When does a person stop acquiring information and make a decision? Remember that the acquisition of infor-

At any rate, if the reader can accept our assumption, he may further recognize that the student will *fully* allocate his resources—i.e., time and material and monetary wealth—and will equate the ratios of the marginal utility of the goods he buys to their respective prices. Including knowledge (k), which is the end product of the learning process as a good that can be "consumed" by the student, the marginal condition is: $MU_a/P_a = MU_k/P_k = \ldots = MU_n/P_n$, where MU denotes marginal utility, the subscript a can represent any good such as an apple, and subscript n can stand for any other good. P denotes price, which in the case of knowledge may mean the money and time expenditure required to obtain a unit of knowledge. If the equality has not been attained and, for example, $MU_k/P_k > MU_a/P_a$, then the student has gotten more utility for the last \$1 (or resource) spent on knowledge than on apples. (For a more detailed explanation, see Chapter 1). He can, consequently, increase his utility by shifting his resources from apples to the acquisition of knowledge. In other words, if he is rational, we can expect him to choose to learn more and to continue to expand his knowledge until equality is attained among the ratios.

Here, knowledge has been treated as a composite good, whereas we know that it comes in many diverse forms. This means that the actual utility maximizing condition is a little more complicated. Letting subscripts e, f, and h denote knowledge in the fields of economics, French, and history, the marginal condition becomes: $MU_a/P_a = MU_e/P_e = MU_f/P_f = MU_h/P_h = \ldots MU_n/P_n$. If, instead, $MU_e/P_e > MU_f/P_f$, the student can increase his utility by learning more economics and less French.

Another way of saying the same thing is that the student will "purchase" knowledge, or any particular kind of knowledge, up to the point that the marginal benefits equal the marginal costs. *He will purchase only so much,* and he will vary his "consumption" of any kind of knowledge, such as economics, not only with the price he himself pays (that is, the demand curve for economic literacy is downward sloping), but also with changes in the marginal utility and price of other goods. For illustrative purposes, suppose that the marginal utility of apples, which, by the way, is totally outside of formal classroom setting, increases; this means that MU_a/P_a will become greater than MU_e/P_e. It would then be rational for the student to consume more apples and less economic knowledge. If on the other hand, P_e were to rise, it would be rational for the student to spend less on economics and more on other goods such as apples or even more on other subjects. If he does not do this, assuming equality among the ratios before the price increase, MU_e/P_e will be less than the other ratios. (To test your understanding of what has been said, what would

---

mation itself can be a rational act. Aside from this issue, one economist, Gary Becker, showed that even if people are irrational in at least one sense of the term, many of the deductions made from an assumption of rationality still hold ("Irrational Behavior and Economic Theory," *Journal of Political Economy*, 70 [February 1962], 1–13).

the student choose to do given the following changes: an increase in MU_e; a reduction in P_f; and an increase in P_a.)

A simple conclusion that deserves special note is that the amount of knowledge the student acquires may not be the same the professor believes he should acquire, or in other terms, any disagreement between what the student does in fact accomplish in class and what the professor expects him to accomplish may simply be due to a difference between what the professor perceives the benefits for the student to be and what the student perceives them to be.[5] Also, recognize that in our view of student behavior the student does not automatically respond to stimuli; rather, he is viewed as receiving information about relative costs and benefits about matters to be learned, weighing it in terms of his own preference, and then choosing an appropriate response. The extent of the student's response depends on what happens to the marginal utilities of the goods as more or less is consumed. For example, going back to the situation in which $MU_e/P_e >$ MU_f/P_f, we concluded that the student would choose to learn more economics, but how much depends on the rate at which MU_e fall as more is consumed. If MU_e diminishes rapidly, the student will learn less additional economics than if the MU diminished slowly. Keep in mind that the student will increase his knowledge in economics until the ratios are equal.[6] This leads to the point that a new classroom device or technique can, from a technical point of view, increase the ability of the student to learn economics. However, because of the cost involved and perceived benefits to the student, the student may *choose* to increase his understanding by less than what is technically possible.

To illustrate this last point with more precision, assume for simplicity that there are two subjects, French and economics, open to the student; that both subjects yield positive benefits to the student; and that the student has allocated a given amount of time to the study of these subjects.[7] In Figure 20–1 we have scaled the student's achievement in economics along the horizontal axis and achievement in French along the vertical axis.

We do not know a great deal about our hypothetical student, but we do know that if he allocates *all* of his time to the study of economics, he can achieve only so much in that field. We have arbitrarily selected E_1 in

---

[5] We also wish to point out that any disagreement could just as easily be due to the fact that the instructor and student do not evaluate the MUs of other goods as being the same. Can you explain why?

[6] We have sidestepped the possibility that MU_f will increase as fewer units of French are learned.

[7] Admittedly, as we have discussed, the amount of time available for educational purposes is not likely to be fixed. However, the assumption does simplify the discussion and does not detract from the limited argument we have in mind. Also, see Robert J. Staaf, "Student Performance and Changes in Learning Technology in Required Courses," *Journal of Economic Education*, 3 (Spring 1972), 124–129.

Figure 20–1 as that limit. We also know that if he chooses to achieve E_1 in economics, he will learn nothing in French. This, of course, assumes that learning French requires some time and that learning economics has nothing to do with learning French. The same can be said about the student's ability to learn French. If he devotes all of his time to the study of French, he can learn only so much; we have indicated this limit by F_1.

FIGURE 20–1

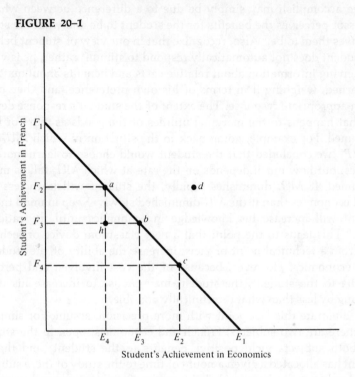

Student's Achievement in Economics

Alternately, the student can choose to divide his time between the study of French and economics in any number of ways, changing the relative achievement in the two subjects. By taking time away from the study of French and applying it to the study of economics, he can increase his achievement in economics while giving up achievement in French (i.e., the cost of achieving in economics). It is from this line of reasoning that we have drawn a line between F_1 and E_1. This line (or more properly, transformation curve) depicts the numerous combinations of French and economics achievement that can be "produced" by the student. The student can, therefore, choose to consume any combination along F_1E_1. Although it does happen, it is doubtful that the typical student will choose either combination F_1 or E_1. Assuming that the student must pass both courses, he cannot afford to have zero achievement in either field.[8] Consequently, we would expect the student to choose some interior combination, such as a, b, or c. Combination d is out of the range of possibilities; it requires the use of more resources than our particular student has available for education. (For some other student who may be more efficient at learning economics and French d might be possible. Why?) If the student chooses combination h, he will not be fully using his resources; he can have more achievement in French and/or economics. Therefore, any combination inside and not on F_1E_1 will not be chosen by the rational student. Hence, the task of the student is to sort through all combinations along F_1E_1 for that one combination that will maximize his own satisfaction. If he chooses b, it must be because it is preferred over a and c.

The task of the professor can be viewed as two-fold. First, the professor of economics can attempt, by various persuasive techniques, to change the student's preferences toward economics. The result may be that the student prefers combination c over b. The student learns more economics, but notice that the greater achievement in economics in this case is at the expense of achievement in French. (The efforts, on the other hand, can induce the student to allocate more time to education in which case the transformation curve will move out to the right).

Second, the economics professor can attempt to increase the efficiency with which the student learns economics. If he accomplishes what he sets out to do, the student can achieve more in economics; the limit of the student's achievement can move, for example, from E_1 to E_2 in Figure 20–2. Assuming that the French professor does nothing to improve learning in his discipline, the student's transformation curve will, pivoting on F_1, move to F_1E_2. The student can then choose any combination along this new curve. He can choose combination r; his achievement in economics increases while his achievement in French remains constant. On the other hand, the student can choose combination s, in which case his achievement in French would rise and his achievement in economics would remain constant. If we had put some leisure activity, such as golf, on the vertical axis instead of achievement in French, the result of the efficiency change in economics could have meant more rounds of golf for the student. The common sense explanation for s is simply that since the student can now learn more economics in the same amount of time, he can reduce the amount of time spent studying economics, learn the same amount and spend the time on some other activity such as golf or studying French.

The student can also choose combination t in which case he increases

---

[8] We recognize that some students come to a class with such a backlog of knowledge in a given subject area that they do not have to do anything to pass the course. Here again, we are attempting to concentrate on the typical student in the typical class.

FIGURE 20–2

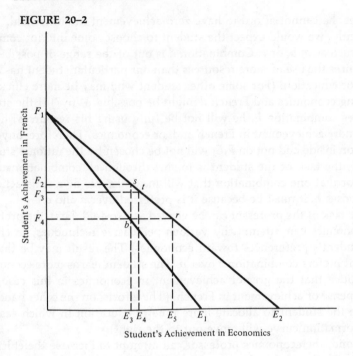

Student's Achievement in Economics

his achievement in both subjects; however, in our example the increase in economics is much smaller than the increase in French. This might be the expected result of the student who is a French major and is taking economics as a means of satisfying his general education requirement.

This analysis suggests a possible explanation for the outcomes of experiments conducted by educators and which appear to have no impact. The researcher can have two classes of students. In one class he teaches the conventional way, and the mean student achievement may be measured at level E_3. In the other class, he does something that is innovative and in effect moves the transformation curve out to F_1E_2. However, he really does not know if or how much the curve has moved. Besides, he may not even think in terms of the students' transformation curves. All he does is measure their mean achievement, which may be E_4. Because the difference between E_3 and E_4 is quite small, he may conclude that the experiment was a failure. While it is possible that what is done did not have any effect on learning efficiency (that is, the curve actually does not move), the failure of the researcher could have been the oversight of the increase in the students' achievement in French or the greater amount of time the student spends "goofing-off" or out on dates. If he had broadened his research and had considered the possibility that students may have been choosing to do something else, his conclusion *may have* been different. This is only a possibility, but one which researchers in education should not pass by lightly.

Before leaving student maximizing behavior, one additional, important point can be made. We have implicitly assumed that the marginal utility of knowledge, MU_k, is positive, which is in accord with the paradigm that there are benefits to education. Therefore, the student is *willing* to pay some price to acquire some finite amount of knowledge. However, some types of knowledge may have no perceivable benefits *to the student*. This may be descriptive of many of the courses included under general education requirements. In such a case, the student must be *paid* before he can be expected to bear freely the cost of learning the subject. Of course, one way of "paying" the student is to impose a cost on him if he does not "voluntarily" learn the material. This can be done by making the coursework a requirement for graduation or entry into a profession. The student can also be penalized with low grades, damaging his future income earning ability. If he takes the coursework, he is permitted to obtain his degree. The degree then becomes the payment. As discussed in the previous chapter, such tie-in sales can be made to the student so long as the price charged students in the form of tuition and fee payments is below the market clearing price.[9]

THE RATIONAL PROFESSOR

The professor can also be viewed as a rational human being and as facing a transformation curve. Consider Figure 20–3. In that graph we have put the leisure time of the professor on the vertical axis; assuming the professor's field is economics, we have scaled the mean achievement of the professor's classes along the horizontal axis. If the professor does nothing with his classes except walk into class, he will have only so much leisure time available for doing other things such as playing golf or undertaking research. We have arbitrarily indicated this limit as L_1. On the other hand, he can use all of the time raising his students' understanding in economics. In this event, the students' mean achievement can rise to E_1. Like the student, the professor can divide his time between leisure activities and increasing his students' achievement, in which case he will have open a number of leisure-achievement combinations which may be described by L_1E_1. Also like the student, the professor is faced with the problem of choosing that combination along L_1E_1 that will maximize his utility. Remember the professor does have "academic freedom" which gives him considerable leeway in deciding how he will use his time.

---

[9] We force sudents to go to public schools. The element of compulsion suggests that the perceived benefits of education for those who actually have to be forced is not sufficient to cover the students' private cost of the education.

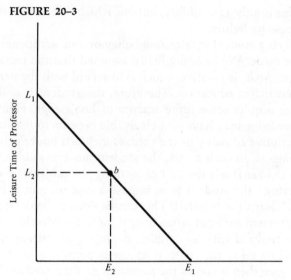

FIGURE 20-3

Mean Achievement of Students in Economics

If he chooses combination b, the students' mean achievement level will be E_2. This implies that the students will, given their abilities and effort, learn only so much, and this is in part the result of the utility maximizing behavior of the professor. If the professor had *chosen* to work harder, the students would have learned more, possibly as much as E_1. However, the professor would have had less leisure time available or less time for research, and he apparently, in this example, did not believe the additional achievement was worth the cost in terms of leisure time.

If we now introduce some innovative technique into the classroom that can improve the efficiency of the learning process, the professor's transformation curve will, pivoting on L_1, shift to L_1E_3 in Figure 20-4. The professor can now choose any combination along this curve. He can choose combination c, in which case the full benefits of the change in classroom efficiency is revealed in student achievement, which rises from E_2 to E_4. On the other hand, the professor can trade some of the gains in learning efficiency for additional leisure time. He can choose combination d, or any other between c and L_1; in this example, the net increase in student achievement from the innovation is very slight. If this were a part of an experiment, the researcher might conclude that the innovation was ineffective. Recognizing the possible choice behavior of the student and faculty and recognizing that most educational experiments are undertaken in public schools and general education courses at the college level, it may be understandable why researchers so often may have found that their experiments have had little effect.

FIGURE 20–4

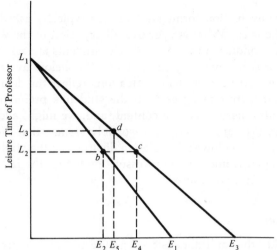

Mean Achievement of Students in Economics

STUDENT EVALUATIONS

Increasingly, universities are turning to student evaluations as a means of evaluating faculty performance. However, the issue of whether or not student evaluations can be influenced by the grades the professor gives his students is unsettled. Allen Kelley, in a study in economic education, found a positive relationship between grades and student evaluations but concluded, "Providing students with high course grades does not appear to exert an important impact on evaluations."[10] Furthermore, he suggests that if the instructor had raised his quality point average from 2.27 to 3:50, the mean ratings for the course would have increased by only two to three percentage points. Conversely, Dennis Capozza, in another study in principles of economics, came to a dramatically different conclusion. "The results indicate that every 10% increase in the amount learned reduces a professor's rating by half a point. On the other hand, if a professor's grades average 3.5 instead of 2.5, he improves his rating by one and a half points. Another way of expressing the relationship would be that if a professor wishes to receive a perfect rating of 1.0, then he should teach nothing and give at least ⅔ of the class As."[11] In this sec-

---

[10] Allen C. Kelley, "Uses and Abuses of Course Evaluations as Measures of Educational Output," *Journal of Economic Education*, 4 (Fall 1972), 13–18.

[11] Dennis R. Capozza, "Student Evaluations, Grades and Learning in Economics," *Western Economics Journal*, 11 (March 1973), 127. For other studies on the same subject, see V. W. Voeks and G. M. French, "Are Student Ratings of Teachers Affected

tion, we will demonstrate what economic (choice) theory can say on the subject.

On student evaluation forms students are typically asked to respond to such questions as "What is your overall appraisal of the way in which your professor conducted the course?" The students are asked to rate the professor on a scale that may range from "far below average" to "far above average." At best, student evaluations reflect the degree to which the course and instructor agree with the student's preference for such factors as grades, leisure, course content, and, we might add, classroom entertainment. We can, therefore, reasonably assume that the higher the *relative* utility (or the lower the relative disutility)[12] the student acquires from attending class under one professor, the higher the relative evaluation of the instructor and course.[13]

Grade Inflation

Setting aside the multidimensional nature of student preference, assume for the time being that all professors, other than the one with which we are concerned, hold their grades constant and that the student is rational and views grades (or quality point average) and leisure time as goods from which he receives some utility. Assume also that higher grades (e.g., As and Bs) are preferred to lower grades and that leisure time (which can be used for anything inside or outside academic life) available to the student is limited to L_1 in Figure 20–5. These assumptions appear to us to be reasonably descriptive of the typical student. Grades (or quality point average) in an economics course is scaled along the horizontal axis.

Given the professor's standards and assuming the student has to work for his grades, we know that the student will have to forgo leisure time to raise his grades. Because other things may be important to him, we would not expect him to spend all of his time studying and attempting to raise his grade to the highest point possible, which in this case is a B.[14] The

---

by Grades?" *Journal of Higher Education*, 31 (June 1960), 330–334; Miriam Rodin and Burton Rodin, "Student Evaluation of Teachers," *Science*, 177 (September 29, 1972), 1164–1166; Alan Nichols and John C. Soper, "Economic Man in the Classroom," *Journal of Political Economy*, 80 (September/October 1972), 1169–1173, and John C. Soper, "Soft Research on a Hard Subject: Student Evaluations Reconsidered," *Journal of Economic Education*, 5 (Fall 1973), 22–26.

[12] The student can possibly dislike all of his instructors; but if asked to rate the instructors, he will give the one whom he dislikes least the highest rating.

[13] These statements seem reasonable to us because if the student is asked to give comparative ratings to different professors in different fields or different courses, he must be able to reduce the comparative problem to one common basis. We use the economist's concept of utility as that common denominator.

[14] For illustrative purposes, we have arbitrarily assumed that this particular student is incapable of making an A under the instructor's initial standards.

FIGURE 20–5

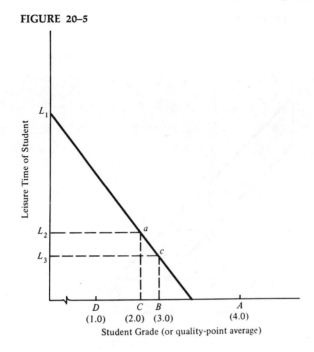

Student Grade (or quality-point average)

student may *choose* combination a, at which he makes a grade of C and has L_2 leisure time available for studying other subjects or going out on dates. (He used the difference between L_1 and L_2 for studying economics.) The student may choose combination c—that is, he could have made a higher grade—however, since he did not, we must assume that the additional time spent studying (L_2-L_3) was worth more to him than the marginal increase in his grade.[15]

The professor can change his grading structure in any number of ways, but to keep the discussion short and simple, we will focus attention on one way and assume that the professor will give the student the opportunity to make a higher grade for the same amount of effort. Furthermore, we assume that he eases up in such a way that the student's transformation curve between grades and leisure time shifts out in a parallel manner, from L_1B to L_3A in Figure 20–6. Given the shift, the student has the opportunity to move from combination a (on L_1B) to any point on L_3A. He can move to b, in which case he will have a higher grade and the same amount of leisure time. This means that his effort (L_1-L_2) and achieve-

[15] A point worth mentioning at this juncture is that if a researcher observes several students making higher grades than others in the class, he cannot on *a priori* grounds expect their ratings of the instructor to be higher for the simple reason that they may have worked harder to obtain their grades and are, therefore, no better off.

FIGURE 20–6

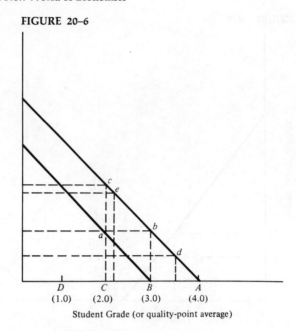

Student Grade (or quality-point average)

ment in the course should remain constant. On the other hand, the student could *choose* combination c; there he would end up with the same grade but with more leisure time. If he chooses c, he will spend less time studying economics and, presumably, will achieve less.

Alternately, the student can choose any combination between c and b and end the course with a higher grade and more leisure time. Since he can have more of both, if he wishes, we must assume that from the student's point of view, he is better off and conclude that the professor's rating will rise because of "reduced standards." How much, however, we cannot say. Even if the student chooses a combination like d, in which event he would have a higher grade but less leisure time, we would still expect the professor's rating to rise. The student can choose, say, combination e—that is, more of both—and in the event he chooses d, we must deduce that d is preferred to e. Since e is obviously preferred to a (because there is more of both at e), d must also be preferred to a. Therefore, the instructor's rating should be up at d. (This is a little tricky and you may want to reread this paragraph to insure that you follow it.)

There are two points that fall out of the graph that need to be especially stressed. First, if the students as a group choose a combination like e, it means that the grade they receive under the new grading structure may rise by an insignificant amount; but the instructor's ratings will still be up. If a researcher correlates the grades that professors give with their student evaluations and never looks at what the student achieves in the course or what he does with his leisure time, he may find very little or no correlation. He may actually conclude that higher student ratings cannot be bought with changes in the grading structure. However, there are professors who in fact may be "buying" higher student ratings with an easing of their standards. The problem is that the researcher has failed to see that students are taking the benefits of the professors' lower standards in terms of more leisure.

Second, as noted above, it is possible for the student to choose a combination like d (less leisure and a higher grade). If he does, he will be studying and achieving more in the course; however, it is interesting to note that Capozza in the study quoted at the first of this section found an inverse relationship between achievement and student evaluations, meaning that the students may be choosing combinations like e (more leisure). The suggested inverse relationship between achievement and student evaluations was also borne out in studies by Attiyeh and Lumsden[16] and by Rodin and Rodin.[17] Interestingly enough, most studies on the relationship between student ratings and grades have been for the most part undertaken in courses like Principles of Economics, which are required for one reason or another. In such courses most students may not want to be there in the first place; and under such conditions, if given the chance, they may move from a to, say, e; that is, they may take the benefits of the higher grading structure in terms of more leisure time. If the course is one students want to take because they like the subject or because they believe the knowledge acquired can be used to bolster their income, then one may more likely find a strong positive relationship between achievement and student ratings of the professors.

Real Grade Inflation

In the foregoing discussion, we explicitly assumed that other professors held their grades constant. However, if all professors inflate their grading structure, which has tended to be the case over the past decade,[18] the value to the student of any absolute grade falls. This is because the student's own ranking among his classmates falls if he continues to receive the same grades while their grades go up. The student's utility from taking a course under a professor who does not inflate should fall and so should the student's rating of the professor. Therefore, if student evalu-

---

[16] Richard Attiyeh and Keith G. Lumsden, "Some Modern Myths in Teaching Economics: The U.K. Experience," *American Economic Review*, 62 (May 1972), 429–433.

[17] Miriam Rodin and Burton Rodin, "Student Evaluations of Teachers," *Science*, (September 29, 1972).

[18] See Roy Burwen, "Institutional Research Notes," San Francisco: Office of Institutional Research, San Francisco State College, March 1971 (unpublished).

ations are used in determining salary increases, the professor who does not inflate can experience a drop in relative income. Also, if grade inflation is the general rule among professors, a professor may, to raise his (relative) ratings, have to inflate his grades relative to the general trend.

At this point, the reader may believe that we look upon student evaluations of professors as a totally perverted device for evaluating teaching. On the contrary, we recognize that students can see good qualities in teachers. We believe that students can fairly accurately tell when a professor is prepared for class and if he is sufficiently competent to teach the course. They can also make judgments about his treatment of themselves and other students. All of these judgments can be reflected in their rating of the professors they have. The main point we have been trying to make in this section is that given the quality of the professor, economic theory suggests that student evaluations can be distorted by the professor's grading structure. If two professors are *equal in every other respect*, we would predict that the professor with the higher grading structure (in the sense that we have used the term in this section) will tend to receive the higher student ratings. In a similar manner, if two professors are distinctly different in the eyes of the students, one being "better" than the other, our analysis suggests that the professor, who would otherwise have the lower rating, can (partially) offset the differential by easing up on his grades.

21

Committees and Comment Pollution

Committees are an integral part of the internal governance of colleges and universities. They are typically delegated major responsibilities such as determining admissions standards, developing curricula, handing out awards, and making policy recommendations on such important matters as internal resources allocation, grading systems, tenure, and other faculty and student welfare measures. Although one may like to think of the committee process as one in which learned men and women, through an in-depth evaluation of a problem area, make sound judgments, faculty members and administrators commonly characterize their committee meetings as dull, boring, and a monumental waste of time. They are also prone to suggest that what may appear to be informed judgments are often (though not always) nothing more than the personal expressions of members who throughout the committee sessions made little or no attempt to come to grips with the issues at hand (and it should be noted that, generally speaking, the larger the committee, the more common the complaints). If these criticisms are correct, not only may the university be employing its resources inefficiently through direct support of the committees themselves, but may be operating on the basis of very poor judgments.

The purpose of the analysis in this chapter is not to suggest that *all* university committees operate, in some sense, badly, but rather to develop an economic explanation as to why there is likely to be an excessive "production" of comments (or "comment pollution") within *many* committee meetings (or why meetings may be long and dull), and why the judgments of the individual members may often (though not always) be uninformed, or why little effort may be made in studying the assigned task of the committee. Once the sources of the problems of the committee are recognized, remedies do emerge, as is indicated below. In developing the argument, we take the usual position that committee members—faculty, administrators, and students—are similar to their counterparts in other walks of life in that they weigh the costs and benefits of taking action, will take an action if the benefits exceed the costs, and will extend "production" of the activity up until the point at which the marginal private benefits of the action equal the marginal private costs. In a word, the committeeman is "rational."[1]

COMMENTS AS PUBLIC GOODS

A comment made by a committeeman in a meeting is a public good (or perhaps, as frequently as not, a public "bad") in much the same sense as is police protection or industrial pollution. (What is a "public good"? A "public bad"?) Take, for example, the situation of the industrial polluter. When he fouls the air, he imposes a cost on persons who may live or work in the surrounding area: the people on the street may experience eye irritation and the housewife may find that the pollution soils the clothes she hangs out to dry. If the property rights to the air are left unassigned (as has been the case in the past), the polluter need not consider these external costs in his production decisions. Consequently, his private costs are less than the social costs of the industrial activity, and we can expect that production (and the emission of pollutants) will be extended beyond the social optimum.[2] It is only through the internalization of the external costs through user charges or taxes that an economically efficient output can be achieved.

In the case of the committeeman's comment, once the comment is made, all members of the committee must hear it. There are external costs (as in

---

[1] The chapter is, in part, the application to a specific problem area the general line of analysis that was developed in Chapters 11 and 12.

[2] The social optimum is the output level at which the marginal *social* costs equals the marginal *social* benefits. The social costs include all costs incurred by those directly involved in a transaction and those, not a party to the transaction, but who are affected indirectly. It is the emission of particles beyond the point of social optimum that economists would call pollution. One Indian can urinate in the Hudson River (as many did for a long time) without affecting, in the sense that anyone is disturbed, the esthetic beauty of the area or the quality of the water. The problem of pollution exists when all people start throwing their waste in the river at basically the same place and same time; that is, they go beyond the social optimum amount of waste disposal.

Problem: Several years ago people who were very concerned about the destruction of the environment gathered on what was then called "Earth Day" at the Washington Monument. After all the speeches on what man was doing to the world were over, they left, leaving the grounds covered with litter. Realizing that the mess was created by "concerned citizens," how could it happen? Would you as an economist have expected them to create the mess? Why?

the case of the industrial production) involved since people other than the one making the comment must, if they are present, spend the time to hear what is said. The private cost to the individual making the comment is mainly equal to the time he himself spends listening to himself.[3] (There may be those who fear making a fool of themselves with their comments; however, we find that there are many in the universities who get a great deal of positive utility in making comments to any group. They enjoy sounding off before the committee in the same way that a musician likes to perform before an audience.) The social costs, on the other hand, is equal to the summation of the opportunity cost incurred (or value of time spent) by all members of the committee listening to the comment, and it needs to be emphasized that the discrepancy between the private and social costs for a comment expands with the size of the committee. The rational committeeman will extend the production of his comments until the marginal *private* benefits equal the marginal *private* costs; and since the private costs are likely to be less than the social costs, we should expect there to be a natural tendency for committees to overproduce comments for the same reason that the industrial producer (when external costs are not internalized) can be expected to pollute.

A solution for efficient operation of a committee is for the chairman to impose costs on members making comments to the extent necessary to achieve equality between the private costs actually considered by each committeeman and the costs to the committee as a whole. This may be easier said than done; however, recognition of the problem of inequality between private and social costs may suggest to the chairman attitudes and devices that have the effect of raising the effective private cost of a comment to the individual.[4] Firmness would indeed be a desirable characteristic of any good chairman, and such a tack may be easier for the chairman to embrace if he understands that controlling the comments of individual members can be desired by all members. It may appear to be

---

[3] The individual who is concerned about the feelings of others may also include in his own calculations the additional factor that his comments may inconvenience others or may lower his stature in their eyes. This still does not mean that the assessed private costs of the individual making the comment are necessarily equal to the social costs as calculated by the other committeemen and that the committee will necessarily work "properly." There are committees that do in some sense work "properly"; however, our purpose here is to develop a model of committee behavior that will enable us to understand why so many committees do not. In addition, full inclusion of all "charitable feelings" in the choice calculus of the individual committeeman makes the model so general that all predictive content is lost. Our assumption regarding the costs that are considered is similar to the assumption of profit maximization in more conventional economic discussions of the firm.

[4] We must hedge the issue at stake here since an economist has no particular expertise in suggesting what may actually constitute an increase in cost, barring the use of such things as taxing income or what can amount to the same thing, charging for each comment made. The authors seriously doubt that such techniques would be acceptable or, necessarily, efficient means of controlling committeeman's behavior.

paradoxical, but it is still the case that even though each individual member may freely choose to "pollute" the committee with comments, he could still desire some form of collective (chairman) control over the comments made by all committee members. The simple reason is that although his own freedom may be restricted, he does not have to endure the "comment pollution" generated by others.[5]

THE JUDGMENT OF COMMITTEEMEN

If a doctoral candidate were to select as his thesis topic the effectiveness of the Interest Equalization Tax Act from July 1963 through December of the following year, he would, no doubt, undertake an exhaustive review of the relevant literature, make a point by point evaluation of the provisions of the act, collect mountains of data and evaluate them in different ways, and end up spending no less than nine months in *concentrated* study. If the same student were hired by a university and appointed to a committee whose function is to make recommendations on the internal allocation of university resources, most of his colleagues (given the typical committee organization) may indeed consider him to be a little unusual (if not queer) if he addressed the task of the committee with the same thoroughness with which he developed his doctoral thesis. He would probably get the same reaction even though the problem confronting the committee were considered by all to be more important than the subject of a doctoral thesis.

One obvious explanation for the disparity in the amount of effort expended on a thesis and committee task is that the committeeman must, once employed, divide his allegiance and work effort among the demands of his students, department chairman, and professional activities: he simply may not have the time for committee work.[6] In addition, he may not have any particular personal interest in the problem facing the committee whereas his doctoral research may have been personally gratifying, and many committee tasks, admittedly, require only that the committee members express their own preferences. Our concern, however, is with those committees that do require study and preparation on the part of the members but yet the effort expended may never come close to being that which may be required; and we seek in this paper explanations for the behavior of committeemen that have largely gone unrecognized by uni-

---

[5] Of course, the most desirable situations for any *individual* committeeman would be for the chairman to permit *him* completely free range in making comments while at the same time restricting the comments of the other members. We are suggesting in the text that the committeeman would be willing to compromise this position to move away from a completely free and open committee session.

[6] It is interesting to note, however, that many faculty members are employed before they finish their doctoral thesis; they (generally speaking) will still make a concentrated effort to complete their thesis.

versity officials, but which are no less important than those reasons frequently cited.

Committee work can be exceedingly costly to committee members. A committeeman, studying the issue of internal resource allocation, for example, can be expected to spend, if he does a good job, five to ten hours a week for a period of a year or more trying to assess the scope of the problem at hand and evaluating current programs on campus. If he has no particular expertise in such areas—for example, he is in English or music—the magnitude of his task is considerably multiplied. This means he must forgo other activities that may have value to him; if he is inclined to operate within the publish-or-perish world or consults a great deal, serious effort on the business of the committee can reduce his future income stream. Otherwise, time spent on committee work can deny him rounds of golf or conversation with students or his family. In short, in absence of compulsion, the decision to undertake committee work at any level is an economic (choice) problem for the individual committeeman.[7] Therefore, to understand his behavior, one must compare the costs with the benefits of committee work as perceived by the individual committeeman.

The cost of a committeeman's work potentially includes the value of the time spent on research, as indicated above, plus the time spent in committee meetings listening to others, relating what he has learned, attempting to synthesize the information he receives from others with that which he has collected, and attempting to convince others of the relative correctness of his own position. There are, in essence, two basic types of potential costs: research costs and costs associated with dealing with the committee. Note that almost all costs are under the control of the committeeman—the exception being the minimum number of times he must attend meetings—and that many of the costs of dealing with the committee escalate exponentially with the size of the committee.[8] As suggested earlier, comment pollution—or the length of the meetings—is likely to rise with the number of members since there are more perspectives and, therefore, potentially more comments to be made. And when there are more members, there are more people to convince that any given position, should be taken.[9] Again, there are more perspectives in

---

[7] Although he may have no choice with regards to whether he is appointed to a particular committee, the committeeman typically has a great deal of latitude in determining how many meetings he will attend, how well prepared he is for the meetings, and how attentive he is during the sessions.

[8] Research costs are more directly related to the assigned task of the committee than to anything else.

[9] Because of the public goods nature of comments made within committee meetings, the cost of persuasion is not likely to rise proportionately with the number of committee members. This does not mean, however, that the cost will not rise.

One of the reasons for forming committees in the first place is to make comments public goods and, therefore, reduce the costs of forming a consensus among a number of people who may represent various aspects of campus life.

the larger committees, which must be won over to a given position, if one is to be taken; and therefore, the variety of tactics required to convince (develop) a winning coalition is likely to be greater.

On the benefit side of the "choice ledger" of the individual committeeman, one can distinguish between indirect and direct benefits of committee work. Indirect benefits may include such factors as the effect a member's work will have on his own income, security, and prestige through the actions taken by the committee. In the case of the committee on internal resource allocation, the committeeman, through his effort, can possibly affect university policy and, therefore, the demands for his own services as a teacher. The direct benefits may include the entertainment value (for want of better words) associated with being in on what is happening on campus, giving the impression that he is doing something, and having interesting conversations with people with whom he does not normally associate.

The amount of work a committeeman is willing to undertake depends on the perceived benefits from his action and how they compare with the cost of achieving those benefits. As we assumed in the beginning, the committeeman will undertake no work unless the benefits exceed the costs, or the payoff is positive. In many instances the indirect benefits from committee work can be quite small for the individual member; the decisions made may have nothing to do with the member's own welfare (but may have a great deal to do with welfare of, say, students). In the event that the effects of the committee decisions are generalized over the entire faculty, the effect can be quite small for any one individual; and if so, he will make his decision on how much research to undertake on the basis of the *individual* benefits he receives and not on the basis of the total effects. Since the decisions of the committee are public goods themselves, the effort expended by each member can easily be sub-optimal.[10] It is indeed apparent that one tends to observe greater effort expended by those committeemen who are directly or indirectly affected substantially by the decisions of the committee.

As for the direct benefits, committee work, and particularly the quality factor, is given very little attention in the evaluation of faculty members. Student credit hours generated and research are by far the dominant considerations. Clearly, the typical department chairman who is primarily responsible for evaluation may never do anything more than count the number of committees his faculty are on; in fact, inquiry into the quality of the individual's committee work can be considered in many circles of academia as a violation of commonly accepted professional ethics.[11] We

---

[10] Gordon Tullock, "Public Decisions as Public Goods," *Journal of Political Economy*, 79 (July/August 1971), 913–918.

[11] It would be in the interest of the faculty member to employ some personal re-

do not mean to suggest that there is never any feedback, but only that it may be so scant that it does not reflect the true effort of the committee-man and may be too unreliable to use as a basis for evaluation.[12] The other direct benefits (entertainment) may explain his attendance at meetings but tend to detract from his research effort.

The work of the committeeman can also be related to committee size, but in an inverse manner: the larger the committee, the smaller the perceived benefits from expended effort. In a large meeting of faculty—take, for example, a faculty meeting as an extreme case—the vote of an individual faculty member is one among many. The probability of his individual vote determining the outcome of the meeting is rather small, and one may add, also, that the probability of what he does or says in the faculty meeting affecting the outcome of the meeting is also rather small (or smaller than for smaller committees). For smaller committee meetings, the probability goes up; however, the rational committeemen will still discount the benefits resulting from the committee actions by (1) the probability that his own vote will be affected by research (A; see below); (2) the probability that his position, determined by his own research, is the correct one (D); (3) the probability that his research will affect the outcome of the committee vote (E); and (4) the probability that the committee decision or vote will actually affect the individual committeeman (F).[13] Even for the smaller committees, it might be deduced that these probabilities and corresponding discounts can be so low that the expected personal benefits, resulting from the research efforts, will have to be far greater than the expected costs, which can in themselves be quite large.

For example, assume that the following values are associated with the probabilities noted above: A = .5, D = .75, E = .2, and F = .5. (These values seem to us to be reasonably generous for purposes of illustration.) The rational committeeman will undertake the cost of research (C) if the discounted benefits (B) are greater than the costs or if (ADEF) (B) − C > 0. *For this example, this means that the expected benefits would have to be greater than $53.33 for each dollar value of research cost incurred.* Even if it were conceded that the probabilities are too low and should be adjusted upward, we should still find that the expected benefits will have to be several times the expected costs. In light of the analysis, it

---

sources attempting to give the impression that he is working harder on his committees than he actually is. It *may be* rational for him to work harder at giving a false impression than on committee business.

[12] Our model of rational behavior would clearly suggest that the committeeman who knew that his work was being scrutinized by those who have power over his income would exhibit more effort.

[13] This last factor must be added since many committees are set up for the purpose of making recommendations and not for taking action directly. In such instances, it is not certain what the committee recommends will actually be adopted as university policy.

is quite understandable why many committee members, even in relatively small committees, do very little to become informed on the subject matter facing them.[14]

The foregoing analysis also suggest several general guidelines for committee organization:

1. University committees that are organized to study a problem for which there is no obvious answer should be kept small. From personal experience, the authors doubt that a committee with more than six members will actually *study* any problem before it. Larger committees should be reserved for those areas of university life for which study is not required or the mere expression of individual preferences toward an issue is the underlying function of the committee. As is now virtually axiomatic within the study of groups, large groups should be used for reaction and not for action.

2. In the interest of reducing the cost of research to the individual committeeman, the task of the committee should be segmented and responsibility for research in the different areas should be delegated to the members. This means that if large committees are thought to be necessary for some political purpose, for example, subcommittees should be organized and clear lines of responsibility should be drawn and made known.[15] Since all members will not be studying the entire problem facing the committee, there is a cost embedded in this suggestion. However, if the entire problem is laid on the committee as a whole, the cost of a complete study of the whole problem *can be* too great for any one to undertake *any* research. In addition, each committee member may attempt to become a "free rider," meaning that no one does anything.

3. Before a committee is organized, there should be a high probability that the recommendations of the committee will be put into action. If an administrator frequently organizes committees and almost as frequently ignores their recommendations, he can expect that his behavior will reduce the diligence with which his committees will tackle any problem that is assigned. In other words, it will reduce the probability that he *can* accept the recommendations of the committees he appoints.

CONCLUDING COMMENTS

There have been two overriding conclusions that come out of the foregoing discussion. First, committee meetings are likely to be "dull and

---

[14] In a large faculty meeting, E would be much smaller than in the example above. If E = 1/500, the benefits would have to be greater than $2,666 for each $1.00 of cost. This would mean that to expect the committeemen to incur $1,000 worth of cost on committee work, one would have to expect $2,666,000 worth of benefits. The obvious paradox is that a few people actually work as hard as they do.

[15] An alternative would be for the committee to be given the authority to hire someone to undertake the research and draw up proposals the committee can approve or disapprove.

boring" because, given their typical organization, there is likely to be an overproduction of comments and these comments are likely to be based on uninformed judgments; this goes for student as well as faculty committee meetings and it is just as applicable to committee meetings that are wrestling with the question of what to do about industrial pollution as well as how to reallocate faculty resources. If the reader has difficulty accepting this as a generality, then it is clear that he has not been on many committees. Second many of the problems universities have experienced in the past may be the result of the extensive use of committees and the general lack of concern over (or understanding of) the operations of the committee. A university may well be advised to be more selective in the use of committees, particularly the larger ones.

part seven

A Final Word

22

Where Do We Stand?

The total social system consists of all the people in the world, all the roles which they occupy, all their patterns of behavior, all their inputs and outputs which are relevant to human beings, and all the organizations and groups that they belong to. This is, of course, a very large, complicated system. Nevertheless, it is convenient to separate it from other systems of the world even though all the world's systems interact and form a total system of the planet. Just as the geologists and oceanographers study the lithosphere and the hydrosphere, meteorologists study the atmosphere, and biologists study the biosphere, so we say that social scientists study the sociosphere, which operates as a system at a somewhat different level of organization from the others.

Kenneth Boulding[1]

The vast expansion of economics as a discipline is one of the more interesting intellectual developments of this generation. The number of economists involved in this expansion and the variety of topics analyzed is on the increase; there is every reason to believe that this trend will continue, blurring the traditional boundaries which have separated economics from the other social sciences. In fact, we encourage the breaking down of these boundaries in order that more cooperation can take place among the different social sciences.

In this book we have outlined the economic approach to the study of human behavior and the social order and have used this approach to discuss a wide range of topics, many of which are not normally thought of as being within the scope of economics as a discipline. We hope that in the

---

[1] Kenneth E. Boulding, *Economics as a Science* (New York: McGraw-Hill Book Company, 1970), p. 1.

261

process we have been able to demonstrate how fruitful this approach can be in terms of improving our understanding of the world around us. More importantly, we hope we have stimulated the reader to employ this approach in his own attempts to come to grips with issues and problems outside the scope of this book.

In considering a wide range of topics with a single approach—that of economics—we are fully aware that at times our efforts may be misunderstood or misinterpreted. A major point of controversy concerns the concept of rationality, which has been at the base of many of our discussions. To be sure, many noneconomists will make the point again and again and again that man is not rational, and hence the economist's assumption of rationality is false. In discussions with people of this persuasion, we have always found that they define "rational" in a way not characteristic of the economist. They have as their idea of a rational man a person who is perfectly informed and cold-blooded, who takes very long views, gives considerable attention to all decisions, and invariably aims at direct, selfish ends. With this interpretation of the word rational, it is easy to demonstrate that men are not rational. Even though we point out that the disagreement amounts to a difference in definitions—and that the economist's definition is relatively immune to such criticism—we expect economic analysis to continue to be attacked at this level.

"Economic man," normally perceived as a money grubbing materialist, is a caricature. Human behavior encompasses the aesthetic, religious, and ethical dimensions, as well as the economic, and a complete understanding of man's existence must account for them all. In this book we have attempted to alert the reader to be mindful of all of these aspects of human experience, and where possible, we have introduced aesthetic and ethical considerations into our discussions. We have concentrated on what may be called the *economic dimension*, broadly defined, because that is our area of expertise and because there is much to be gained by the clear recognition of the economic motive in all areas of human experience.

By the same token, much work needs to be done in the way of exploring the full dimensions of human behavior and integrating them to a greater degree than social scientists are presently capable of doing. The problems of doing this are indeed formidable. In general, we need to know much more about value formation. More specifically, ethics is an area of human behavior which has been barely touched by economists; we know very little about how ethics emerge, become altered, and, consequently, how they affect social order. If we are in an "ethical crisis," as many suggest, we need to know why. Much has been done over the past decade on the economics of politics, but much remains to be understood regarding the limitations of political order. We need to know more about how the market, politics, and ethics are interrelated as social organizers. It has been only recently that such economists as Kenneth Boulding have begun to address the roles that love, fear, benevolence, and malevolence play in the social order.

Perhaps, many more economists, as well as other social scientists, will search these problems, and by the time this book is rewritten we will be able to add more insight into what we already understand about social order. Although many new tools and techniques of analysis may be necessary, we suspect that the economic approach to problems, which has been at the heart of all that we have written, will play a significant role in our attempts to address ever more complex problems, and it is this prospect that makes economics an exciting field to be in.

Index

Index

This book has been set in 10 and 9 point Palatino, leaded 2 points. Part numbers and chapter titles are in 20 point Palatino. Part titles are in 30 point Palatino italic and chapter numbers in 42 point Palatino italic. The size of the type page is 27 × 45½ picas.